CONTINUE

A Biblical Journey in Personal Discipleship

"If ye continue in my word, then are ye my disciples indeed…"–JOHN 8:31

Paul Chappell

First published in 2015 by Striving Together Publications, a ministry of Lancaster Baptist Church, Lancaster, CA 93535. Striving Together Publications is committed to providing tried, trusted, and proven books that will further equip local churches to carry out the Great Commission. Your comments and suggestions are valued.

Striving Together Publications
4020 E. Lancaster Blvd.
Lancaster, CA 93535
800.201.7748

Contributions from Tim Christoson, Tobias England, Jerry Ferrso, Mike Lester, Gabe Ruhl, and Jim Schettler
Writing assistance by Monica Bass and Robert Byers
Cover design by Keenan Sultanik and Andrew Jones
Layout by Craig Parker
Special thanks to our proofreaders

The author and publication team have put forth every effort to give proper credit to quotes and thoughts that are not original with the author. It is not our intent to claim originality with any quote or thought that could not readily be tied to an original source.

ISBN 978–1-59894–284–2
Printed in the United States of America

TABLE OF CONTENTS

An Introduction to Mentors v

Week One—**The Word of God** 1

Week Two—**Knowing God** 25

Week Three—**Who Is Jesus?** 49

Week Four—**Your Salvation** 75

Week Five—**Developing a Prayer Life** 97

Week Six—**Your Relationship with God's Word** 119

Week Seven—**The Holy Spirit** 137

Week Eight—**The Life of a Disciple** 157

Week Nine—**The Local Church** 179

Week Ten—**Your Place in Your Church Family** 203

Week Eleven—**Financial Stewardship** 223

Week Twelve—**Go and Tell the Good News** 241

Week Thirteen—**Living in Light of Eternity** 259

Week Fourteen—**Continue** 281

Appendix A—**Answer Key for Fill-In-The-Blanks** 291

Appendix B—**Answers for Lesson Review Questions** 295

Appendix C—**Topical Verses for Bible Memory** 309

Appendix D—**Understanding Bible Translations** 315

Appendix E—**Bible Reading Schedules** 321

AN INTRODUCTION TO MENTORS

Thank you for your heart to invest in new and growing Christians! This truly is one of the greatest life investments you can make. It is a joy to come alongside a new Christian and help ground him in God's Word, encourage his faith, and mentor him in Christian living.

As we have written and compiled *Continue*, we have taken care to make this resource easy to understand and use. Below are a few introductory explanations that may be a help to you:

Weekly Package—Each week contains the lesson itself followed by five daily devotional readings along with seven daily passages of Scripture reading. The lesson is designed to be covered in one sitting and then the devotional readings give further information and encouragement to the disciple as he develops a habit of daily reading God's Word.

Lesson Components—Every lesson covers a specific topic of basic doctrine and Christian living. It contains an introduction and three main points followed by an application and assignment.

Verse Lookups—One of the benefits of discipleship is that a new Christian gains experience in looking up verses in the Bible and thus learning the order of the books and how to readily find passages. This takes time and is developed over the course of several weeks. Each lesson in this course includes around twenty references in bold, without the text of the verse. These references are key verses to the topic and are designed for you and the disciple to look up in the Bible.

Conversation Starters—Throughout the lessons you'll find "conversation starters" in the margins. These are designed to spark conversation that leads to personal examples or practical application. As a mentor, these conversation starters are something you'll want to look at in advance so you will have already considered if you have personal input at these moments. Feel free to add your own as well.

Session Time—Each lesson is written with a 45–60 minute time frame in mind. Some lessons may take less time and some more, depending on the questions the disciple has and the amount of material you add as you teach the lesson. As a mentor, it is helpful if you look over the lesson in advance so you know if you will be adding personal illustrations or Bible passage context in one part of the lesson and you may want to skip a conversation starter earlier in the lesson in order to complete the lesson in one sitting. If you have a week or two where you are not able to complete the lesson in one sitting, simply pick up where you left off the following week.

Devotional Readings—At the end of each lesson are five daily readings. The first four are devotional, and the fifth is review questions from the lesson. As you begin the next lesson, take a moment to ask how the daily readings went, to review the answers to the questions, and to ask if your disciple has any additional questions regarding the previous week's material.

Questions—A key element to learning is asking questions. Be sure to provide time for the person you are discipling to ask questions. You will not know the answer to every question, and that's okay. When a question is asked to which you don't know a biblical answer, simply say that you're not sure and will come back with an answer the following week. In the coming week, be sure to study Scripture for the answer or to ask your pastor or another mature Christian for help.

Mentoring—Biblical discipleship is not merely a once-per-week meeting; it is a way of life. As you work through the material in *Continue* together, think of yourself not so much as a teacher (although you are teaching) but as a mentor. Your role is to come alongside, invest yourself into, and mentor another Christian in the joy of continuing in a walk with God.

Ministry Involvement—One of the vital aspects of Christian growth is personal involvement in soulwinning and in serving the Lord through local church ministry. We recommend that as you complete Lesson 10, you work toward involving the disciple in a regular church ministry. In this lesson, he is encouraged to discover his spiritual gifts, and this is a good time to find out what area of ministry interests him. Also, we recommend that you, as his mentor, invite him to participate with you in times of soulwinning and gospel outreach.

After the course is completed—Completing a discipleship course is only the beginning of what we pray will be a lifetime of closely walking with God for a new Christian. After you complete this book, take care to continue the mentoring relationship you have formed with the disciple. Spiritual maturity is the work of the Holy Spirit and doesn't necessarily take place in fourteen sessions. Continue to encourage spiritual growth through times of fellowship, mentoring, and serving the Lord together. Be ready (after first discussing with your pastor) to encourage the disciple to consider mentoring another new Christian when you sense he has reached a point of spiritual maturity with a consistent Christian testimony, and he could lead someone else through this book.

Mentoring through discipleship is part of Christ's Great Commission of *"Teaching them to observe all things whatsoever I have commanded you…"* (Matthew 28:20). The Apostle Paul emphasized to Timothy the importance of discipling new Christians: *"And the things that thou hast heard of me among many witnesses, the same commit thou to faithful men, who shall be able to teach others also"* (2 Timothy 2:2).

Thank you for investing yourself to commit God's Word to others so they can continue the process!

DISCIPLESHIP LESSONS & DAILY DEVOTIONS

1 THE WORD OF GOD

INTRODUCTION

Welcome to the discipleship journey! Discipleship is an exciting process of growing in God's grace and in your relationship with your Saviour.

2 PETER 3:18
But grow in grace, and in the knowledge of our Lord and Saviour Jesus Christ.

Of course, a personal relationship with God begins with salvation. If you are not sure that you have been saved or don't fully understand what that means, ask the person you are meeting with to explain it to you.

Once a person is saved, discipleship is the _____ of learning what it means to follow Jesus in obedience and growth.

JOHN 8:31
Then said Jesus to those Jews which believed on him, If ye continue in my word, then are ye my disciples indeed;

CONVERSATION
STARTER

Take a moment to
hear each other's
salvation testimony.

Simply put, a disciple is a _____ of Jesus Christ. Thus, *discipleship* is learning what it means to follow Jesus fully.

What you will learn

Over the next fourteen weeks, we'll study together some of the most vital truths of God's Word. Below is a summary of the topics we'll cover:

_____*:* We'll begin with learning a little bit about the Bible itself—who wrote it, how we know it is accurate, and why we believe it.

Who _____ *Is:* We'll cover the nature of God, understand who Jesus is, and how the Holy Spirit guides us in the Christian life.

Bible Reading and _____*:* In these lessons you'll learn more about how God speaks to us through the Bible and how we communicate with Him through prayer.

Christian _____*:* As Christians, our lifestyle should point others to our God. This lesson covers the practical aspects of how that takes place.

The Local _____*:* Discover why Jesus established the church, why it is so precious, and how and where you fit in here in this local body of believers.

_____ *Stewardship:* Learn God's promises and principles for handling your finances with wisdom.

_____ *to Others:* Learn how to share your faith with those who do not know the Lord and how to become a discipler, helping others become grounded in God's Word.

All scripture is given by inspiration of God, and is profitable for doctrine, for reproof, for correction, for instruction in righteousness:—2 Timothy 3:16

BIBLE (3)

What you can expect

Meeting one-on-one with another Christian who knows and loves the Lord is an opportunity to have a personal mentor who desires to be available to help you both in and outside of discipleship times.

Your _____ is there to come alongside you and teach you from the Bible what it means to be a committed follower of Jesus Christ. Discipleship is also an awesome opportunity to ask questions as you study God's Word, and your discipler is available to help you find the answers.

In each weekly discipleship meeting, you'll learn an important truth for the Christian life from the Bible and then have the opportunity to apply it to your life through short assignments. Additionally, you are provided with five daily devotional readings each week that will help you become _____ in God's Word and further apply the truths from the previous lesson.

What you should commit

We ask that you begin this dicipleship course as a serious commitment in the following ways:

A commitment to meet* _____ *week to finish the course: There are fourteen lessons in this course, so it's about a four-month commitment. It's important that you are committed to meeting each week until you have finished the lessons.

***A commitment to regular church* _____:** One of the most significant ways that God strengthens our faith is through the preaching of God's Word. Discipleship is an exciting time to study the Bible, but it can never be a substitute for attending the regular preaching services of our church.

NOTES

A commitment to complete the _____*:* Each lesson has assignments for you to work through during the week. These are in the form of five daily readings or questions for you to answer. We pray these assignments are the beginning of daily time in God's Word for you even after you complete discipleship.

Becoming a committed follower of Jesus Christ is—in many ways—a journey of a lifetime. But there is no better time than today to get started.

Welcome to an incredible journey!

—————— LESSON ONE ——————

We begin our journey learning about the Book that will be our guide through this course—in fact, through our entire Christian life: the _____.

In this lesson, you'll learn some of the most important truths related to the Bible—who wrote it, why we believe it, and what impact it has on our daily living.

First, take a moment to see how your Bible is put together.

It contains _____ books.

It is divided into _____ sections—the Old Testament and the New Testament.

The Old Testament was recorded _____ Jesus came to earth.

The _____ Testament tells about when Jesus was on earth and the spread of the gospel through the first-century churches after He returned to Heaven.

SEE IT FOR
YOURSELF

Open your Bible to the Table of Contents in the front. Use it as a reference point as you read about how the Bible is put together.

All scripture is given by inspiration of God, and is profitable for doctrine, for reproof, for correction, for instruction in righteousness:—2 Timothy 3:16

BIBLE 5

The Bible is not arranged in chronological order, but according to _____. There are groupings of books on history, literature, prophets, gospels, and epistles.

Use the Table of Contents in the front of your Bible to help you find passages until you become familiar enough with the order of the books that you can find them on your own.

God Wrote the Bible

God is the sole _____ of the Bible.

There are two words we use to describe how God got the Bible to man:

_____: This is God communicating previously unknown truth.

_____: This is God having His truth recorded.

God has revealed Himself to man in many ways, including creation, our conscience, and history. (We'll look at these in our next lesson.) But the clearest way He has revealed Himself is through the pages of _____.

▶ **2 Peter 1:19–21**

In this passage, the Apostle Peter—who saw Jesus in His glorified state—explains that the Word of God is a "more sure word of prophecy." In other words, by having God's revelation of Himself _____ for us in black and white, we know it is true and that we can depend upon it.

Peter also describes the process by which God recorded the Bible.

NOTES

Let's break this verse down:

The Bible did not originate with _____: *"came not…by the will of man."*

Men of God _____ the words of the Bible: *"holy men of God spake…"*

God is the _____ of the Bible: *"as they were moved by the Holy Ghost."*

The Bible word for this process is _____.

▶ **2 Timothy 3:16**

To better understand this process, you should understand the meaning of the word *inspiration*.

***What Bible inspiration is** _____:* Sometimes we use the word *inspiration* to refer to an idea or the motivation to do something creative or artistic. For instance, we might say, "Michelangelo was inspired to paint the ceiling of the Sistine Chapel" or "Shakespeare was inspired as he wrote *Romeo and Juliet.*"

***What Bible inspiration** _____:* There is another definition for *inspiration* that we don't use often. It is "the drawing of air into one's lungs; inhaling." This is the inspiration spoken of in 2 Timothy 3:16. The phrase *"given by inspiration of God"* literally means "_____." In other words, God breathed the words of the Bible to human penmen who wrote them down.

Because of these two truths—revelation and inspiration—the Bible is literally the _____. It is God's words to us.

Jesus Himself specifically stated that God's Word was divinely inspired by God.

All scripture is given by inspiration of God, and is profitable for doctrine, for reproof, for correction, for instruction in righteousness:—2 Timothy 3:16

BIBLE 7

▶ **Matthew 4:4**

The Bible is the most amazing book of all time:

God used more than _____ different men from a variety of backgrounds over a timespan of _____ years to record each word.

The writing took place on _____ different continents (Asia, Africa, and Europe) and in _____ different languages (Hebrew, Aramaic, and Greek).

Yet, the entire book completely agrees and has been validated time and again by history, archaeology, and science.

If you asked ten contemporary authors to individually write their viewpoint on just one controversial subject, you would come up with a wide range of conflicting opinions. And yet, the Bible covers hundreds of controversial subjects by many different writers—and the entire book agrees. There can be only one reason for this: the Bible has just one Author—God.

God Has Preserved the Bible

So we now know that God moved human penmen to write the words in the Bible. But that leads to the question, how do we know these words are preserved for us today?

God _____ to preserve His Word.

▶ **Psalm 12:6–7**

▶ **Psalm 119:89, 152, 160**

▶ Isaiah 40:8 (Interestingly, the Apostle Peter quoted from this very passage in 1 Peter 1:25: "But the word of the Lord endureth for ever. And this is the word which by the gospel is preached unto you.")

▶ Matthew 24:35

God tells us the _____ by which He has preserved His Word.

God specifically told people to _____ His Word:

Moses
Exodus 17:14
And the Lord said unto Moses, Write this for a memorial in a book, and rehearse it in the ears of Joshua…

Isaiah
Isaiah 8:1
Moreover the Lord said unto me, Take thee a great roll, and write in it with a man's pen concerning Maher-shalal-hash-baz.

Isaiah 30:8
Now go, write it before them in a table, and note it in a book, that it may be for the time to come for ever and ever:

Jeremiah
Jeremiah 30:2
Thus speaketh the Lord God of Israel, saying, Write thee all the words that I have spoken unto thee in a book.

Habakkuk
Habakkuk 2:2
And the Lord answered me, and said, Write the vision, and make it plain upon tables, that he may run that readeth it.

All scripture is given by inspiration of God, and is profitable for doctrine, for reproof, for correction, for instruction in righteousness:—2 Timothy 3:16

BIBLE 9

God specifically told people to _____ His Word.

Fathers
DEUTERONOMY 6:7–9

And thou shalt teach them diligently unto thy children, and shalt talk of them when thou sittest in thine house, and when thou walkest by the way, and when thou liest down, and when thou risest up. And thou shalt bind them for a sign upon thine hand, and they shall be as frontlets between thine eyes. And thou shalt write them upon the posts of thy house, and on thy gates.

Priests & Kings
DEUTERONOMY 17:18

And it shall be, when he sitteth upon the throne of his kingdom, that he shall write him a copy of this law in a book out of that which is before the priests the Levites:

So in Old Testament times, God used the home (fathers), the government (kings), and religion (priests) to multiply copies of His Word for the next generation.

In the New Testament, God has chosen to use the _____ to preserve His Word. Consider this process:

God's Word is _____.
JOHN 17:17

Sanctify them through thy truth: thy word is truth.

The _____ is the "pillar and ground of the truth."
1 TIMOTHY 3:15

…the house of God, which is the church of the living God, the pillar and ground of the truth.

Those who have been saved are instructed to _____ what has been preserved to others.

MATTHEW 28:19–20

Go ye therefore, and teach all nations, baptizing them in the name of the Father, and of the Son, and of the Holy Ghost: Teaching them to observe all things whatsoever I have commanded you: and, lo, I am with you alway, even unto the end of the world. Amen.

Historically, there is _____ that God has preserved His Word.

There are over five thousand preserved manuscripts of the New Testament alone—all tediously copied with the utmost care—dating all the way back to approximately AD 130.[1] This is more evidence than any secular author such as Pliny or Aristotle have that their work is credible and authentic. The New Testament is the most well-attested to piece of ancient literature in the world.

Additionally, Scripture has historically been received as authoritative by Christians throughout the centuries. Although Christians have not always obeyed God's Word, there is no period of church history in which the Bible was questioned as being divinely inspired.

Some religions and false teachers say that the Bible has been so corrupted over the centuries that it cannot be trusted. They have then rewritten the Bible according to their religious teachings, or they have additional books they insist you must read along with the Bible to properly understand it. These claims go directly against what God has promised concerning preserving His Word for us. We can trust the Bible!

---

1. Matt Slick, "Manuscript evidence for superior New Testament reliability," http://carm.org/manuscript-evidence (accessed January 7, 2015).

All scripture is given by inspiration of God, and is profitable for doctrine, for reproof, for correction, for instruction in righteousness:—2 Timothy 3:16

BIBLE 11

God's Word has not only been preserved through copies, but it has been _____ into thousands of languages.

Perhaps you have wondered why there are many different versions of the Bible in English. We examine this question more closely in Appendix D. In our church we use the King James Version of the Bible, and we believe this is God's preserved Word for English-speaking people.

God Uses the Bible Today

God has recorded His Word through human authors and preserved it for us through the centuries. But that's not where it stops. The Word of God has power in our lives today!

The Holy Spirit _____ us.

In our next lesson, we'll see that the Holy Spirit is God. He is part of what the Bible calls the "Godhead." As God, the Holy Spirit wrote the Bible. (We saw that earlier in 2 Peter 1:21.) Now, He helps us to understand the Bible.

▶ 1 Corinthians 2:12–14

The unsaved person ("natural man") cannot thoroughly understand the Bible.

The saved person has the Holy Spirit to illuminate—shed light on—the truths found in God's Word.

▶ John 16:13

The Bible tells us what is _____.

▶ John 17:17

The Bible tells us how the _____ should operate.

We believe that the Bible—not tradition or personal preferences—should be our final authority for what we believe and what we practice. (In Lesson 9, we will see many of God's specific instructions to local churches and how they impact everything we do, from our structure to our teaching to our worship.)

▶ 2 Timothy 3:16

The Bible instructs us in every area of _____.

Our lifestyle should match what we believe. God's Word gives us instruction in the practical areas of life, such as relationships, raising children, finances, and even our service for God. We'll explore many of these areas in future lessons.

The Word of God brings _____.

▶ 1 Peter 2:2

The Word of God gives us God's _____.

▶ 2 Peter 1:4

The Word of God helps us resist _____.

▶ Psalm 119:11

The Word of God has the power to _____ our lives.

▶ Hebrews 4:12 (**Note:** The word *quick* in this verse is an Old English word meaning "alive.")

All scripture is given by inspiration of God, and is profitable for doctrine, for reproof, for correction, for instruction in righteousness:—2 Timothy 3:16

BIBLE 13

We are responsible to read, study, and _____ the Bible.

When we learn and apply its truths to our lives, God promises to bless us.

▸ **2 Timothy 2:15**

▸ **Joshua 1:8**

———— **APPLICATION** ————

The Bible that you hold in your hands is a great treasure. It is literally God's Word to you—written by God Himself and preserved for you.

The Bible is vital to your Christian growth. Through it, you learn about your Saviour, and you learn how to live in a way that is pleasing to God.

There are two decisions you can make right now that will set the direction for the rest of your Christian life:

First, determine that you are committed to obey whatever is _____ in Scripture. Throughout the rest of your life, you will be discovering the treasures of God's Word. But you will find those discoveries enhanced as you determine that you will respond to what you know to be true from the Bible.

Second, determine that you will make God's Word a _____ _____ of your life. God promises to bless those who read, study, and obey His Word. Begin with reading a short passage—maybe even just one verse—every day and thinking on it throughout the day. *Continue* daily devotions will help you get started!

THIS STUDY IN REVIEW

1. God Wrote the Bible
2. God Has Preserved the Bible
3. God Uses the Bible Today

NOTES

———— **ASSIGNMENTS** ————

Write 2 Timothy 3:16 in the space below, and plan to memorize this verse so you can quote it to your discipler next week.

_____

_____

_____

_____

Read the five daily readings throughout this coming week, including answering the questions on day five. These questions are where you will pick up with your discipleship meeting next week.

Choose one of the three Bible reading plans from the following daily reading pages. Begin discovering God's Word for yourself! (Although there are only five devotional lessons each week, be sure to read the Scripture for days 6 and 7.)

- **Topical** covers two or three verses each day that relate to the lessons we are studying.

- **New Testament in a Year** is a day-by-day journey through the entire New Testament.*

- **Entire Bible in a Year** is a day-by-day journey through the entire Bible.*

   *Because this course is just fourteen weeks, there are schedules in Appendix E (pages 321–324) where you can keep track of your progress for a full year.

DAY 1

God's Promises for You

In hope of eternal life, which God, that cannot lie, promised before the world began;—**Titus 1:2**

[BIBLE READING]

Topical
2 Timothy 3:16; 2 Peter 1:21

New Testament in a Year
Matthew 1

Entire Bible in a Year
Genesis 1–3; Matthew 1

One of the most exciting conclusions of understanding that God wrote the Bible and that it is preserved for us today is that we can trust its many promises!

All of us have been lied to by another person. We've had people misrepresent facts or tell us they would do something that they never followed through to completion. The Bible tells us, however, not only that God will not lie, but that He cannot lie. Everything God has promised is absolutely true.

Consider just a few promises of God that can bring peace to your life. (You could even look these up in your Bible and highlight them.)

You have eternal life that can never be taken away.
And I give unto them eternal life; and they shall never perish, neither shall any man pluck them out of my hand.—**John 10:28**

God will never leave you, and He will be your helper.
…he hath said, I will never leave thee, nor forsake thee. So that we may boldly say, The Lord is my helper, and I will not fear what man shall do unto me.—**Hebrews 13:5–6**

Anything is possible with God.
But Jesus beheld them, and said unto them, With men this is impossible; but with God all things are possible.—**Matthew 19:26**

NOTES

God will give you the strength you need for each challenge of life.
Fear thou not; for I am with thee: be not dismayed; for I am thy God: I will strengthen thee; yea, I will help thee; yea, I will uphold thee with the right hand of my righteousness.—**Isaiah 41:10**

God's grace is sufficient for your every need.
And he said unto me, My grace is sufficient for thee: for my strength is made perfect in weakness. Most gladly therefore will I rather glory in my infirmities, that the power of Christ may rest upon me.
—**2 Corinthians 12:9**

God will give you guidance.
Trust in the LORD with all thine heart; and lean not unto thine own understanding. In all thy ways acknowledge him, and he shall direct thy paths.—**Proverbs 3:5–6**

God will give you wisdom.
If any of you lack wisdom, let him ask of God, that giveth to all men liberally, and upbraideth not; and it shall be given him.—**James 1:5**

God will reward your faithfulness.
And let us not be weary in well doing: for in due season we shall reap, if we faint not.—**Galatians 6:9**

_____

_____

_____

_____

_____

DAY 2

The Uniqueness of God's Word

For ever, O LORD, thy word is settled in heaven. —**Psalm 119:89**

[BIBLE READING]

Topical
Matthew 4:4; Isaiah 40:8

New Testament in a Year
Matthew 2

Entire Bible in a Year
Genesis 4–6; Matthew 2

The Bible is a book unlike any other. As the only book God ever wrote, it stands above every other book. Consider just a few of the ways in which the Bible is unique:

The Bible is unique in its composition. Composed of sixty-six books, written over a 1,500 year time span by forty different human writers on three different continents and in three different languages, there is no other book like it!

The Bible is unique in its unity. Even with the diverse human elements mentioned above, there is an overriding unity throughout the entire Bible. It does not disagree with itself, and it has a central message revealing who God is and how we can have a relationship with Him.

The Bible is unique in its relevance. Although the Bible is centuries old, it is still read regularly all around the world. Rich and poor, educated and ignorant, kings and paupers—people from every background and in all types of circumstances read it and gain help through its pages.

The Bible is unique in its circulation. The Bible was the first major book printed on the Gutenberg Press, and still today it is printed and circulated by the millions. It has been translated into many languages, and over 2,800 languages have at least a portion of the Bible.[1]

---

1. Wycliffe Bible Translators, Scripture and Language Statistics 2014, http://resources.wycliffe.net/statistics/2014_Scripture_and_Language_Statistics_EN.pdf.

NOTES

The Bible is unique in its survival. Written on perishable material millennia ago, we still have accurate copies of it. This is even more remarkable when you consider how it has been attacked. It has been hunted down to be burned, and skeptics have tried to limit its influence. Yet we still have it, and it still changes lives.

The Bible is unique in its literary character. How do farmers, shepherds, fishermen, kings, tax collectors…people from all different backgrounds and levels of literacy write a unified book that even the secular world recognizes as literary genius?

The Bible is unique in its accuracy. Although the Bible is not a history or science book, when it speaks to these subjects, it is accurate. Time and again, archeologists, historians, and scientists have discovered the accuracy of God's Word as they've made discoveries that have lined up with the statements of Scripture from hundreds of years previous.

The Bible is unique in its prophecies. No other book—religious or secular—can even hold a candle to the approximately *two thousand* accurately fulfilled prophecies in the Bible.

But the best way to discover the uniqueness of God's Word is to read and apply it, and see for yourself how God works in *your* life through it!

_____

_____

_____

_____

_____

DAY 3

Can We Trust the Bible?

*But sanctify the Lord God in your hearts: and be ready always to give an answer to every man that asketh you a reason of the hope that is in you with meekness and fear:—***1 Peter 3:15**

[BIBLE READING]

Topical
Psalm 12:6–7;
Matthew 24:35

New Testament in a Year
Matthew 3

Entire Bible in a Year
Genesis 7–9; Matthew 3

There are many books today that claim to be the Word of God. Intelligent scholars have written books that attempt to discredit the authority of the Bible. This should not surprise us, for Satan has been trying to cast doubt on the Bible since the beginning of time.

Satan's first words to Eve in the Garden of Eden were in the form of a question, attempting to cast doubt on Eve's faith in God: "*Now the serpent was more subtil than any beast of the field which the LORD God had made. And he said unto the woman, Yea, hath God said, Ye shall not eat of every tree of the garden?*" (Genesis 3:1).

The world is in rebellion against God, and worldly people under the influence of Satan seek to destroy your faith. To counter this attack and the doubts that may come, it is important for you to have an answer that will enable you to make a solid defense of your faith.

Proving the trustworthiness of the Bible is not difficult. In the last devotion, we looked at the Bible's uniqueness. Let's look closer at its accuracy in archaeology, history, science, and prophecy.

Historical and Archaeological Evidence—Skeptics have often pointed to unsubstantiated details in the Bible to claim that it is inaccurate. And time and again, archaeological evidence has later been uncovered that supported the biblical record and embarrassed the skeptics.

One example of this is King Belshazzar, mentioned in the book of Daniel. For many years, skeptics pointed out his name as an "error" in the Bible because historians had a complete listing of Babylonian kings, and Belshazzar was not on this list. Then, in the late 1800s, archaeology unearthed a document that showed King Nabonidus made his son, Belshazzar, the co-regent of the kingdom. This also explains why when Belshazzar honored Daniel, he made him third highest in the kingdom. Thus, not only was Scripture accurate, but it was accurate down to the details.

Scientific Evidence—A few of the scientific facts mentioned in Scripture—hundreds of years before scientists came to understand them—include that the earth is round (Isaiah 40:22), that it hangs on nothing (Job 26:7), that there are an innumerable number of stars (Genesis 15:5), and that there are water currents in the seas (Psalm 8:8).

In addition to these, God gave His people basic sanitation laws, including burying their waste (Deuteronomy 23:13), not touching dead bodies (Numbers 19:11), and more, thousands of years before modern medicine discovered germs and understood the spread of disease.

Although these kinds of evidences are strong proof for the Bible, the primary reason we believe God's Word is accurate is because God Himself said so! The Bible is our final authority regardless of the evidence.

_____

_____

_____

_____

DAY 4

How Jesus Used the Bible

But he answered and said, It is written, Man shall not live by bread alone, but by every word that proceedeth out of the mouth of God.
—**Matthew 4:4**

[BIBLE READING]

Topical
John 16:13; John 17:17

New Testament in a Year
Matthew 4

Entire Bible in a Year
Genesis 10–12; Matthew 4

We see an example in the life of Christ of how to use the Bible. Although Jesus was God, He was also fully man, and thus He experienced the same temptations we experience today (Hebrews 4:15). When Jesus was tempted in the wilderness, He did not rely on His own strength to overcome, but He quoted from the Old Testament. (You can read the full account in Matthew 4:1–11.)

In fact, Jesus used the phrase, "It is written," over a dozen times. This phrase always referred to what was written in the Old Testament. Notice what Jesus believed and taught about the Bible:

• **The Bible is reliable.**

  But how then shall the scriptures be fulfilled, that thus it must be?—**Matthew 26:54**

• **The Bible is authoritative.**

  But he answered and said, It is written, Man shall not live by bread alone, but by every word that proceedeth out of the mouth of God.…Jesus said unto him, It is written again, Thou shalt not tempt the Lord thy God.…Then saith Jesus unto him, Get thee hence, Satan: for it is written, Thou shalt worship the Lord thy God, and him only shalt thou serve.—**Matthew 4:4, 7, 10**

• **The Bible is sufficient.**

And he said unto him, If they hear not Moses and the prophets, neither will they be persuaded, though one rose from the dead. —**Luke 16:31**

- **The Bible is indestructible.**

  Think not that I am come to destroy the law, or the prophets: I am not come to destroy, but to fulfil. For verily I say unto you, Till heaven and earth pass, one jot or one tittle shall in no wise pass from the law, till all be fulfilled.—**Matthew 5:17–18**

- **The Bible is unified and clear.**

  Then he said unto them, O fools, and slow of heart to believe all that the prophets have spoken: Ought not Christ to have suffered these things, and to enter into his glory? And beginning at Moses and all the prophets, he expounded unto them in all the scriptures the things concerning himself....And he said unto them, These are the words which I spake unto you, while I was yet with you, that all things must be fulfilled, which were written in the law of Moses, and in the prophets, and in the psalms, concerning me. —**Luke 24:25–27, 44**

As you read the Bible, realize you are reading a book that Jesus Himself verified as accurate. Jesus not only *wrote* the Bible (John 1:1), but He *used* the Bible. If Jesus used the Bible, how much more do we need it in our daily lives?

_____

_____

_____

_____

_____

DAY 5
Review of Week One

The questions below cover the material we studied in this lesson and are given here to help you cement these truths in your mind and heart. Feel free to look back over previous pages as you answer these questions. When you begin the next lesson with your discipler, take a few minutes to discuss any questions you have from this week's material.

1. What is a disciple? _____
    _____
    _____
    _____

2. What is the clearest way that God has revealed Himself? _____
    _____
    _____
    _____

3. Who is the author of the Bible? _____
    _____
    _____
    _____

4. What does the word *inspiration* mean in the Bible? _____
    _____
    _____
    _____

[BIBLE READING]

Topical
1 Peter 2:2; Psalm 119:105

New Testament in a Year
Matthew 5:1–26

Entire Bible in a Year
Genesis 13–15;
Matthew 5:1–26

DAY 6

Topical
Joshua 1:8

New Testament in a Year
Matthew 5:27–48

Entire Bible in a Year
Genesis 16–17;
Matthew 5:27–48

DAY 7

Topical
Matthew 5:17–18

New Testament in a Year
Matthew 6:1–18

Entire Bible in a Year
Genesis 18–19;
Matthew 6:1–18

NOTES

5. How do we know that the Bible is preserved for us? _____
   _____
   _____
   _____

6. What are some ways that the Word of God has power in our lives today? _____
   _____
   _____
   _____

7. What is our responsibility as disciples concerning God's Word? _____
   _____
   _____
   _____

② KNOWING GOD

REVIEW

Take a few moments to review together last week's study, memory verse, and the daily readings. You can use these questions to spark dialogue:

1. What truth or principle stood out to you most in last week's study and/or devotional readings?

2. Since we last met, have you had opportunity to apply or share a truth from the previous study?

3. Do you have any questions related to last week's devotional readings or assignment?

INTRODUCTION

One of the most exciting and humbling truths of the Christian life is that God desires to have a relationship with us. We are made to know Him. Even after we trust Him as our Saviour, He wants us to grow in our knowledge of Him and our experience with Him.

JOHN 17:3

And this is life eternal, that they might know thee the only true God, and Jesus Christ, whom thou hast sent.

In this lesson, we learn about who God is and how we deepen our relationship with Him.

—————— **LESSON TWO** ——————

God Has Revealed Himself to Us

God does not expect us to just figure out for ourselves who He is. He has specifically _____ Himself to us.

Notice just a few of the ways God has made Himself known to mankind:

He reveals Himself through _____.

We have simply to look around us to see evidence of an all-powerful God.

▶ **Psalm 19:1**

Even as an intricately-crafted clock points to a skilled maker, so a perfectly-synchronized solar system and universe points to a Creator.

The very first verse of the Bible tells us that God made the world.

▶ **Genesis 1:1**

Incredibly, God made the entire world out of nothing—simply by speaking it into existence.

▶ **Genesis 1:3, 6, 9, 11, 14, 20, 24**

For there are three that bear record in heaven, the Father, the
Word, and the Holy Ghost: and these three are one.—1 John 5:7

GOD 27

In the summary of God's creation, we read that He made it all
"very good."

▶ **Genesis 1:31**

(It wasn't until sin entered the world, as we find in Genesis 3, that
pain, suffering, and death came as well. We'll look at this more
closely in Lesson 4.)

Although many people have tried to discredit the Creation account
of Genesis 1–2, there is no science that can prove or disprove the
_____ of the universe. Scientists who believe the
Bible (and there are many) interpret data from a biblical worldview
that includes belief in a Creator and a worldwide flood.[1] To them,
the evidence and the conclusions clearly match. Similarly, scientists
who believe in the evolutionary process likewise approach data with
their worldview, and to them, the data suggests another conclusion.
The truth is, since no one was there to witness the beginning of the
universe, both conclusions are accepted by faith.

Indeed, the Bible tells us that believing God created the world we
see out of nothing is a matter of _____.

Hebrews 11:3
*Through faith we understand that the worlds were framed by the word
of God, so that things which are seen were not made of things which
do appear.*

Believing in creation is faith in a _____, while
believing in evolution is faith in _____.

---

1. The Genesis 6 account of a worldwide flood answers many of the questions
   raised by scientists and archeologists. Simply put, the fossils that evolutionary
   scientists suggest support the evolutionary process exactly fit the evidence of
   what we would see if there were a worldwide flood, as Scripture records.

Knowing God is our Creator leads to an important conclusion: We are created for Him, not for ourselves.

REVELATION 4:11
Thou art worthy, O Lord, to receive glory and honour and power: for thou hast created all things, and for thy pleasure they are and were created.

We do not exist to_____ ourselves, but to please God.

He has revealed Himself throughout _____.

There were two times in world history when the entire world knew the revealed truth of who God is.

In the Garden of _____

▶ **Genesis 2:15–17**

In _____ day

▶ **Genesis 7:1**

Before the worldwide flood that God sent as judgment on the earth, God made a way for everyone alive to escape His judgment. Noah preached, warning everyone, that God's judgment would come and that they could find refuge in the ark. Sadly, only Noah and his family believed God and were saved by their faith.

2 PETER 2:5
And spared not the old world, but saved Noah the eighth person, a preacher of righteousness, bringing in the flood upon the world of the ungodly;

For there are three that bear record in heaven, the Father, the Word, and the Holy Ghost: and these three are one.—1 John 5:7

GOD 29

He has revealed Himself through the human

_____.

Interestingly, the Bible never sets out to prove the existence of God. It simply assumes His existence.[2]

GENESIS 1:1

In the beginning God created the heaven and the earth.

This biblical assumption is because God hardwired the knowledge of Himself into our hearts when He made us.

▶ **Romans 2:14–15**

It has been wisely observed that no one is born an atheist. All around the world, people know there is some God, and they have a sense of right and wrong. That sense may be molded (and in some cases twisted or silenced) by their environment, but it is there, nonetheless.

Scripture tells us it is _____ who has placed within us the gift of conscience which testifies of God, of sin, and of our need for Him.

JOHN 1:9

That was the true Light, which lighteth every man that cometh into the world.

People can—and do—reject the knowledge of God. But it is not because there is no evidence—from both within and without—to support the truth of God's existence.

_____

2. This is not to say that there is no evidence or philosophical evidence for the existence of God. Many great thinkers, including previous atheists and agnostics, have concluded that there is a God based on the overwhelming cosmological, philosophical, and moral evidence in the world around us.

PSALM 14:1

The fool hath said in his heart, There is no God. They are corrupt, they have done abominable works, there is none that doeth good.

He has revealed Himself through the _____.

While nature gives us general revelation of God (i.e. that there is a God), the Bible gives us specific revelation of God (i.e. exactly who He is and what He is like). We saw this in Lesson 1, and we will look at many specific verses throughout this lesson.

He has revealed Himself through His _____.

Jesus Christ came as God in the flesh to reveal to us who God is.

▶ 1 Timothy 3:16

And so, in creation, throughout history, embedded into our conscience, and through His Word and His Son, God has revealed Himself to us. He wants us to know Him!

God Exists as a Trinity

The Bible clearly tells us that there is _____ true God.

▶ Mark 12:29

Notice these verses as well that emphatically state there is one God.

ISAIAH 45:5

I am the LORD, and there is none else, there is no God beside me…

EPHESIANS 4:6

One God and Father of all, who is above all, and through all, and in you all.

For there are three that bear record in heaven, the Father, the
Word, and the Holy Ghost: and these three are one.—1 John 5:7

GOD 31

JAMES 2:19

Thou believest that there is one God; thou doest well…

But the Bible also tells us that this God exists as a _____
—literally a tri-unity, or three in one. Scripture refers to this as
the "Godhead."

▶ **Acts 17:29**

▶ **Romans 1:20**

We see throughout Scripture that the Father, the Son, and the Holy
Spirit are all God—although there is but one God.

1 JOHN 5:7

*For there are three that bear record in heaven, the Father, the Word,
and the Holy Ghost: and these three are one.*

Note: "the Word" in this verse refers to Jesus Christ. Compare to
John 1:1, 14. We'll study this further in our next lesson.

There is one God who exists simultaneously in three
_____. Each is coequal, copowerful, and coeternal.

The _____ is God.

▶ **Romans 1:7**

The _____ is God.

▶ **Hebrews 1:8**

(Our next lesson is dedicated to learning more about God the
Son—Jesus.)

The _____ is God.

▶ **Acts 5:3–4**

NOTES

(We'll learn more about the Holy Spirit and how He works in our lives in Lesson 7.)

The Trinity is impossible to explain, but it is vital to believe. We see it all throughout the Bible. Notice these verses that refer to all three parts of the Trinity at the _____ time:

MATTHEW 3:16–17
And Jesus, when he was baptized, went up straightway out of the water: and, lo, the heavens were opened unto him, and he saw the Spirit of God descending like a dove, and lighting upon him: And lo a voice from heaven, saying, This is my beloved Son, in whom I am well pleased.

MATTHEW 28:19
Go ye therefore, and teach all nations, baptizing them in the name of the Father, and of the Son, and of the Holy Ghost:

2 CORINTHIANS 13:14
The grace of the Lord Jesus Christ, and the love of God, and the communion of the Holy Ghost, be with you all. Amen.

We are made in the _____ of God.

One of the earliest revelations of the Trinity was given in the very first chapter of the Bible. Notice the use of God speaking in the plural "us" in this verse:

▸ **Genesis 1:26**

And there, even as God began to reveal His Trinity, He also revealed that He made us in His image. He made us to _____ Himself.

We don't resemble God in physical characteristics, for God is a Spirit and does not require a body.

For there are three that bear record in heaven, the Father, the
Word, and the Holy Ghost: and these three are one.—1 John 5:7

GOD 33

JOHN 4:24

NOTES

*God is a Spirit: and they that worship him must worship him in spirit
and in truth.*

Rather, we resemble Him in the sense that we have a body, soul, and
spirit; we have physical and immaterial components to our being. We
were created in His likeness mentally, socially, morally, and spiritually.

Mentally, we were created with intelligence and rationale—an ability
to reason and choose.

Socially, we were created with a need for interaction and fellowship.

Morally, we were created with responsibility to live according to right
and wrong.

Spiritually, we were created with a spirit that will live forever even
after our bodies die and with the capacity to have a relationship
with God.

All of these areas of our _____ to God's image are seen
in Genesis 2 and 3:

We see Adam's **mental** intelligence in that he named all of the animals
(Genesis 2:19).

We see Adam and Eve's **social** need in their relationship with each
other (Genesis 2:18).

We see their **moral** responsibility in that God gave them a specific
command and the free will to choose to obey or disobey (Genesis 2:16–17)
and in the fact that they indeed made a choice (Genesis 3:6).

We see their **spiritual** capacity in their personal relationship with
God, which was later severed through sin (Genesis 3:8).

NOTES

God is so much _____ than our minds can comprehend. And yet, He made us in His image and for a relationship with Him.

The Bible Tells Us about God's Characteristics

In addition to the truth that God is a Trinity—three in one—the Bible tells us much more about our God and His characteristics. We often refer to these as God's _____.

Some of God's attributes are _____ to God alone.

Theologians call these characteristics "non-communicable." In other words, we will never become like God in these ways, because these belong to God alone.

Notice a few of the amazing, awesome attributes of our God:

_____ (completely sinless and absolutely unique)

Isaiah 6:3
And one cried unto another, and said, Holy, holy, holy, is the Lord of hosts: the whole earth is full of his glory.

_____ (all-present, or present everywhere at the same time)

Proverbs 15:3
The eyes of the Lord are in every place, beholding the evil and the good.

Jeremiah 23:24
Can any hide himself in secret places that I shall not see him? saith the Lord. Do not I fill heaven and earth? saith the Lord.

For there are three that bear record in heaven, the Father, the
Word, and the Holy Ghost: and these three are one.—1 John 5:7

GOD 35

_____ (all-powerful)

PSALM 33:9
For he spake, and it was done; he commanded, and it stood fast.

JEREMIAH 32:17
*Ah Lord GOD! behold, thou hast made the heaven and the earth by
thy great power and stretched out arm, and there is nothing too hard
for thee:*

_____ (all-knowing)

HEBREWS 4:13
*Neither is there any creature that is not manifest in his sight: but all
things are naked and opened unto the eyes of him with whom we have
to do.*

_____ (cannot and will not change)

MALACHI 3:6
*For I am the LORD, I change not; therefore ye sons of Jacob are
not consumed.*

HEBREWS 13:8
Jesus Christ the same yesterday, and to day, and for ever.

_____ (ruler of all)

ISAIAH 46:10
*Declaring the end from the beginning, and from ancient times the
things that are not yet done, saying, My counsel shall stand, and I will
do all my pleasure:*

1 TIMOTHY 6:15
*Which in his times he shall shew, who is the blessed and only Potentate,
the King of kings, and Lord of lords;*

_____ (eternal with no beginning and no end and without measure or limit)

PSALM 90:2
Before the mountains were brought forth, or ever thou hadst formed the earth and the world, even from everlasting to everlasting, thou art God.

Some of God's attributes He wants to develop _____ us

The previous characteristics belong to God alone. And yet, there are some of God's characteristics that He wants to develop in us. (We call these communicable attributes. They are the moral characteristics of God.)

Even as God created us in His image in certain capacities, He desires to make us in His image by developing His characteristics in our _____.

A partial list of some of these attributes is called the "_____ of the Spirit" in the book of Galatians. We'll study this list and how the Holy Spirit develops these characteristics in us more thoroughly in Lesson 7.

▶ **Galatians 5:22–23**

The Bible promises us that _____ God allows in our lives He can use for the purpose of conforming—or molding—us to the image of Jesus Christ.

▶ **Romans 8:28–29**

The exciting thing about knowing God is that the _____ we learn about who He is, the more we can become like Him in His moral attributes.

For there are three that bear record in heaven, the Father, the Word, and the Holy Ghost: and these three are one.—1 John 5:7

GOD 37

—————— **APPLICATION** ——————

These three truths summarize how what we have studied in this lesson can help us grow in our relationship with God:

God has revealed Himself to us because He _____ **a relationship with us.** After you trust Christ as your Saviour, He wants you to continue growing in your relationship with Him. He wants you to get to know Him better day by day even as you would in a close friendship with another person.

Growth in your Christian life _____ **through growth in your relationship with God.** As you read the Bible, read it to understand who God is. Even as you can't have a close human relationship with someone you don't really know, you won't grow in your relationship with God unless you grow in knowing God personally.

Growth in your Christian life is _____ **by becoming more like Christ.** God does not want us to know Him purely for head knowledge. He wants to make us like Him in our daily lives. You will know that you are growing as a Christian as you become more like your Heavenly Father in day-to-day situations.

NOTES

Q

THIS STUDY IN REVIEW

—————

1. God Has Revealed Himself to Us
2. God Exists as a Trinity
3. The Bible Tells Us about God's Characteristics

—————

NOTES

PREVIOUS MEMORY
VERSES

2 Timothy 3:16

—————— ASSIGNMENTS ——————

Write 1 John 5:7 in the space below, and plan to memorize this verse so you can quote it to your discipler next week.

_____

_____

_____

_____

Read the five daily readings throughout this coming week, including answering the questions on day five. These questions are where you will pick up with your discipleship meeting next week.

DAY 1

A Language Everyone Hears

The heavens declare the glory of God; and the firmament sheweth his handywork. Day unto day uttereth speech, and night unto night sheweth knowledge. There is no speech nor language, where their voice is not heard. — **Psalm 19:1–3**

[BIBLE READING]

Topical
Hebrews 11:3;
Revelation 4:11

New Testament in a Year
Matthew 6:19–34

Entire Bible in a Year
Genesis 20–22;
Matthew 6:19–34

If you had a message that was so significant that you wanted everyone in the world to hear, what language would you use?

Perhaps as a child you composed a secret language or code with your friends. You scrambled letters or symbols to represent other letters so only the people who had "the code" would be able to decipher your message. Your goal was to conceal your messages.

But what if you wanted to reveal a message—even to people who didn't know "the code"?

This is exactly what God did. He has delivered a message to the world that is so plain it crosses every language barrier. It is literally written in the sky. It is creation itself.

Look again at Psalm 19:1–3 above. It's true: Regardless of what language you speak, where on this planet you live, what your background is, or any other incidental details of your life, you are surrounded by the majesty of nature, and your life is regulated by the intricacies of God's creation.

- The sun and moon regulate day and night.

- The orbit of the earth in relation to the sun creates months and years as well as seasons.

- The moon provides gravity.

- The stars give unwavering anchor points for navigation.

- The planets remain in perfectly synchronized orbit.

- The atmosphere gives oxygen to all living species.

And all of this continues day after day, night after night, with no human intervention or force. Indeed, the heavens declare God's glory.

Everyone in the world sees (or experiences the results of) God's handiwork above them. God put them there to show His glory and to reveal His majesty to mankind.

Romans 1:20 tells us that these things we can see reveal to us a God we cannot see: *"For the invisible things of him from the creation of the world are clearly seen, being understood by the things that are made, even his eternal power and Godhead…"*

Although everyone sees the majesty of the heavens, not everyone interprets it the same way. Some, rejecting the truth of God, choose to see the amazingly crafted world around them as a random product of chance. Others see the wonders of creation and understand the message it speaks: There is a God. He created the world and His glory far surpasses anything we can fathom.

Today, as you go about your day, notice the world around you. See in it the greatness and majesty of God. And give God praise for who He is and what He has made.

_____

_____

_____

_____

_____

DAY 2

Three in One

For there are three that bear record in heaven, the Father, the Word, and the Holy Ghost: and these three are one. —**1 John 5:7**

[B I B L E   R E A D I N G]

Topical
1 Timothy 3:16;
1 John 5:7

New Testament in a Year
Matthew 7

Entire Bible in a Year
Genesis 23–24; Matthew 7

One of the greatest mysteries of theology is the Trinity—that God is three in one. This truth is so beyond our comprehension that even to illustrate it is difficult.

Throughout the centuries, people have proposed various illustrations:

An equilateral triangle—This type of triangle has three equal angles and sides. If you remove any one angle, you do not have a triangle. Yet the triangle is one shape.

An egg—There are three distinct parts: the shell, the white, and the yolk. Yet it is one object.

Fire—It must have three elements to exist: fuel, heat, and oxygen. They are all distinct, yet without any one of them, there will be no fire.

A three-stranded rope—It has three strands, yet it is one rope.

A tree—A tree is composed of roots, branches, and leaves. All three are necessary for its survival.

Water—Water molecules have three forms: solid (ice), liquid, and steam. All three have the same essence and are H_2O.

Time—It is comprised of the past, present, and future. All three are distinct, yet time needs them all to be measured as time.

These illustrations can help to a degree, but they all have their weaknesses. For instance, a two-stranded rope would still be a rope.

Water does not retain its three forms all at the same time. No physical object can fully capture the mystery of the Trinity.

If there is one truth we do learn through these objects, however, it is that creation itself reflects the nature of its Creator. Although the illustrations fall short, they do have a certain resemblance to God's triune nature.

Scripture provides a few examples of all three Persons of the Trinity appearing at the same time:

The creation of the world: *"And God said, Let us make man in our image, after our likeness…"*—GENESIS 1:26

The baptism of Jesus: *"And Jesus, when he was baptized, went up straightway out of the water: and, lo, the heavens were opened unto him, and he saw the Spirit of God descending like a dove, and lighting upon him: And lo a voice from heaven, saying, This is my beloved Son, in whom I am well pleased."*—MATTHEW 3:16–17

Paul's benediction: *"The grace of the Lord Jesus Christ, and the love of God, and the communion of the Holy Ghost, be with you all. Amen."*—2 CORINTHIANS 13:14

Although we cannot fully understand or explain the Trinity, in the end, we believe it is true because we see it in Scripture, and we accept it by faith.

_____

_____

_____

_____

_____

DAY 3

Do You Know Him?

That I may know him, and the power of his resurrection, and the fellowship of his sufferings, being made conformable unto his death;—**Philippians 3:10**

[BIBLE READING]

Topical
Matthew 28:19;
2 Corinthians 13:14

New Testament in a Year
Matthew 8:1–17

Entire Bible in a Year
Genesis 25–26;
Matthew 8:1–17

If you were shown three pictures side by side and were asked to pick out which was the president of the United States, you would likely recognize the likeness in the photo and be able to identify which one was the president. In fact, you probably know enough information about the president to give several additional details:

- Name of spouse
- Number of children (if any)
- Year elected
- Home state

But if someone asked you, "Do you know the president?" most likely (unless you happen to be a close friend!) you couldn't truthfully answer "yes." Although you may know about the president, you don't actually know the president.

Too many Christians are content to live their entire Christian life knowing about God without really knowing God.

Based on our study this week alone, you could give many facts about God:

- He has revealed Himself through the Bible.
- He exists as a Trinity.
- He created the world.
- He loves you.

You could make this list infinitely longer, but you get the idea. All of these are facts about God. Furthermore, they are true and are vital for us to know. We don't want to stop, however, by knowing about God. We want to really know Him personally.

Personal experience with God, of course, begins at salvation. When we received Christ as our Saviour, the barrier of sin between us and God was removed, and our spirits were born again that we might have personal fellowship with God.

Knowing God begins at salvation, but it shouldn't end there. Day by day, year by year, our relationship with God should be growing fuller and stronger. Just as a relationship with a dear friend continues growing over the years, so our relationship with God should grow.

We see this in the example of the Apostle Paul. Paul told many other people about Christ as he preached the saving power of the gospel. He labored for Christ fervently. But that wasn't enough to him. As we see in Philippians 3:10, he wanted to know Christ personally.

Our relationship with God deepens as we seek Him with our whole heart (Jeremiah 29:13), learn who He is through His Word (the primary means by which He reveals Himself to us), and communicate with Him through prayer.

We'll learn more about these truths in upcoming weeks, but it all begins with having a hunger in your heart to not just know about God, but to know Him. Ask the Lord today to continue to cultivate that hunger in your heart.

_____

_____

_____

_____

_____

DAY 4

True Transformation

And we know that all things work together for good to them that love God, to them who are the called according to his purpose. For whom he did foreknow, he also did predestinate to be conformed to the image of his Son, that he might be the firstborn among many brethren. —**Romans 8:28–29**

[BIBLE READING]

Topical
Genesis 1:26; John 4:24

New Testament in a Year
Matthew 8:18–34

Entire Bible in a Year
Genesis 27–28;
Matthew 8:18–34

Our ultimate purpose in life is to bring God glory. Revelation 4:11 says, "*Thou art worthy, O Lord, to receive glory and honour and power: for thou hast created all things, and for thy pleasure they are and were created.*"

As we saw in this week's study, God made us in His image. Because of sin, however, we are very unlike God in our daily living. Our natural responses to life are selfish and are more about bringing ourselves glory than bringing God glory.

Thus, God's goal for our lives is to transform us into Christlike believers. We will never have the attributes of God that are unique to Him alone, but He desires for our daily lives to reflect how Jesus lived while on this earth. In fact, God says that He has predestinated us "to be conformed to the image of His Son." That means He will make it happen.

The Bible tells us that in Heaven we actually will be like Christ: "*…we know that, when he shall appear, we shall be like him; for we shall see him as he is*" (1 John 3:2).

Between now and then, however, we should be becoming like Jesus. As we see in Romans 8:28–29, God will use every event of our lives and make it work together for good—for the purpose of making us like Jesus.

NOTES

Thankfully, becoming like Jesus is not a job that we have to accomplish on our own. Philippians 2:13 tells us, *"For it is God which worketh in you both to will and to do of his good pleasure."*

Although this transformation is the work of God, He has given us tools to cooperate with Him in the process:

The Word of God: Especially, as we read the Gospels (Matthew, Mark, Luke, and John), we see what Jesus is like. As we read God's Word and apply its truths to our lives, we find ourselves becoming like Jesus.

The work of the Holy Spirit: Galatians 5:22–23 tell us the Holy Spirit will bear godly fruit in our lives—the fruit of love, joy, peace, and more. These spiritual fruits are actually characteristics of Jesus Himself. As we yield to the Holy Spirit, He develops this fruit from within.

Difficulties of life: God allows difficult situations in our lives to increase our dependence upon Him. During these times, we often see the ungodly responses of our heart rise to the surface, and we turn to the Lord to cleanse and change us.

Thus, as we read and apply God's Word and—through both the good times and the bad—let the Holy Spirit develop fruit in our lives, God slowly but surely transforms us to the image of Christ.

_____

_____

_____

_____

_____

DAY 5

Review of Week Two

The questions below cover the material we studied in this lesson and are given here to help you cement these truths in your mind and heart. Feel free to look back over previous pages as you answer these questions. When you begin the next lesson with your discipler, take a few minutes to discuss any questions you have from this week's material.

1. Believing that God created the world is a matter of what? _____

    _____

    _____

    _____

2. What are the two times in world history when the entire world knew the revealed truth of who God is? _____

    _____

    _____

    _____

3. What does the word *trinity* mean? What are the three Persons in the Godhead that make up the Trinity? _____

    _____

    _____

    _____

4. Give some examples of God's many attributes. What are some that you want to see God develop in your life? _____

    _____

    _____

    _____

[BIBLE READING]

Topical
Isaiah 6:3; Jeremiah 23:24

New Testament in a Year
Matthew 9:1–17

Entire Bible in a Year
Genesis 29–30;
Matthew 9:1–17

DAY 6

Topical
Psalm 33:9; Jeremiah 32:17

New Testament in a Year
Matthew 9:18–38

Entire Bible in a Year
Genesis 31–32;
Matthew 9:18–38

DAY 7

Topical
Hebrews 13:8; Psalm 90:2

New Testament in a Year
Matthew 10:1–20

Entire Bible in a Year
Genesis 33–35;
Matthew 10:1–20

NOTES

5. Everything God allows in our lives He uses for the purpose of molding us to what? _____

_____

_____

_____

6. Why has God revealed Himself to us? _____

_____

_____

_____

7. How is growth in our Christian life measured? _____

_____

_____

_____

3 WHO IS JESUS?

REVIEW

Take a few moments to review together last week's study, memory verse, and the daily readings. You can use these questions to spark dialogue:

1. What truth or principle stood out to you most in last week's study and/or devotional readings?

2. Since we last met, have you had opportunity to apply or share a truth from the previous study?

3. Do you have any questions related to last week's devotional readings or assignment?

INTRODUCTION

About halfway through Jesus' ministry on earth, He asked His disciples an important question:

MATTHEW 16:13–14
When Jesus came into the coasts of Caesarea Philippi, he asked his disciples, saying, Whom do men say that I the Son of man am? And they said, Some say that thou art John the Baptist: some, Elias; and others, Jeremias, or one of the prophets.

NOTES

After the disciples answered Jesus' question, Jesus asked an even more vital question—a question that you and I must answer today as well:

MATTHEW 16:15

He saith unto them, But whom say ye that I am?

As in the first century, people today have many views of who Jesus is. Some say that He was a good man, even a great teacher. Others say that He was an impostor—a man who claimed to be God but was not. Still others suggest He was a prophet.

The important thing, however, is that you and I know who Jesus is. Peter gave the right answer to Jesus' question:

MATTHEW 16:16–17

And Simon Peter answered and said, Thou art the Christ, the Son of the living God. And Jesus answered and said unto him, Blessed art thou, Simon Barjona: for flesh and blood hath not revealed it unto thee, but my Father which is in heaven.

Indeed, Jesus is God. We call this truth the "_____ of Christ."

But why does it matter so much that we know this?

Knowing who Jesus is guards us against _____ teachers. There are entire religions that teach Jesus is not really God in the flesh. The Bible tells us plainly that these religions are not of God.

▶   1 John 4:3

Knowing who Jesus is helps us as we share the _____ with others.

And every spirit that confesseth not that Jesus Christ is come in the flesh is not of God: and this is that spirit of antichrist, whereof ye have heard that it should come; and even now already is it in the world.—1 John 4:3

JESUS 51

Our salvation depends on the fact that Jesus, as God, came to pay for our sins. When we understand what the Bible teaches about the deity of Christ, we can help answer the questions other people have.

▶ **Romans 5:8**

Knowing who Jesus is allows us to know and _____ Him. During Jesus' ministry, He healed the sick and the lame, and even raised a few people from the dead. As you can imagine, many people followed Him. But at one point, when Jesus clearly claimed to be God, many people forsook Him.

Jesus then turned to His disciples and asked a piercing question:

▶ **John 6:67–69**

Once again, Peter knew the right answer. He knew that if Jesus is God, He is worthy to be followed.

In this lesson, we'll learn more about who Jesus is, how we know it, and what that means for us.

—————— **LESSON THREE** ——————

Jesus Is God

The fact that Jesus is indeed God is revealed all throughout Scripture. Notice just a few of the ways that we see Jesus' deity.[1]

His deity is shown through His _____.

---

1. Additional references include: John 20:28; 1 Timothy 3:16; Titus 2:13; Romans 9:3–5; 1 John 3:16, 5:20; Revelation 1:8, 21:6–7.

NOTES

He is called God.[2]

ISAIAH 9:6

For unto us a child is born, unto us a son is given: and the government shall be upon his shoulder: and his name shall be called Wonderful, Counseller, The mighty God, The everlasting Father, The Prince of Peace.

JOHN 20:28

And Thomas answered and said unto him, My Lord and my God.

He claims to be the Jehovah[3] of the Old Testament (noted in the King James Version with the all caps spelling LORD*).*[4]

Compare John 8:58 to Exodus 3:14:

JOHN 8:58

Jesus said unto them, Verily, verily, I say unto you, Before Abraham was, I am.

EXODUS 3:14

And God said unto Moses, I AM THAT I AM: and he said, Thus shalt thou say unto the children of Israel, I AM hath sent me unto you.

Compare John 17:5 to Isaiah 42:8:

JOHN 17:5

And now, O Father, glorify thou me with thine own self with the glory which I had with thee before the world was.

---

2. Additional references include: Hebrews 1:8; 1 Timothy 3:16; Titus 2:13; Romans 9:3–5; 1 John 3:16, 5:20; Revelation 1:8, 21:6–7; Colossians 2:9.
3. **Note:** The name Jehovah in the Old Testament was the specific name for the one, true God. Much like our English word "God" can be use specifically (to refer to God Himself) or generically (to refer to, for instance, the god of money), so the Hebrew word for God could be used either way. Using the word "Jehovah" was one way of adding clarity to particular passages.
4. Additional references include: John 10:11 (c.f. Psalm 23:1); Matthew 25:31–32 (c.f. Joel 3:12); John 8:12 (c.f. Psalm 27:1); Revelation 1:17 (c.f. Isaiah 44:6).

And every spirit that confesseth not that Jesus Christ is come in the flesh is not of God: and this is that spirit of antichrist, whereof ye have heard that it should come; and even now already is it in the world.—1 John 4:3

JESUS 53

ISAIAH 42:8

I am the LORD: that is my name: and my glory will I not give to another, neither my praise to graven images.

He is called the Son of God.

JOHN 3:16

For God so loved the world, that he gave his only begotten Son, that whosoever believeth in him should not perish, but have everlasting life.

Sometimes this title is misunderstood as suggesting inferiority. However, we should always study the Bible in its own cultural context, instead of our culture. The Jews very clearly understood this title as being equal to God, not inferior to God.

JOHN 5:17–18

But Jesus answered them, My Father worketh hitherto, and I work. Therefore the Jews sought the more to kill him, because he not only had broken the sabbath, but said also that God was his Father, making himself equal with God.

His deity is shown through His _____.

Jesus performs works that only God can do.

He creates.

JOHN 1:3

All things were made by him; and without him was not any thing made that was made.

He preserves all things.

HEBREWS 1:3

Who being the brightness of his glory, and the express image of his person, and upholding all things by the word of his power, when he had by himself purged our sins, sat down on the right hand of the Majesty on high;

He forgives sins.
MARK 2:7–11
Why doth this man thus speak blasphemies? who can forgive sins but God only? And immediately when Jesus perceived in his spirit that they so reasoned within themselves, he said unto them, Why reason ye these things in your hearts? Whether is it easier to say to the sick of the palsy, Thy sins be forgiven thee; or to say, Arise, and take up thy bed, and walk? But that ye may know that the Son of man hath power on earth to forgive sins, (he saith to the sick of the palsy,) I say unto thee, Arise, and take up thy bed, and go thy way into thine house.

He gives eternal life.
JOHN 17:2
As thou hast given him power over all flesh, that he should give eternal life to as many as thou hast given him.

His deity is shown through _____.

The Bible tells us plainly that we are to worship God only.

▶ **LUKE 4:8**

Yet, throughout the Gospels, we see many people worship Jesus, and He never stopped a single one of them. Later in the New Testament, we even see that God the Father commands the angels to worship Him.

Wise men come to worship Him.
MATTHEW 2:2
Saying, Where is he that is born King of the Jews? for we have seen his star in the east, and are come to worship him.

And every spirit that confesseth not that Jesus Christ is come in the flesh is not of God: and this is that spirit of antichrist, whereof ye have heard that it should come; and even now already is it in the world.—1 John 4:3

JESUS 55

Those in a ship worship Him.

MATTHEW 14:33

Then they that were in the ship came and worshipped him, saying, Of a truth thou art the Son of God.

A healed blind man worships Him.

JOHN 9:38

And he said, Lord, I believe. And he worshipped him.

The Father commands the angels to worship Him.

HEBREWS 1:6

And again, when he bringeth in the firstbegotten into the world, he saith, And let all the angels of God worship him.[5]

His deity is shown through His _____.

In our previous lesson, we saw some of the attributes that belong to God alone. Here we see that Jesus also has these attributes, meaning that He is God.

Omnipotence

MATTHEW 28:18

And Jesus came and spake unto them, saying, All power is given unto me in heaven and in earth.

Omniscience

JOHN 16:30

Now are we sure that thou knowest all things, and needest not that any man should ask thee: by this we believe that thou camest forth from God.

---

5. Additional references include Matthew 8:2, 9:18, 15:25, and 28:17.

Jesus even predicted His own death—when He would die, how He would die, and that He would rise again:

MATTHEW 16:21
From that time forth began Jesus to shew unto his disciples, how that he must go unto Jerusalem, and suffer many things of the elders and chief priests and scribes, and be killed, and be raised again the third day.

Omnipresence
MATTHEW 28:20
…and, lo, I am with you alway, even unto the end of the world. Amen.

Eternality
JOHN 1:1
In the beginning was the Word, and the Word was with God, and the Word was God.

Immutability
HEBREWS 13:8
Jesus Christ the same yesterday, and to day, and for ever.

Holiness
HEBREWS 7:26
For such an high priest became us, who is holy, harmless, undefiled, separate from sinners, and made higher than the heavens;

As mentioned earlier, there are some people who say Jesus was merely a good teacher or a great prophet, but that He was not God. We see, however, that the Bible explicitly states that He _____ God. Also, because Jesus Himself claimed to be God, He could not be just a good teacher. If He is not God, He was either a _____ (claiming to be what He was not) or a _____ (confused

And every spirit that confesseth not that Jesus Christ is come in the flesh is not of God: and this is that spirit of antichrist, whereof ye have heard that it should come; and even now already is it in the world.—1 John 4:3

JESUS 57

about who He really was). Neither of these describes the Jesus of the Bible. He was neither a liar nor a lunatic; He is the _____!

Jesus Is the Saviour of the World

The Bible tells us that not only is Jesus God, but that He humbled Himself to come to this earth, take on human flesh, die on the cross for our sins, and rise from the dead as our risen Saviour.

▶ **Philippians 2:5–11**

Let's look specifically at what this means:

He came to _____.

The baby born in a Bethlehem manger was God, who clothed Himself in human flesh.

▶ **John 1:1, 14**

Jesus entered our world through a virgin's womb.

▶ **Luke 1:26–36**

This virgin birth was prophesied hundreds of years earlier through the prophet Isaiah.

Isaiah 7:14
Therefore the Lord himself shall give you a sign; Behold, a virgin shall conceive, and bear a son, and shall call his name Immanuel.

The name *Immanuel*, spelled *Emmanuel* in the New Testament, literally means, "God _____ us." Notice the fulfillment of the Isaiah 7:14 prophecy:

Matthew 1:23

Behold, a virgin shall be with child, and shall bring forth a son, and they shall call his name Emmanuel, which being interpreted is, God with us.

Even the place of Jesus' birth had been prophesied _____ years before He was born. Only God could predict the location for where He would choose to be born—and then fulfill that prediction!

Micah 5:2

But thou, Bethlehem Ephratah, though thou be little among the thousands of Judah, yet out of thee shall he come forth unto me that is to be ruler in Israel; whose goings forth have been from of old, from everlasting.

Because Jesus came and lived in our world, He knows our feelings, needs, and temptations not only by His omniscient knowledge, but also by _____.

Hebrews 4:15–16

For we have not an high priest which cannot be touched with the feeling of our infirmities; but was in all points tempted like as we are, yet without sin. Let us therefore come boldly unto the throne of grace, that we may obtain mercy, and find grace to help in time of need.

Even though Jesus experienced the same temptations we face, He never _____—because He is God.

He _____ for us.

We saw in our previous lesson that God created a perfect world without sin. It wasn't until sin entered the world that death and suffering followed.

And every spirit that confesseth not that Jesus Christ is come in the flesh is not of God: and this is that spirit of antichrist, whereof ye have heard that it should come; and even now already is it in the world.—1 John 4:3

JESUS 59

▶ **Romans 5:12**

The Bible tells us also that the payment of sin is eternal death.

▶ **Romans 6:23**

Yet God, because of His love for us, proved this love by coming and paying our penalty for sin.

▶ **Romans 5:8**

One of the reasons the truth of Jesus' deity is so important is because if Jesus were not God, He could not have paid for the sins of the world. He would have been paying for His own sin. But as God, His blood is powerful enough to cover the sins of the entire world.

1 John 2:2
And he is the propitiation for our sins: and not for ours only, but also for the sins of the whole world.

He _____ us.

Jesus died for the sins of every person in the world, and He will save anyone who calls on Him from the penalty of eternal death.

Three words describe this: *call, turn, trust.*

You call out to the Lord for His gift. You turn from self-effort. And you trust the payment Jesus already made. In the language of the Bible this is "repentance toward God [turning from self], and faith toward our Lord Jesus Christ [trusting what He has done on your behalf]" (Acts 20:21).

God gives a direct promise that He will save anyone who thus calls out to Him for salvation.

NOTES

▶ **Romans 10:13**

JOHN 1:12
But as many as received him, to them gave he power to become the sons of God, even to them that believe on his name:

1 JOHN 4:14
And we have seen and do testify that the Father sent the Son to be the Saviour of the world.

In the first lesson, you shared with your discipler when and where you were saved. But if, as you have seen these verses now, you have any doubt about that, ask your discipler to help you.

Also, these verses are helpful verses to use when you are showing someone else how to be saved.

Jesus Is the Risen Lord

The most spectacular evidence of Jesus' deity was His bodily _____ from the dead.

▶ **Luke 24:1–7**

The resurrection of Jesus Christ is, as one man put it, "the crowning proof of Christianity."[6]

Jesus didn't rise from the dead secretly. In the Bible, there are over _____ different recorded appearances of Jesus after He rose from the dead.[7]

---

6. Henry M. Morris, *Many Infallible Proofs: Evidences for the Christian Faith* (New Leaf Publishing Group, 1974), 97.
7. See John 20:11–18; Matthew 28:1–10; 1 Corinthians 15:5; Luke 24:13–35; John 20:19–24, 26–28, 21:1–23; 1 Corinthians 15:6–7; ACTS 1:3–10, 9:3–9.

And every spirit that confesseth not that Jesus Christ is come in the flesh is not of God: and this is that spirit of antichrist, whereof ye have heard that it should come; and even now already is it in the world.—1 John 4:3

JESUS 61

▶ **Acts 1:3**

He showed Himself multiple times—one of which was to a gathering of over _____ people who testified as eyewitnesses.

▶ **1 Corinthians 15:6**

Jesus not only died, but He rose from the grave with a glorified body. He has forever conquered death, so we who have trusted Him as our Saviour can know with certainty that we will live in Heaven forever.

▶ **2 Corinthians 5:8**

What does the resurrection of Christ mean in our lives on a daily basis?

Jesus will build the _____.

At the beginning of this lesson, we saw Peter's declaration that Jesus is, in fact, God. It is on this truth that Jesus said He would build His church.

▶ **Matthew 16:18**

We will come back to this in Lesson 9. But for now, notice that Jesus purchased the church when He died on the cross, and because of His resurrection, He is the head of the church.

ACTS 20:28
Take heed therefore unto yourselves, and to all the flock, over the which the Holy Ghost hath made you overseers, to feed the church of God, which he hath purchased with his own blood.

NOTES

COLOSSIANS 1:18
And he is the head of the body, the church: who is the beginning, the firstborn from the dead; that in all things he might have the preeminence.

Jesus should be Lord of our _____.

When you trusted Jesus as your Saviour, you believed that you were a sinner in need of a Saviour and your good works were not enough to get you to Heaven, but that Jesus died on the cross to pay for your sins. You believed in Him and received the gift of eternal life.

ROMANS 6:23
For the wages of sin is death; but the gift of God is eternal life through Jesus Christ our Lord.

But your relationship with the Lord doesn't end there. He wants to not only be your Saviour, but also to be the Lord—the Master—of your life.

▶ **Luke 6:46**

The Bible tells us that _____ to the Word of God is a characteristic of a true believer in Jesus. If we love the Lord, we will gladly obey Him.

▶ **John 14:15**

We are not to simply study God's Word for _____, but for _____.

▶ **James 1:22**

And every spirit that confesseth not that Jesus Christ is come in the flesh is not of God: and this is that spirit of antichrist, whereof ye have heard that it should come; and even now already is it in the world.—1 John 4:3

JESUS 63

— APPLICATION —

The truth about who Jesus is has important applications for every Christian:

Reject any teacher who _____ or questions Jesus' deity. Often after someone becomes a Christian, those around that person—seeing his new spiritual interests—will try to draw him into their religious teachings. The Bible tells us that there are false religions that are actually of Satan and that any religion that does not teach that Jesus is God in the flesh is not of God. (For further study, see 2 Corinthians 11:3–4 and 1 John 4:3.)

Look for opportunities to tell _____ about who Jesus is and how they can be saved. In Lesson 12, you'll learn how to share the gospel with others, but you don't have to wait until then. You can simply share with someone else why Jesus died on the cross, and then tell them what He did for you when you asked Him to save you!

Pray about the burdens and temptations you are facing, and remember that He is _____ you. Because Jesus came to live in human flesh, He understands what we face and the struggles we feel. But because He is God, He can give us more than empathy; He can give us help! (See also Hebrews 4:15–16.)

NOTES

THIS STUDY IN REVIEW

1. Jesus Is God
2. Jesus Is the Saviour of the World
3. Jesus Is the Risen Lord

NOTES

Write 1 John 4:3 in the space below, and plan to memorize this verse so you can quote it to your discipler next week.

_____

_____

_____

_____

PREVIOUS MEMORY VERSES

———————————

2 TIMOTHY 3:16
1 JOHN 5:7

———————————

Read the five daily readings throughout this coming week, including answering the questions on day five. These questions are where you will pick up with your discipleship meeting next week.

DAY 1

The Names of God

For unto us a child is born, unto us a son is given: and the government shall be upon his shoulder: and his name shall be called Wonderful, Counsellor, The mighty God, The everlasting Father, The Prince of Peace. —**Isaiah 9:6**

[BIBLE READING]

Topical
Matthew 16:13–17;
1 John 4:3

New Testament in a Year
Matthew 10:21–42

Entire Bible in a Year
Genesis 36–38;
Matthew 10:21–42

Though God is one God, He identifies Himself by many names throughout the Bible. These names reveal to us some of the aspects of His personality and the ways in which He deals with us. We see several of these names in one verse—which gives prophetic descriptions of Jesus.

Wonderful—Though Jesus laid aside His glory when He came to earth, that was only a temporary veiling. Jesus is filled with all of the beauty and majesty of God, and He is wonderful.

For in him dwelleth all the fulness of the Godhead bodily.
—**Colossians 2:9**

Counsellor—All of us need advice and counsel as we go through life. All of the wisdom that we will ever need is available to us through Jesus Christ.

But of him are ye in Christ Jesus, who of God is made unto us wisdom, and righteousness, and sanctification, and redemption:
—**1 Corinthians 1:30**

Mighty God—This is an expression of the power that Jesus possesses. Far from being just a good man or a great teacher, He was also completely God with all power and authority.

NOTES

For by him were all things created, that are in heaven, and that are in earth, visible and invisible, whether they be thrones, or dominions, or principalities, or powers: all things were created by him, and for him:—**Colossians 1:16**

Everlasting Father—Jesus is not a created being. He is eternal, and equal with the Father. He has always been God, and always will be.

I beheld till the thrones were cast down, and the Ancient of days did sit, whose garment was white as snow, and the hair of his head like the pure wool: his throne was like the fiery flame, and his wheels as burning fire.—**Daniel 7:9**

Prince of Peace—Jesus provides us with a peace that is not dependent on our circumstances but on His love and presence.

Peace I leave with you, my peace I give unto you: not as the world giveth, give I unto you. Let not your heart be troubled, neither let it be afraid.—**John 14:27**

What an incredible God we serve!

_____

_____

_____

_____

_____

DAY 2

Power to Forgive

When Jesus had lifted up himself, and saw none but the woman, he said unto her, Woman, where are those thine accusers? hath no man condemned thee? She said, No man, Lord. And Jesus said unto her, Neither do I condemn thee: go, and sin no more.
—**John 8:10–11**

[BIBLE READING]

Topical
Romans 5:8; John 6:67–69

New Testament in a Year
Matthew 11

Entire Bible in a Year
Genesis 39–40; Matthew 11

When the Pharisees wanted to trap Jesus, they often tried to place Him in a position where He would have to choose between following the Law given to Moses by God and the law of the Romans who ruled Israel. The story of a woman taken in adultery is one such example.

In John 8, the Jews brought to Jesus a woman whom they said they caught in an adulterous act. Under Old Testament law, adultery was a capital offense, punishable by stoning. Yet under first-century Roman occupation, the Jews were forbidden from carrying out capital punishment for violations of Jewish law. Thus in order to trap Jesus, they asked Him what should be done to her.

Jesus saw right through their trap and issued His directive: *"So when they continued asking him, he lifted up himself, and said unto them, He that is without sin among you, let him first cast a stone at her"* (John 8:7). The men who were trying to trap Jesus could not face Him, and walked away. That left Jesus with a woman who knew she had done wrong.

The response Jesus made to her reveals so much about the way God treats us. He told her not to continue her sinful life, but He also forgave her. Many people live in bondage because of what they have done in the past. Yet one of the most wonderful truths of Scripture

NOTES

is that while there may be lingering consequences because of our sin, when God forgives, He never holds the past against us.

People may not let us off the hook, but God forgives completely. *"For I will be merciful to their unrighteousness, and their sins and their iniquities will I remember no more"* (Hebrews 8:12). The devil likes to remind us of what we did or failed to do, but God does not treat us that way. The blood that Jesus shed on the cross is a complete covering for all of our sins, both past and future. John wrote, *"But if we walk in the light, as he is in the light, we have fellowship one with another, and the blood of Jesus Christ his Son cleanseth us from all sin"* (1 John 1:7).

God knows everything we do—we cannot hide our sin from Him. Ever since the Garden of Eden when Adam and Eve tried to hide so God would not know they had eaten the forbidden fruit, people have been trying to cover sin. Yet when we come to God, He offers forgiveness. Rather than living with a broken relationship, we should run to Him for mercy. *"Let the wicked forsake his way, and the unrighteous man his thoughts: and let him return unto the Lord, and he will have mercy upon him; and to our God, for he will abundantly pardon"* (Isaiah 55:7).

_____

_____

_____

_____

_____

DAY 3

Choosing Your Own Parents

But when the fulness of the time was come, God sent forth his Son, made of a woman, made under the law, To redeem them that were under the law, that we might receive the adoption of sons.
—**Galatians 4:4–5**

[BIBLE READING]

Topical
John 3:16; John 1:3

New Testament in a Year
Matthew 12:1–23

Entire Bible in a Year
Genesis 41–42;
Matthew 12:1–23

There are dozens of Messianic prophecies in the Old Testament, many of them relating to the birth of Jesus Christ. From the first promise of a Saviour given to Adam and Eve and recorded in Genesis 3:15, there was an eager expectation for the coming of the Lord. As time passed, first years, then centuries and then millennia, there were still faithful people waiting and watching for His coming. Just as with everything God does, it did not happen according to man's schedule. It was only *"when the fulness of time was come"* that Jesus was born.

Just as one example, events were orchestrated that literally put the world in motion as the government in Rome declared a census which required people to return to their ancestral home town to be registered. That order from an occupying foreign power was probably a source of great frustration and annoyance to the people of Israel, but it was necessary to get Mary and Joseph from Nazareth to Bethlehem so that Jesus could be born there and the prophecy would be fulfilled. God is not bound by time as we are, and He is willing to wait and work behind the scenes to bring everything together in His perfect timing.

Mary and Joseph were not chosen at random or by accident. They were selected by God for the roles they would play in Jesus' life. Both of them were descendants of Israel's King David, but through different lines of the royal family. Joseph's ancestor had been cursed

NOTES

because of his evil life so that none of his descendants could ever be king. If Joseph had actually been Jesus' father, not only would Jesus have inherited a sin nature, but His ancestry would disqualify Him from taking the throne of David. But through His mother Mary, Jesus has a blood claim to be the ruler of Israel.

Every promise concerning Christ's coming was fulfilled to the letter. The time and place of His birth were specified by different men prophesying decades apart in different countries. There is no way for so many details to fall into place accidentally—God was at work. The fulfilled prophecies demonstrate that Jesus truly was the Messiah and the Son of God. And the knowledge that it all happened as it was foretold gives us full assurance that all of the things the Bible tells us about the future and the Second Coming of Christ will happen just as God says they will.

_____

_____

_____

_____

_____

DAY 4

Since He Is Lord

Jesus answered and said unto him, If a man love me, he will keep my words: and my Father will love him, and we will come unto him, and make our abode with him. He that loveth me not keepeth not my sayings: and the word which ye hear is not mine, but the Father's which sent me. —**John 14:23–24**

[BIBLE READING]

Topical
Luke 4:8; Matthew 28:18

New Testament in a Year
Matthew 12:24–50

Entire Bible in a Year
Genesis 43–45;
Matthew 12:24–50

We are saved by grace through faith alone—it is not the result of anything we do or don't do. Yet the fact that we do not earn our salvation does not mean that we are freed from all responsibility and obligation to obey. Jesus is not just our Saviour, He is also our Lord. Those who say that they love Him but do not obey His commands do not demonstrate genuine love. It is a contradiction to say, "No, Lord." As Lord, Jesus has full right to command us and expect to be obeyed.

When Ronald Reagan was president, he met with a Republican senator who was not willing to vote for a bill that Reagan very much wanted passed. After their conversation had been going on for a while, the senator said, "Mr. President, I would jump out of an airplane without a parachute if you said to, but…" President Reagan interrupted him with a single word, "Jump!" and the man reversed his position and cast his vote for the bill. He could not legitimately profess support without being willing to follow through and do what he was told.

The concept of a Christian who ignores what the Bible teaches may be acceptable to our society where rebellion and people deciding for themselves what is right and wrong is the common standard, but it is not acceptable to God. As Sovereign Lord, He demands and expects us to do what He says. Jesus told His disciples, "*If ye love me,*

NOTES

keep my commandments" (John 14:15). This is the motivation for our obedience—not fear or advancement, but love.

The Bible tells us that we are to not be content with our current spiritual state but are to be maturing. *"But grow in grace, and in the knowledge of our Lord and Saviour Jesus Christ. To him be glory both now and for ever. Amen"* (2 Peter 3:18). A vital part of our spiritual development is our growing level of obedience to the Lord. The more we do what He says, the more closely our lives will follow the pattern and example that Jesus set for us. Jesus said, *"And he that sent me is with me: the Father hath not left me alone; for I do always those things that please him"* (John 8:29). There is no Christian walk apart from obedience.

_____

_____

_____

_____

_____

DAY 5

Review of Week Three

[BIBLE READING]

Topical
Romans 5:12;
Romans 6:23

New Testament in a Year
Matthew 13:1–30

Entire Bible in a Year
Genesis 46–48
Matthew 13:1–30

The questions below cover the material we studied in this lesson and are given here to help you cement these truths in your mind and heart. Feel free to look back over previous pages as you answer these questions. When you begin the next lesson with your discipler, take a few minutes to discuss any questions you have from this week's material.

1. Why is it vital that we believe in the deity of Christ—that Jesus is God? _____
   _____
   _____
   _____

DAY 6

Topical
Romans 5:8;
1 John 2:2

New Testament in a Year
Matthew 13:31–58

Entire Bible in a Year
Genesis 49–50;
Matthew 13:31–58

2. What does the name *Emmanuel* mean? _____
   _____
   _____
   _____

DAY 7

Topical
John 1:12; 1 John 4:14

New Testament in a Year
Matthew 14:1–21

Entire Bible in a Year
Exodus 1–3;
Matthew 14:1–21

3. What verse tells us that Jesus understands our feelings, needs, and temptations not only by omniscient knowledge, but also by experience? _____
   _____
   _____
   _____

4. How did God prove His love for us? _____
   _____
   _____
   _____

NOTES

5. Why is it important in relation to Jesus' death for our sin that He actually is God? _____

_____

_____

_____

6. There are many evidences in Scripture for Jesus' deity, but what is the most spectacular? _____

_____

_____

_____

7. What is one of the ways we know someone is a false teacher and that we should reject their teaching? _____

_____

_____

_____

REVIEW

Take a few moments to review together last week's study, memory verse, and the daily readings. You can use these questions to spark dialogue:

1. What truth or principle stood out to you most in last week's study and/or devotional readings?

2. Since we last met, have you had opportunity to apply or share a truth from the previous study?

3. Do you have any questions related to last week's devotional readings or assignment?

INTRODUCTION

What a wonderful day it was in your life when you trusted Jesus as your Saviour, turning exclusively to Christ for your redemption. The Bible uses rich metaphors to describe that moment:

You passed from darkness to light.

ACTS 26:18

To open their eyes, and to turn them from darkness to light, and from the power of Satan unto God, that they may receive forgiveness of sins, and inheritance among them which are sanctified by faith that is in me.

You were born again.

JOHN 3:3

Jesus answered and said unto him, Verily, verily, I say unto thee, Except a man be born again, he cannot see the kingdom of God.

1 PETER 1:23

Being born again, not of corruptible seed, but of incorruptible, by the word of God, which liveth and abideth for ever.

You have been redeemed—bought back.

1 PETER 1:18–19

Forasmuch as ye know that ye were not redeemed with corruptible things, as silver and gold, from your vain conversation received by tradition from your fathers; But with the precious blood of Christ, as of a lamb without blemish and without spot:

You are adopted into God's family.

ROMANS 8:15

For ye have not received the spirit of bondage again to fear; but ye have received the Spirit of adoption, whereby we cry, Abba, Father.

All of that took place at the _____ you called on the Lord for salvation!

In this lesson, we'll look at some questions you may have about your salvation. For instance, can you lose your salvation? What if you don't *feel* saved? And is there anything you should do now that you are saved?

As we answer these questions from the Bible, you'll see some wonderful truths about the gift of salvation!

—————— LESSON FOUR ——————

Can I Lose My Salvation?

Sometimes after a person trusts Christ as Saviour, they begin to worry that maybe something they do wrong will make them _____ the promise of eternal life.

Thankfully, it is not _____ to ever lose your salvation. Here's why:

God's _____ is forever.

When God gives a gift, it's for keeps! And the gift of salvation is the gift of eternal life.

▶ **John 10:28–29**

By definition, *eternal* life can never end. It is yours forever.

▶ **John 5:24**

A gift is free, and once it has been received, it cannot be taken back. Salvation is God's gift to us that we possess for all of eternity.

▶ **Romans 6:23**

▶ **John 3:16**

Our _____ is sure.

When we accept Christ, we are born again into the family of God. Once we become a child of God, we remain His child for all of eternity. There is nothing we can do to cause God to disown us.

▶ John 6:37[1]

We have a "_____ deposit."

Like the "earnest money" you may be asked to put down when getting a loan to buy a house, so God has given us an "earnest" to assure us that He is going to follow through on giving us a home in Heaven.

▶ 2 Corinthians 1:22; 5:5

▶ Ephesians 1:13–14

The Holy Spirit will never leave you. You are _____ by Him.

So can you lose your salvation? _____. A thousand times no.

CONVERSATION STARTER

Describe a situation when your feelings didn't match reality—perhaps on a roller coaster, in an unfounded fear, or as a result of misinformation.

What If I Don't Feel Saved?

Sometimes our emotions don't match _____.

Sometimes a Christian may not *feel* saved and thus may doubt that they ever truly were saved.

God wants you to have _____ of your salvation —knowing that you are His child.

---

1. Additional references include John 1:12 and Galatians 4:5–7.

How can we have this assurance?

We have assurance because of God's _____.

God promised that anyone who calls on Him for salvation _____ (not *might*) be saved.

▶ **Romans 10:13**

The God who has promised to give us eternal life is a God who _____ lie. He always keeps His promises.

▶ **Titus 1:2**

We have assurance because of God's _____.

As mentioned a moment ago, the moment you trusted Christ as your Saviour, the Holy Spirit took up residence in you. The Bible tells us that the Holy Spirit assures our hearts of our relationship with God.

ROMANS 8:16

The Spirit itself beareth witness with our spirit, that we are the children of God:

We'll see in a later lesson that the Holy Spirit also convicts us when we do wrong so we will change.[2] But we can resist His voice. One of the dangers of that, however, is that if we refuse to listen to His voice convicting us, we may find that we don't hear His voice reassuring us of our salvation. Thus, sometimes Christians doubt their salvation because they have blocked the voice of the Holy Spirit giving them assurance.

---

2. See John 16:8 and Ephesians 4:30.

1 John 3:24

And he that keepeth his commandments dwelleth in him, and he in him. And hereby we know that he abideth in us, by the Spirit which he hath given us.

We have assurance because of God's _____.

There is absolutely _____ we—or any other person or thing—can do to separate us from our Heavenly Father's love.

▶ Romans 8:35–39

We have assurance because of God's _____ in our lives.

When we trust Christ as our Saviour, we are made a new person.

▶ 2 Corinthians 5:17

God begins to work in our lives in specific ways. As we see His work unfolding, we know it is the hand of God. Notice these evidences of salvation in a Christian's life:

Hunger for the Word of God
1 Peter 2:2

As newborn babes, desire the sincere milk of the word, that ye may grow thereby:

Growing obedience to God's commandments
1 John 2:3

And hereby we do know that we know him, if we keep his commandments.

Love for other Christians

1 JOHN 2:10

He that loveth his brother abideth in the light, and there is none occasion of stumbling in him.

As these evidences of salvation develop in our lives from the inside out, we have assurance that God is working in our lives.

We have assurance because of God's _____.

We will never lose our salvation because we sin. Since we cannot earn salvation by anything we do, we cannot lose it by what we do (or don't do) either.

Just as a child who disappoints their parents through something they do is still the parents' child, so the child of God who sins is still God's child. The Father/child relationship is still real, but the fellowship becomes strained.

It is not okay for us to just keep sinning without caring. In fact, as a loving Heavenly Father, God _____ us when we sin —and that correction is proof that we are His children.

▶ **Hebrews 12:5–11**

The very fact that God corrects us when we sin, with the goal of restoring our fellowship with Him, gives us assurance that we belong to Him.

So we see, God wants us to not only be saved, but to have assurance of our salvation—to have absolute _____ in our hearts that we have a sure relationship with Him.

CONVERSATION STARTER

Have you noticed a difference in how you feel when you sin before and after your salvation? Before you were saved, your conscience may have made you feel a little guilty when you sinned, but after you were saved, there is the added pain of the Holy Spirit convicting and chastening you when you sin.

Why Should I Be Baptized?

Baptism is an exciting step of _____ after you are saved because it is an outward expression of your inward decision. It is in no way part of your salvation, but it is one of the first ways we can demonstrate that we want to obey our Lord's commands.

JOHN 15:14
Ye are my friends, if ye do whatsoever I command you.

While baptism is not part of salvation, it is an important step of obedience to Christ. By following the Lord in believer's baptism, you are obeying Christ and showing others that you are _____ He is your Saviour.

Notice these important truths regarding baptism:

CONVERSATION STARTER

What group or passion or team do you like to be identified with? Perhaps a sports team or hobby. How do you let others know that you consider yourself part of that group? How is that similar or dissimilar to publicly identifying with Christ and His church through baptism?

Baptism is an _____.

The Bible teaches that baptism is a symbol—an outward expression of an inward decision.

In the life of every Christian, baptism is an important first step of obedience to God that declares to others your faith in Christ.

Just as a wedding ring identifies a husband with his wife, baptism identifies a Christian with Christ. That identity is with Christ's death, burial, and resurrection.

▶ **Romans 6:3–5**

Baptism is your way of saying to everyone, "Jesus saved me, and I'm not ashamed of Him. I want to live now for Him."

Baptism also identifies a Christian with the local church and its doctrine. In the New Testament, people who were baptized were added to the church.

▶ **Acts 2:41–42**

Baptism is for _____ Christian.

The Bible teaches that baptism is for anyone who has personally accepted Christ as Saviour. Baptism does not save or wash away sins. It simply shows on the outside what Jesus already did on the inside.

▶ **Acts 8:36–38**

There are three important reasons to be baptized:

Christ commands it. *Go ye therefore, and teach all nations, baptizing them in the name of the Father, and of the Son, and of the Holy Ghost:*—**Matthew 28:19**

Christ was our example. *Then cometh Jesus from Galilee to Jordan unto John, to be baptized of him.*—**Matthew 3:13**

Believers in the Bible practiced it. *Then they that gladly received his word were baptized: and the same day there were added unto them about three thousand souls.*—**Acts 2:41**

If you have trusted Christ as your Saviour and have not been baptized since, you should choose to be baptized as soon as you can.

Baptism should be by _____.

The word *baptize* literally means "to plunge or to dunk." The Bible teaches that you should be baptized in water by immersion rather than by sprinkling. Because baptism is a picture of Christ's death, burial, and resurrection, only immersion correctly pictures this.

Notice these Bible examples:

▶ **Mark 1:9–10**

▶ **Acts 8:38–39**

Other passages in Scripture that speak of baptism, use the word *buried*, showing that baptism in Bible days was understood to be by immersion.

ROMANS 6:4
Therefore we are buried with him by baptism into death: that like as Christ was raised up from the dead by the glory of the Father, even so we also should walk in newness of life.

COLOSSIANS 2:12
Buried with him in baptism, wherein also ye are risen with him through the faith of the operation of God, who hath raised him from the dead.

Baptism should take place _____ after salvation.

In the Bible, baptism always took place right after salvation. It was an immediate and glad response of someone who found salvation and wanted to publicly identify with Jesus.

▶ Acts 16:30–33

▶ Acts 2:41

Even if you were baptized before your salvation, you need to be baptized in accordance with Scripture _____ your salvation.

NOTES

The Christian who _____ to be baptized could be compared to a wife who refuses to accept her wedding ring. How can a Christian's relationship with Christ start off right if they refuse to follow Him or are ashamed of Him before others?

When a Christian is not willing to be baptized, they are missing the blessing of committing themselves to Christ through obedience and losing the _____ they might have through public identification with Him.

James 4:17

Therefore to him that knoweth to do good, and doeth it not, to him it is sin.

Baptism is an exciting step of obedience to your Saviour. If you have not been baptized since your salvation, make plans to do so soon!

APPLICATION

Salvation is the greatest gift any person has ever been given. But Satan will do everything he can to cause you to question if you are really a child of God.

To avoid or counter those doubts, there are three important steps you can take:

1. Settle in your own heart that salvation is forever. Record the date when you trusted Jesus as your Saviour somewhere where you will see it regularly (perhaps in the front of your Bible). Review the verses in this lesson and even memorize some of them. That way, if doubts begin to come to your mind, you have truth to use as ammunition against them.

THIS STUDY IN REVIEW

1. Can I Lose My Salvation?
2. What If I Don't Feel Saved?
3. Why Should I Be Baptized?

2. Share your testimony and your doubts (if and when they arise) with a mature Christian. (Your pastor or the person who is discipling you would be a good person to share this with.) Not every Christian encounters times of doubt concerning their salvation, but some do. Satan would have you think that you are all alone and that "real Christians" wouldn't have those questions. That is simply not true. Sharing these kinds of struggles with a mature Christian gives you a prayer partner—and someone to remind you of God's promises!

3. Publicly declare your salvation by being baptized. Baptism not only identifies you with Christ to others, but it has a way of cementing in your own heart the truth that Jesus has saved you—forever.

———— ASSIGNMENTS ————

Write Romans 8:16 in the space below, and plan to memorize this verse so you can quote it to your discipler next week.

_____

_____

_____

_____

Read the five daily readings throughout this coming week, including answering the questions on day five. These questions are where you will pick up with your discipleship meeting next week.

DAY 1

Your Spiritual Birthday

Verily, verily, I say unto you, He that heareth my word, and believeth on him that sent me, hath everlasting life, and shall not come into condemnation; but is passed from death unto life. —**John 5:24**

[BIBLE READING]

Topical
1 Peter 1:23

New Testament in a Year
Matthew 14:22–36

Entire Bible in a Year
Exodus 4–6;
Matthew 14:22–36

It is very important for us to understand that salvation is a one-time event, not a process. We are not being saved gradually, getting better and better until we reach a point where God sees that our good outweighs our bad and accepts us into His family. Salvation happens immediately in the moment when we place our faith in Christ alone for our salvation.

Jesus declared that those who believe—not believe that Jesus existed or was a good teacher, but put their trust in Him as the only hope of salvation—already have everlasting life. It is not something that we will get one day. Salvation is ours already. We sometimes speak of this as being "born again." This is a term that Jesus used to describe salvation: *"Jesus answered and said unto him, Verily, verily, I say unto thee, Except a man be born again, he cannot see the kingdom of God"* (John 3:3).

We do not remember our physical birth, but it is a single event that happened on a certain day in a specific place at a specific time. Our spiritual birthday, the day when we were born again, is likewise a single event that took place at a specific time. It is a day that we should never forget. Most people don't have trouble remembering when their birthday each year comes around (even though some may not want to admit how many they have had). A vital part of the assurance of our salvation is knowing when that wonderful event happened.

NOTES

Salvation is not something we have to wonder about. In fact, God does not want us to be confused or worried about whether we are saved. John wrote, *"These things have I written unto you that believe on the name of the Son of God; that ye may know that ye have eternal life, and that ye may believe on the name of the Son of God"* (1 John 5:13). Since salvation is not our doing, but all of God, and since He always keeps His promises, we have nothing to doubt.

Evangelist D. L. Moody said, "If someone asks if my name is Moody and I reply, 'I hope so' that would be very strange. I don't say 'I'm trying to be' I say 'I am.' If someone asks if I am a Christian, I ought to be able to give him a reason." Once you have trusted Christ as Saviour, don't allow anything to shake your faith that He has saved you just as He promised.

_____

_____

_____

_____

_____

DAY 2

Restoring Fellowship

Behold, the LORD'S hand is not shortened, that it cannot save; neither his ear heavy, that it cannot hear: But your iniquities have separated between you and your God, and your sins have hid his face from you, that he will not hear. — **Isaiah 59:1–2**

[BIBLE READING]

Topical
Romans 8:15

New Testament in a Year
Matthew 15:1–20

Entire Bible in a Year
Exodus 7–8;
Matthew 15:1–20

Nothing that we do or don't do can change our position in the family of God once we have been saved. Just as we did not get saved by our works, we do not maintain our salvation by our works. While it would be nice if we could reach a point where we always do the right thing and don't ever sin, that will not happen while we are here on earth. And while our sin does not change our standing with God, it certainly changes our relationship with Him.

All of us who have children know the experience of them doing something we told them not to do or failing to do what we have instructed. Are we disappointed and saddened? Of course. But they are still our children, and they do not stop being part of our family. Jesus said of His children, *"And I give unto them eternal life; and they shall never perish, neither shall any man pluck them out of my hand"* (John 10:28).

The knowledge of our security is wonderful, but it does not mean that we should take God's grace for granted. No child who loves his father or mother is content with a broken relationship with them. So what do we do to restore the relationship with God when we sin?

We must admit what we have done. Proverbs 28:13 says, *"He that covereth his sins shall not prosper: but whoso confesseth and forsaketh them shall have mercy."* The Bible concept of confession is not just

NOTES

saying that we have done something, but actually agreeing with God that what we did was wrong.

As long as we are trying to justify or excuse our actions, our relationship with God will continue to be hindered. The wonderful thing about God is that even though He knows everything, He doesn't hold things against us. Once we have confessed and forsaken our sin, as far as He is concerned it is over forever. He tells us, *"…for I will forgive their iniquity, and I will remember their sin no more"* (Jeremiah 31:34).

_____

_____

_____

_____

_____

DAY 3

Nothing Can Separate

For I am persuaded, that neither death, nor life, nor angels, nor principalities, nor powers, nor things present, nor things to come, Nor height, nor depth, nor any other creature, shall be able to separate us from the love of God, which is in Christ Jesus our Lord. —**Romans 8:38–39**

[BIBLE READING]

Topical
John 10:28–29

New Testament in a Year
Matthew 15:21–39

Entire Bible in a Year
Exodus 9–11;
Matthew 15:21–39

Being a Christian does not mean that things will always be easy for us. In fact, bad things happen to good people all the time. The difference for a believer is that we are never alone when difficult times come. In Romans 8:35 Paul lists seven calamities that come into our lives. *"Who shall separate us from the love of Christ? shall tribulation, or distress, or persecution, or famine, or nakedness, or peril, or sword?"* But he concludes that none of these can create a separation between us and God's love.

Paul was not speaking theoretically when he talked about trouble. He was beaten repeatedly, thrown into jail in more than one city, shipwrecked, and stoned. Eventually he would be killed in Rome for his faithful Christian witness. Yet despite all those troubles and the very real suffering he endured, Paul was not defeated or discouraged. He considered himself a victor. *"Nay, in all these things we are more than conquerors through him that loved us"* (Romans 8:37).

God does not measure triumph and defeat by the world's standards. He gives us the ultimate example of victory through what appears to be defeat with the cross. Satan no doubt rejoiced when Jesus died, but that was simply a necessary part of God's plan for our salvation. Every event that happens in our lives has a purpose, and no event that happens in our lives can defeat God's overwhelming love for us.

There are battles in the Christian life as we strive to live in a way that honors and pleases God in a fallen world. But there is nothing we face that can take us away from the love of God. That assurance sustains us through whatever trials we endure, and reminds us that no matter what, we are on the winning side.

None of us enjoy going through suffering and trials. Yet they are a normal and natural part of life. Peter wrote, *"Beloved, think it not strange concerning the fiery trial which is to try you, as though some strange thing happened unto you:"* (1 Peter 4:12). Instead of griping and complaining, we should go to God for the comfort and strength to endure what has come, trusting in His unfailing love to be our strength through the storms.

_____

_____

_____

_____

_____

DAY 4

I'm With Him

But ye are a chosen generation, a royal priesthood, an holy nation, a peculiar people; that ye should shew forth the praises of him who hath called you out of darkness into his marvellous light: Which in time past were not a people, but are now the people of God: which had not obtained mercy, but now have obtained mercy.
—1 Peter 2:9–10

[BIBLE READING]

Topical
Titus 1:2

New Testament in a Year
Matthew 16

Entire Bible in a Year
Exodus 12–13; Matthew 16

Dr. Robert Cialdini, a research scientist who teaches at Arizona State University, conducted a study to determine the impact of the school's football team on the attitude of the student body. What he found was that when the team won, students put on jerseys and school shirts and talked about how "we" won the game. When the team lost, school gear was hard to find, and the conversation revolved around how "they" blew it. In short, most students were only willing to identify with the team when it was winning.

God has called us as His children to be set apart from the world and clearly identified as His children. We should never "take off our jerseys" to hide that we are Christians. We should be proud to carry His name, and we should live in such a way that we bring honor and glory to our Father in Heaven. There are many ways in which we can identify ourselves as Christians.

Baptism. When Philip, one of the deacons in the early church, led a high ranking official from the government of Ethiopia to the Lord, the new believer immediately wanted to be baptized as a sign of his faith: *"And as they went on their way, they came unto a certain water: and the eunuch said, See, here is water; what doth hinder me to be baptized? And Philip said, If thou believest with all thine heart, thou* *mayest. And he answered and said, I believe that Jesus Christ is the Son of God"* (Acts 8:36–37).

Church membership. The Lord has given us the church for many reasons, and one of the most important is that it is a place of fellowship and encouragement. *"Not forsaking the assembling of ourselves together, as the manner of some is; but exhorting one another: and so much the more, as ye see the day approaching"* (Hebrews 10:25).

Love for each other. The way we treat other believers is one of the most important evidences to the world that we are Christians. Jesus said, *"By this shall all men know that ye are my disciples, if ye have love one to another"* (John 13:35).

When our Christianity is more about the way that we live than the title we carry and we are openly identified with Jesus, the world will see that there is something different about us—just as God intends.

_____

_____

_____

_____

_____

DAY 5

Review of Week Four

The questions below cover the material we studied in this lesson and are given here to help you cement these truths in your mind and heart. Feel free to look back over previous pages as you answer these questions. When you begin the next lesson with your discipler, take a few minutes to discuss any questions you have from this week's material.

1. What are some of the metaphors the Bible uses to describe the time you trusted Jesus as your Saviour? _____

    _____

    _____

    _____

2. Why is it impossible to ever lose your salvation? _____

    _____

    _____

    _____

3. How can we have assurance of our salvation? _____

    _____

    _____

    _____

4. Who assures our hearts of our relationship with God? _____

    _____

    _____

    _____

[BIBLE READING]

Topical
Romans 8:35–39

New Testament in a Year
Matthew 17

Entire Bible in a Year
Exodus 14–15; Matthew 17

DAY 6

Topical
Romans 6:3–5

New Testament in a Year
Matthew 18:1–20

Entire Bible in a Year
Exodus 16–18;
Matthew 18:1–20

DAY 7

Topical
James 4:17

New Testament in a Year
Matthew 18:21–35

Entire Bible in a Year
Exodus 19–20;
Matthew 18:21–35

5. What are the evidences of salvation in a Christian's life? _____

_____

_____

_____

6. What is the first way we can demonstrate that we want to obey our Lord's commands? _____

_____

_____

_____

7. What are three important reasons to be baptized? _____

_____

_____

_____

5 DEVELOPING A PRAYER LIFE

REVIEW

Take a few moments to review together last week's study, memory verse, and the daily readings. You can use these questions to spark dialogue:

1. What truth or principle stood out to you most in last week's study and/or devotional readings?

2. Since we last met, have you had opportunity to apply or share a truth from the previous study?

3. Do you have any questions related to last week's devotional readings or assignment?

INTRODUCTION

There are not enough words to describe the wonder and privilege of prayer. Prayer is how we bring our needs to God. It is how we unburden our hearts before Him. And it is one of the ways that we strengthen our relationship with Him.

Prayer is one of the earliest spiritual exercises you learn, and it is one that you will grow in throughout your entire Christian life.

In this lesson, we'll look at some of the basic truths regarding how to pray, what to pray for, and how to keep our prayer life strong.

LESSON FIVE

Prayer Is an Invitation

For the child of God, prayer is an invitation to the very throne room of Heaven.

▶ **Hebrews 4:15–16**

God invites us to bring our needs and requests to Him in prayer.

Prayer is _____ to God.

Sometimes people worry about what words to say when they pray. But at the most basic level, prayer is simply talking to God.

▶ **Jeremiah 33:3**

Prayer is _____ for our needs.

Amazingly, God cares about every need in our lives and invites us to bring them to Him in prayer.

▶ **Matthew 6:26**

God hears us.

NOTES

1 John 5:14

And this is the confidence that we have in him, that, if we ask any thing according to his will, he heareth us:

God cares about our troubles.

1 Peter 5:7

Casting all your care upon him; for he careth for you.

God desires to grant our requests.

Matthew 7:7

Ask, and it shall be given you; seek, and ye shall find; knock, and it shall be opened unto you:

Our needs may be physical, financial, emotional, or spiritual. In any and every case, God wants us to bring our needs to Him in prayer.

CONVERSATION STARTER

Share with one another an answer to prayer you have recently seen in your life.

Prayer Is a Command

God not only *invites* us to pray; He *tells* us to pray!

Colossians 4:2

Continue in prayer, and watch in the same with thanksgiving;

In fact, He even assumes that we will pray. Notice how when Jesus instructed His disciples concerning prayer He said "_____ ye pray," not "_____ ye pray."

Luke 11:2

And he said unto them, When ye pray, say, Our Father which art in heaven, Hallowed be thy name. Thy kingdom come. Thy will be done, as in heaven, so in earth.

So how should we pray?

Pray _____.

The best way to develop a meaningful prayer life is to pray on a regular, daily basis.

PSALM 5:3

My voice shalt thou hear in the morning, O LORD; in the morning will I direct my prayer unto thee, and will look up.

Prayer is not something we run to only in times of emergency. It is to be our regular communication with God.

Pray _____.

Although having a regular, established prayer time is important, we can (and should) pray at any time and any place.

1 THESSALONIANS 5:17

Pray without ceasing.

EPHESIANS 6:18

Praying always with all prayer and supplication in the Spirit, and watching thereunto with all perseverance and supplication for all saints;

Pray with _____.

Pray knowing that your Heavenly Father wants you to pray, hears your requests, and will do what is best for you.

HEBREWS 11:6

But without faith it is impossible to please him: for he that cometh to God must believe that he is, and that he is a rewarder of them that diligently seek him.

Matthew 21:22

And all things, whatsoever ye shall ask in prayer, believing, ye shall receive.

Pray with right _____.

God wants us to bring our personal and family needs to Him. But asking for our needs is different than asking with selfish motives.

James 4:2–3

Ye lust, and have not: ye kill, and desire to have, and cannot obtain: ye fight and war, yet ye have not, because ye ask not. Ye ask, and receive not, because ye ask amiss, that ye may consume it upon your lusts.

Pray according to _____ will.

God always answers our prayers, but His answers are not always "yes." Like a good parent, sometimes our Heavenly Father knows that what we want may not be best for us. Thus, sometimes He does not give us what we ask for, or He does not give it to us right away.

1 John 5:14

And this is the confidence that we have in him, that, if we ask any thing according to his will, he heareth us:

Luke 18:1

And he spake a parable unto them to this end, that men ought always to pray, and not to faint;

Pray in _____ name.

Praying in Jesus' name is praying by His will and authority.

JOHN 14:13
And whatsoever ye shall ask in my name, that will I do, that the Father may be glorified in the Son.

Pray with other _____.

The early church prayed together. Prayer with other Christians has a way of strengthening our faith and our boldness.

ACTS 1:14
These all continued with one accord in prayer and supplication, with the women, and Mary the mother of Jesus, and with his brethren.

ACTS 2:42
And they continued stedfastly in the apostles' doctrine and fellowship, and in breaking of bread, and in prayers.

Pray _____.

In addition to corporate prayer, every Christian should daily have a time of private prayer.

MATTHEW 6:5–6
And when thou prayest, thou shalt not be as the hypocrites are: for they love to pray standing in the synagogues and in the corners of the streets, that they may be seen of men. Verily I say unto you, They have their reward. But thou, when thou prayest, enter into thy closet, and when thou hast shut thy door, pray to thy Father which is in secret; and thy Father which seeth in secret shall reward thee openly.

Pray _____.

The opportunity and privilege of prayer is not something to be taken lightly. We don't pray, simply as a "religious exercise." We pray as one who is presenting their requests to God!

JAMES 5:16

…The effectual fervent prayer of a righteous man availeth much.

MATTHEW 6:7–8

But when ye pray, use not vain repetitions, as the heathen do: for they think that they shall be heard for their much speaking. Be not ye therefore like unto them: for your Father knoweth what things ye have need of, before ye ask him.

Pray with a _____ .

When Jesus' disciples asked Him to teach them how to pray (see Luke 11:1), He gave them a model for what to pray about.

▶ **Matthew 6:9–13**

These verses are not given so we repeat them every day as our prayer. They are given so we know what to pray for.

- *Our Father which art in heaven*—Pray in confidence of your relationship with the Father.

- *Hallowed be thy name*—Worship God in your prayer time.

- *Thy kingdom come*—Pray wanting God's kingdom to be advanced.

- *Thy will be done in earth, as it is in heaven*—Pray with submission to God's will.

- *Give us this day our daily bread*—Ask God to meet your needs and the needs of others.

- *And forgive us our debts, as we forgive our debtors*—Don't harbor bitterness or unforgiveness in your heart.

NOTES

- *And lead us not into temptation, but deliver us from evil:*—Ask God to help you overcome temptation.

- *For thine is the kingdom, and the power, and the glory, for ever. Amen.*—Pray with a heart for God's glory to be advanced.

Some people have found the following acrostic of the word *ACTS* helpful to guide them in their prayer time:

A stands for **adoration:** Praise God for who He is. Tell Him how thankful you are for His goodness to you, His holiness, etc.

C stands for **confession:** Ask God to bring to mind any sins you've not already confessed to Him, and ask Him to forgive you.

T stands for **thanksgiving:** Thank God for recent blessings and answers to prayer He has given.

S stands for **supplication:** Bring your requests before the Lord, praying for your needs as well as the needs of others.

As you begin to spend regular time in prayer, you will find that your prayer life will grow.

Prayer Is Fellowship with God

Prayer is not simply a method of transaction for asking and getting. It is part of our needful communication with God. Because communication is part of a _____, it is vital that we keep that relationship right.

Beware of _____ to prayer.

The Bible tells us of specific ways our prayers become hindered.

- _____ sin hinders our prayers.

  PSALM 66:18

  If I regard iniquity in my heart, the Lord will not hear me:

  ISAIAH 59:1–2

  Behold, the LORD's hand is not shortened, that it cannot save; neither his ear heavy, that it cannot hear: But your iniquities have separated between you and your God, and your sins have hid his face from you, that he will not hear.

- _____ hinders our prayers.

  MARK 11:25

  And when ye stand praying, forgive, if ye have ought against any: that your Father also which is in heaven may forgive you your trespasses.

  1 PETER 3:7

  Likewise, ye husbands, dwell with them according to knowledge, giving honour unto the wife, as unto the weaker vessel, and as being heirs together of the grace of life; that your prayers be not hindered.

- _____ for God's Word hinders our prayers.

  PROVERBS 28:9

  He that turneth away his ear from hearing the law, even his prayer shall be abomination.

NOTES

Restore _____ through prayer.

When we realize we have a hindrance in prayer in our lives, how do we remove it? Through prayer!

1 JOHN 1:9

If we confess our sins, he is faithful and just to forgive us our sins, and to cleanse us from all unrighteousness.

We simply confess our sin to the Lord and ask Him to forgive us. Thankfully, God is faithful to always forgive us when we do.

——— APPLICATION ———

What a privilege God has given us through prayer!

One of the most important steps in your Christian life is to begin praying on a regular basis. You will find that prayer is both a relief (allowing you to unburden your heart to the Lord) and a blessing (as you see God answer your prayers).

There are two vital steps that you can take to begin developing a meaningful prayer life:

1. **Plan a regular prayer** _____. To pray with consistency requires a plan. Set aside a time of day—like you would for important appointments—when you can pray for specific requests to the Lord. Begin with a small amount of time, perhaps five or ten minutes, and increase it as you find your need to pray increasing.

    My daily prayer time: _____

2. **Begin a prayer** _____. The best way to remember the important requests in your life and in the lives of those you love is to write down a list of whom and what you are praying for. This can be as simple as a handwritten list in a notebook, or it can be typed in an electronic program. In whatever way you create your list, be sure to leave room by each request to record when and how God answers that prayer!

NOTES

THIS STUDY IN REVIEW

1. Prayer Is an Invitation
2. Prayer Is a Command
3. Prayer Is Fellowship with God

NOTES

**PREVIOUS MEMORY
VERSES**

2 Timothy 3:16
1 John 5:7
1 John 4:3
Romans 8:16

———— ASSIGNMENTS ————

Write Jeremiah 33:3 in the space below, and plan to memorize this verse so you can quote it to your discipler next week.

_____

_____

_____

_____

Read the five daily readings throughout this coming week, including answering the questions on day five. These questions are where you will pick up with your discipleship meeting next week.

DAY 1

He Cares for You

For he knoweth our frame; he remembereth that we are dust. As for man, his days are as grass: as a flower of the field, so he flourisheth. For the wind passeth over it, and it is gone; and the place thereof shall know it no more. But the mercy of the LORD is from everlasting to everlasting upon them that fear him, and his righteousness unto children's children; —**Psalm 103:14–17**

[BIBLE READING]

Topical
Hebrews 4:15–16

New Testament in a Year
Matthew 19

Entire Bible in a Year
Exodus 21–22; Matthew 19

One of the greatest blessings that we have as Christians is that we are part of God's family. God is not a distant figure far off in Heaven who does not care about what happens on earth. He is personally, intimately involved in our lives every day, and He cares about us. No challenge or problem that we face is too great for Him to handle, and no difficulty or obstacle we face is too small for Him to care—we are His children and He loves us.

Peter wrote, *"Casting all your care upon him; for he careth for you"* (1 Peter 5:7). All of us understand the joy of being able to meet a need for someone we love. When we are able to provide a treasured toy for a young child or meet a substantial need for a friend, we feel a very real sense of pleasure that is beyond what we would experience if we used those same resources on ourselves. God has all of the resources necessary to meet every need that we have.

There is no part of our lives that is not important to Him. We rightfully go to Him with great needs, pleading for healing or the salvation of a loved one, as well as those needs that might seem small to others but matter greatly to us, asking for help completing a difficult task or guidance in making a decision. There is no topic that is off-limits to prayer.

NOTES

Hezekiah prayed for healing. *"Then Hezekiah turned his face toward the wall, and prayed unto the* Lord, *And said, Remember now, O* Lord, *I beseech thee, how I have walked before thee in truth and with a perfect heart, and have done that which is good in thy sight. And Hezekiah wept sore"* (Isaiah 38:2–3).

Elijah prayed about the weather. *"Elias was a man subject to like passions as we are, and he prayed earnestly that it might not rain: and it rained not on the earth by the space of three years and six months"* (James 5:17).

Jesus prayed in thanks for food. *"And he commanded the multitude to sit down on the grass, and took the five loaves, and the two fishes, and looking up to heaven, he blessed, and brake, and gave the loaves to his disciples, and the disciples to the multitude"* (Matthew 14:19).

So pray about everything, remembering that God cares for you!

_____

_____

_____

_____

_____

DAY 2

The Antidote to Worry

Therefore take no thought, saying, What shall we eat? or, What shall we drink? or, Wherewithal shall we be clothed? (For after all these things do the Gentiles seek:) for your heavenly Father knoweth that ye have need of all these things. But seek ye first the kingdom of God, and his righteousness; and all these things shall be added unto you. — **Matthew 6:31–33**

[BIBLE READING]

Topical
Jeremiah 33:3

New Testament in a Year
Matthew 20:1–16

Entire Bible in a Year
Exodus 23–24;
Matthew 20:1–16

A study in 2012 revealed that one in five adult Americans was taking some kind of medication for fear, worry, depression, or anxiety. Spending for these types of drugs amounted to more than 33 billion dollars that year. Worry is a very real part of life, and it can lead to profound physical and emotional difficulties.

Thankfully, God's Word tells us how our minds can be filled with peace rather than consumed by worry. Philippians 4:6–7 says, *"Be careful* [filled with worry] *for nothing; but in every thing by prayer and supplication with thanksgiving let your requests be made known unto God. And the peace of God, which passeth all understanding, shall keep your hearts and minds through Christ Jesus."* Instead of being overcome with worry, we have the choice to trust in God and to take our problems to Him in prayer. When we worry we are saying that we do not believe that God loves us enough to meet our needs. When we pray we are saying that we fully trust Him to give us whatever He knows is best.

We see this illustrated in the life of Daniel. Though he was a foreigner, he rose to a high position in the Persian empire. His enemies conspired against him, getting a law passed to make it illegal to pray to anyone except the king. Daniel kept right on praying anyway. When he was arrested, he was thrown into a den of lions, but God delivered him from what seemed to be certain death. Throughout his ordeal Daniel never exhibited fear. The secret is that he "prayed," "gave thanks," and was "making supplication" (Daniel 6:10–11) instead of worrying.

Years ago, someone sold a poster with a picture of a panda bear. The bear is shown looking at the camera with what appears to be a bemused expression. The caption reads: "Don't tell me worry doesn't do any good. The things I worry about never happen." In truth, worry does nothing to help and much to hinder. It takes a toll on us physically, emotionally, and spiritually. When we trust God instead of worrying, He provides a peace that is beyond human explanation.

_____

_____

_____

_____

_____

DAY 3
What to Pray For

And when the disciples saw it, they marvelled, saying, How soon is the fig tree withered away! Jesus answered and said unto them, Verily I say unto you, If ye have faith, and doubt not, ye shall not only do this which is done to the fig tree, but also if ye shall say unto this mountain, Be thou removed, and be thou cast into the sea; it shall be done. And all things, whatsoever ye shall ask in prayer, believing, ye shall receive. —**Matthew 21:20–22**

[BIBLE READING]

Topical
1 John 5:14

New Testament in a Year
Matthew 20:17–34

Entire Bible in a Year
Exodus 25–26;
Matthew 20:17–34

Sometimes we are tempted to believe we should only pray about the "really big" needs—or that maybe we shouldn't pray for ourselves at all, but only for others. Sometimes we think that our daily needs and concerns are beneath God's notice or attention. But God loves us and delights in doing things for us. In fact, the Bible gives us an open invitation to enter God's presence through prayer and to seek His help: *"Let us therefore come boldly unto the throne of grace, that we may obtain mercy, and find grace to help in time of need"* (Hebrews 4:16).

During Jesus' life, a prominent man named Jairus had a daughter who was sick. He came to ask Jesus for help, but before they reached his house, word came that the daughter had died. Listen to how this message was presented. *"While he yet spake, there cometh one from the ruler of the synagogue's house, saying to him, Thy daughter is dead; trouble not the Master"* (Luke 8:49). What a sad view of God to think that we are a nuisance when we pray. We don't trouble God with our prayers—we delight Him with our presence. Jesus went to the house and brought the little girl back to life.

Dr. John Rice said, "The way to live is to pray day by day and take all your burdens to the Lord and ask whatever you want. God is not

NOTES

old and tired. Ask whatever you want. He loves you. Remember He said in Romans 8:32, '*He that spared not his own Son, but delivered him up for us all, how shall he not with him also freely give us all things?*' Oh, then take your burden to the Lord. Set out to pray about everything. Pray for money when you need money. Pray for food when you need food. Let your requests be made known to God—whatever you need. Oh, you have not because you ask not!"

It is a tragedy for Christians to have needs that go unmet simply because they do not pray. Relying on our Father's love for us as His children, we should trust His promises and make our petitions known to Him. "*Trust in him at all times; ye people, pour out your heart before him: God is a refuge for us. Selah*" (Psalm 62:8).

_____

_____

_____

_____

_____

DAY 4

Promises for Prayer

For every one that asketh receiveth; and he that seeketh findeth; and to him that knocketh it shall be opened. Or what man is there of you, whom if his son ask bread, will he give him a stone? Or if he ask a fish, will he give him a serpent? If ye then, being evil, know how to give good gifts unto your children, how much more shall your Father which is in heaven give good things to them that ask him?—**Matthew 7:8–11**

[BIBLE READING]

Topical
1 Peter 5:7

New Testament in a Year
Matthew 21:1–22

Entire Bible in a Year
Exodus 27–28;
Matthew 21:1–22

There are two conditions that have to be met for a promise to be of any value. First, the person who makes the promise has to be able to do what he promises. If someone who is flat broke promises to give you a million dollars, that isn't very meaningful. Second, the person who makes the promise has to be willing to do what he promises. Having the resources to fulfill a promise doesn't matter if the person will not do it even though he could.

Thankfully, when it comes to God's promises, both of those conditions are met. He is able to supply any need that we have from His unlimited resources and is willing to meet our needs and to hear and answer our prayers because of His great love for us. A Christian who does not pray is missing out on so many blessings and benefits simply through not asking. James wrote, *"Ye lust, and have not: ye kill, and desire to have, and cannot obtain: ye fight and war, yet ye have not, because ye ask not"* (James 4:2).

Notice these promises from God's Word, and let them encourage you as you pray!

Promise for provision: *"But my God shall supply all your need according to his riches in glory by Christ Jesus"* (Philippians 4:19).

NOTES

Promise for power: *"If ye then, being evil, know how to give good gifts unto your children: how much more shall your heavenly Father give the Holy Spirit to them that ask him?"* (Luke 11:13).

Promise for joy: *"Hitherto have ye asked nothing in my name: ask, and ye shall receive, that your joy may be full"* (John 16:24).

Promise for deliverance: *"And call upon me in the day of trouble: I will deliver thee, and thou shalt glorify me"* (Psalm 50:15).

Promise for revival: *"If my people, which are called by my name, shall humble themselves, and pray, and seek my face, and turn from their wicked ways; then will I hear from heaven, and will forgive their sin, and will heal their land"* (2 Chronicles 7:14).

_____

_____

_____

_____

_____

DAY 5

Review of Week Five

The questions below cover the material we studied in this lesson and are given here to help you cement these truths in your mind and heart. Feel free to look back over previous pages as you answer these questions. When you begin the next lesson with your discipler, take a few minutes to discuss any questions you have from this week's material.

1. What can we talk to God about in prayer? _____
   _____
   _____
   _____

2. When should we pray? _____
   _____
   _____
   _____

3. Where should we pray? _____
   _____
   _____
   _____

4. What is one way of strengthening our faith and our boldness
   in prayer? _____
   _____
   _____
   _____

[BIBLE READING]

Topical
Matthew 7:7

New Testament in a Year
Matthew 21:23–46

Entire Bible in a Year
Exodus 29–30;
Matthew 21:23–46

DAY 6

Topical
Ephesians 6:18

New Testament in a Year
Matthew 22:1–22

Entire Bible in a Year
Exodus 31–33;
Matthew 22:1–22

DAY 7

Topical
Hebrews 11:6

New Testament in a Year
Matthew 22:23–46

Entire Bible in a Year
Exodus 34–35;
Matthew 22:23–46

NOTES

5. What are some of the things that can be a hindrance to our prayers? _____

    _____

    _____

    _____

6. How do we get rid of these hindrances? _____

    _____

    _____

    _____

7. What are a few ways you can begin developing a meaningful prayer life? _____

    _____

    _____

    _____

6 YOUR RELATIONSHIP WITH GOD'S WORD

REVIEW

Take a few moments to review together last week's study, memory verse, and the daily readings. You can use these questions to spark dialogue:

1. What truth or principle stood out to you most in last week's study and/or devotional readings?

2. Since we last met, have you had opportunity to apply or share a truth from the previous study?

3. Do you have any questions related to last week's devotional readings or assignment?

INTRODUCTION

In our first study, we saw that God's Word is infallible and unchanging. It was written by God through human authors and has been preserved for us. In this study, however, we will see our relationship to God's Word—how it touches us personally.

NOTES

God's Word is not only true; it is life changing. It can meet the deepest needs of your life and answer the greatest questions of your heart. In this study, let's examine how God's Word meets your needs, how you can access its power and wisdom, and how it will transform your life.

—————— LESSON SIX ——————

God's Word Can Meet Your Needs

The Bible is _____ for your life.

The Bible has the answers to guide us in every area of life.

▶ **2 Timothy 3:16**

Notice these four areas in which God's Word helps us.

Doctrine—It teaches us what to believe.

Reproof—It shows us where we are wrong.

Correction—It tells us how to get back on track when we are wrong.

Instruction—It gives direction for daily living the truth.

Every one of these are vital for a Christian who wants to build their life upon a foundation of truth.

The Bible nourishes your spiritual _____.

Just as a baby will not grow without milk, so a Christian will not grow without taking in God's Word. We should hunger for God's Word spiritually, just as we hunger for food physically.

▶ **1 Peter 2:2**

NOTES

Lasting growth in a Christian's life can only come through the transforming power of God's Word. Let's now look at how we can make God's Word part of our regular routines of life.

God's Word Should Be in Your Routines

For the Word of God to impact you personally, you must encounter it regularly. In other words, it must be part of your daily living.

There are several ways that God instructs us to include God's Word as part of our lives.

_____ it daily.

Even as we need physical nourishment daily, so we should be daily taking in the nourishment of God's Word.

▶ **Job 23:12**

One of the best habits you can develop to help your spiritual growth is to set aside time to daily read the Word of God. This is not simply a three-month assignment for a discipleship course; it is a lifelong habit of growing Christians.

Here are some brief tips to help you gain the most from your Bible reading:

1. Set a time and place to read regularly.

2. Follow a Bible reading plan.

3. Ask God to guide you before you read. (See Psalm 119:18)

4. Ask questions about what you read.

5. Keep a journal or notebook to record verses and passages that the Holy Spirit applies to your life.

CONVERSATION STARTER

What Bible reading plan are you using right now? Have you tried using a journal? Share ideas with one another for how you remember what you've read throughout the day.

NOTES

_____ it consistently.

In addition to your daily Bible reading, you need to hear the preaching and teaching of God's Word at church.

▶ **Romans 10:17**

▶ **Hebrews 10:25**

_____ on it continually.

Refuse to simply let God's Word go in one ear and out the other. The key to letting God's Word transform your heart, mind, and actions is to meditate—to think—on it so we can obey it.

▶ **Joshua 1:8**

▶ **Psalm 1:2–3**

CONVERSATION STARTER

What is an area of your life or spiritual growth that you would benefit by having specific verses to address? Take a few minutes together—either now or at the end of this lesson—to look up verses from Appendix C, so you can begin memorizing and applying them.

One of the disciplines of meditation is to begin _____ Scripture so you have it available to think on.

▶ **Psalm 119:11**

You are already beginning to memorize Scripture in your weekly assignments. Determine now that you will make Scripture memory (and ongoing review of what you have learned) a lifelong habit.

Choose verses to memorize based on what you are learning or areas you know you need growth in. For instance, if you are struggling with worry, you might memorize Philippians 4:6 and 1 Peter 5:7 so you have those verses in your mind and heart to think on when you begin to worry. God's Word has the truths you need for every area of your life! In Appendix C there is a list of verses related to various topics that you may find helpful.

_____ it regularly.

In addition to your Bible reading, church attendance, and Bible memory, you will come across times in your life or areas of confusion when you need to know what the Bible says about a particular topic or truth.

Although you may not dig deeper into Bible study every day, have times in your life when you do study God's Word beyond simply reading it.

This kind of Bible study often takes place in adult Bible classes at church. It is also something you should do on your own with various topics or words. You can use the concordance in the back of your Bible to help.

▶ **2 Timothy 2:15**

_____ it faithfully.

When it comes to the Bible, it's not just about what we _know;_ it is about what we _do_ with what we know.

▶ **James 1:22–25**

So, read it, hear it, memorize and meditate on it, and study it. But don't neglect to _____ it!

God's Word Will Transform Your Life

As you grow in your knowledge and application of God's Word, you will find that it will literally transform your life.

▶ **Romans 12:2**

NOTES

God's plan for our transformation as Christians is that it would come from the _____, that as our minds are _____ by the truths of the Word of God, those truths would then impact our actions and change our lives.

God's Word is to be so much a part of our lives, particularly our _____, that it is like a branch engrafted into a tree.

▶ **James 1:21**

There are many ways that God's Word can transform our lives, but notice three in particular.

_____ the Bible increases your knowledge of God.

We don't read God's Word merely like a textbook. We read it to know our Lord better.

▶ **2 Peter 3:18**

_____ the Bible produces Christlike maturity.

When you become a Christian, you are "born again" into the family of God. From that point forward, God desires for you to be on a path of spiritual maturity, becoming more like Jesus Christ. As you let the Holy Spirit use God's Word to transform your life, you become more and more like Jesus.

▶ **2 Corinthians 3:18**

_____ of the Bible produces spiritual discernment.

As you continue to read, study, meditate on, and obey God's Word, your ability to apply it to specific life situations and to discern right from wrong in sensitive areas of your life will develop.

▶ **Hebrews 5:13–14**

Always remember that the goal of reading, studying, and memorizing God's Word is not merely knowledge; it is _____. A growing Christian will always be able to point to recent transformation in their life that has come about by the Word of God.

NOTES

CONVERSATION STARTER

Share a recent way God's Word has worked in your life—perhaps giving you comfort, encouragement, or change.

APPLICATION

One of the key decisions a Christian can make to continue growing in their walk with God is to make God's Word part of the regular routines of life.

Set a regular time for reading your Bible. Have a daily time and place that you read the Word of God. If possible, it's good to combine this with the prayer time that you began last week. Prayer and Bible reading go hand in hand because they are both communication with God. Prayer is our way of talking to God, and Bible reading is His way of talking to us.

My daily time to read God's Word: _____

Develop a habit of applying God's Word. It is not enough to simply read or hear the Word of God. We must apply it to our lives. Begin a habit of asking yourself the question, "How can I apply this today?" after you read God's Word or hear it preached.

THIS STUDY IN REVIEW

1. God's Word Can Meet Your Needs
2. God's Word Should Be in Your Routines
3. God's Word Will Transform Your Life

NOTES

Make Scripture memory an ongoing practice in your life.
Memorizing God's Word allows us to meditate on it throughout
the day and to use it when we don't have ready access to our Bibles.
Some Christians feel that Bible memory is difficult or impossible
for anyone older than school-aged. In reality, however, we all
memorize things that are important to us. (You know your phone
number and address and probably some favorite sports teams.)
Scripture memory is always worth the effort. It just requires patient
discipline and commitment.

ASSIGNMENTS

Write 1 Peter 2:2 in the space below, and plan to memorize this verse
so you can quote it to your discipler next week.

_____

_____

_____

_____

Consider pausing your current Bible plan for the next few weeks to
begin writing out the book of 1 John. This short epistle is packed
with practical truths for Christian growth and contains only 105
verses. Writing just 3–5 verses per day will allow you to complete
it in less than a month. One benefit to writing out portions of
God's Word is that it helps you focus on each word and phrase,
which increases your understanding and ability to make practical
applications to your life.

Read the five daily readings throughout this coming week, including
answering the questions on day five. These questions are where you
will pick up with your discipleship meeting next week.

**PREVIOUS MEMORY
VERSES**

2 TIMOTHY 3:16
1 JOHN 5:7
1 JOHN 4:3
ROMANS 8:16
JEREMIAH 33:3

DAY 1
Daily Nourishment

Wherefore laying aside all malice, and all guile, and hypocrisies, and envies, and all evil speakings, As newborn babes, desire the sincere milk of the word, that ye may grow thereby: If so be ye have tasted that the Lord is gracious. —**1 Peter 2:1–3**

[BIBLE READING]

Topical
2 Timothy 3:16

New Testament in a Year
Matthew 23:1–22

Entire Bible in a Year
Exodus 36–38;
Matthew 23:1–22

One thing that you never have to teach a healthy newborn is to want to eat. From the very first day of life, a baby wants food —and if it doesn't get that food right away, you will know about it! The Bible describes new believers as baby Christians. In the same way that regular intake of good food is essential to healthy physical development, regular intake of the Word of God is essential to healthy spiritual development.

In the Old Testament, when God delivered the Israelites from Egypt, they had to cross a great wilderness. They were a large group, and there were no natural food sources available to provide for them. God provided miraculously through a food called manna. Each morning it would appear on the ground outside the camp. The people were instructed to go out and gather it, and that would be their food for the day.

The Bible says, *"And they gathered it every morning, every man according to his eating: and when the sun waxed hot, it melted"* (Exodus 16:21). Notice that they had to go out early in the morning to gather the manna because if they waited until the sun had fully risen and the day had gotten hot, it would melt away. Likewise, morning is a great time to gather spiritual nourishment from God's Word.

They were also told that they could not save any for the next day. New manna fell every morning, and it had to be gathered anew each day. When some of the people decided to save some instead of going out the next day to gather more, the manna they kept developed worms and started to stink and they had to throw it out. There is a vital principle here—our spiritual food has to be gathered day after day. We cannot store up enough Bible once or twice a week to make it through our daily lives.

In His model prayer, Jesus instructed us to pray: *"Give us this day our daily bread"* (Matthew 6:11). This is not just true for our physical provision. We need new spiritual food every day, and God provides it for us in the pages of His Word. We simply have to put forth the effort to gather what we need from the Bible.

_____

_____

_____

_____

_____

DAY 2

Beware of Junk Food

This book of the law shall not depart out of thy mouth; but thou shalt meditate therein day and night, that thou mayest observe to do according to all that is written therein: for then thou shalt make thy way prosperous, and then thou shalt have good success. Have not I commanded thee? Be strong and of a good courage; be not afraid, neither be thou dismayed: for the LORD thy God is with thee whithersoever thou goest. —**Joshua 1:8–9**

[BIBLE READING]

Topical
1 Peter 2:2

New Testament in a Year
Matthew 23:23–39

Entire Bible in a Year
Exodus 39–40;
Matthew 23:23–39

A 2012 study revealed that Americans ate more than 10 billion donuts the previous year. That is about three dozen donuts for every man, woman, and child living in the country. We also consume vast amounts of fast food—with much of it eaten in cars as we rush from one place to the next. It is no wonder that Americans are growing more and more obese. One of the worst things about eating junk food is that it destroys our appetite for healthy food.

The same thing is true in the spiritual realm. The victorious and successful Christian life requires repeated and sustained intake of the Word of God. There are many things other than the Word of God that people are filling up on, leaving them little time or interest in becoming serious students of Scripture. If our minds and hearts are filling up on music, media, and relationships that are dishonoring to God, we will have less of an appetite for growing our relationship with God. To take it a step further, if our minds and hearts are filled up with even "innocent" entertainment that consumes our focus, we'll struggle to have a real hunger for the spiritual nourishment we need. It's like eating several donuts before dinner.

NOTES

Jesus promised that the Holy Spirit would equip us to understand the Word of God. He said, *"Howbeit when he, the Spirit of truth, is come, he will guide you into all truth: for he shall not speak of himself; but whatsoever he shall hear, that shall he speak: and he will shew you things to come"* (John 16:13). The Bible is God's truth, and the Holy Spirit who lives within every believer helps us understand what God is saying and how it applies to our lives.

One of the things that Christians today need the most is a steady diet of the Word of God rather than mental junk food. If we spend less time filling up on fluff that may be fun but has little lasting value, we will find that we have more time and desire for a serious look at the Bible, and that spiritual growth in our lives will follow.

_____

_____

_____

_____

_____

DAY 3

Tools for Memory

Blessed is the man that walketh not in the counsel of the ungodly, nor standeth in the way of sinners, nor sitteth in the seat of the scornful. But his delight is in the law of the LORD; and in his law doth he meditate day and night. And he shall be like a tree planted by the rivers of water, that bringeth forth his fruit in his season; his leaf also shall not wither; and whatsoever he doeth shall prosper.
—**Psalm 1:1–3**

[BIBLE READING]

Topical
Romans 10:17

New Testament in a Year
Matthew 24:1–28

Entire Bible in a Year
Leviticus 1–3;
Matthew 24:1–28

The Bible talks often of the importance of meditating on God's Word. This is not the "empty your mind" kind of meditation that is popular in so many circles but a focused meditation that involves focused thinking about what the Bible says. Even as we go about other tasks, we can have the messages of Scripture running through our minds. However, meditation requires that we first have the Word of God in our minds. Too many Christians regard Bible memorization as something for children, but it is a powerful and important spiritual discipline for adults as well.

The Psalmist wrote, "*Thy word have I hid in mine heart, that I might not sin against thee*" (Psalm 119:11). Hiding God's Word in our hearts is simply a metaphor for memorizing the Bible so that we have it with us even when we do not have access to the words on a printed page or an electronic device. We never know when temptation will come, so we need the Bible in our hearts. Here are some practical steps to help you memorize Scripture:

Write it down. If you take the time to write out a verse on a note card or a small piece of paper, it will help you fix the words in your mind. You may even want to get a larger sheet of paper and write a single verse a number of times.

NOTES

Say it out loud. If you have your verse cards with you, take one out and read the verse out loud a few times. This way you are both seeing and hearing the words, and this will help you reinforce your learning of the verse.

Repeat it often. At different times throughout the day, review the verse. At first you can simply read it; then as you become more familiar with the words, start trying to recall as much of the verse as you can without looking at what you have written down.

Go over the verse just before bed. Many of us learned in college that a quick review of notes just before going to sleep helped us remember things more clearly the next day. Ending the day with a verse of Scripture is a great way to clear your mind of the troubles of the day as well.

_____

_____

_____

_____

_____

DAY 4

In One Ear and Out the Other

For if any be a hearer of the word, and not a doer, he is like unto a man beholding his natural face in a glass: For he beholdeth himself, and goeth his way, and straightway forgetteth what manner of man he was. But whoso looketh into the perfect law of liberty, and continueth therein, he being not a forgetful hearer, but a doer of the work, this man shall be blessed in his deed. —**James 1:23–25**

[BIBLE READING]

Topical
Hebrews 10:25

New Testament in a Year
Matthew 24:29–51

Entire Bible in a Year
Leviticus 4–5;
Matthew 24:29–51

Jerome Moody should have been safe that summer day in 1985. He was attending a party held by the New Orleans Recreation Department attended by more than one hundred lifeguards. They were gathered to celebrate a year in which no one had drowned in any of the city pools. But when the lifeguards began clearing the pool (there were four on duty in addition to all those attending the party as guests), they found the body of the thirty-one-year-old man drowned at the bottom of the pool. What began as a celebration ended as a tragedy.

Knowing the truth and receiving warnings about the dangers of evil is not the same thing as heeding the truth and changing our behavior as a result. We can understand the importance of filling our minds with Scripture, we can attend church regularly and hear the Word preached and taught, we can even agree that what we are hearing and learning is true and important. But unless we actually act on what we learn is true, we are missing out on God's protection and blessing.

One of the greatest tests of whether we have the right relationship with the Word of God is whether it is consistently and continually changing our thinking and our actions. If we read the Bible without anything being altered, we may be hearers, but we are not doers.

NOTES

The Bible is a living, active, convicting and life-changing book given to us not just for instruction but for improvement. *"For the word of God is quick, and powerful, and sharper than any twoedged sword, piercing even to the dividing asunder of soul and spirit, and of the joints and marrow, and is a discerner of the thoughts and intents of the heart"* (Hebrews 4:12).

When people can read the Bible without it bringing about change in their lives, they are in a dangerous position. Paul warned us regarding what happens to those who continue to reject the Word: *"...having their conscience seared with a hot iron"* (1 Timothy 4:2). We need to be quick to respond to whatever God convicts us of in His Word.

_____

_____

_____

_____

_____

DAY 5

Review of Week Six

The questions below cover the material we studied in this lesson and are given here to help you cement these truths in your mind and heart. Feel free to look back over previous pages as you answer these questions. When you begin the next lesson with your discipler, take a few minutes to discuss any questions you have from this week's material.

1. As listed in 2 Timothy 3:16, what are the four areas that are vital for Christians who wants to build their life upon a foundation of truth? _____

_____

_____

_____

2. What are some ways you can include the Bible in your routine? _____

_____

_____

_____

3. What is God's plan for our transformation as Christians? _____

_____

_____

_____

4. What are three ways that God's Word can transform our lives?

_____

_____

_____

[BIBLE READING]

Topical
Joshua 1:8

New Testament in a Year
Matthew 25:1–30

Entire Bible in a Year
Leviticus 6–7;
Matthew 25:1–30

DAY 6

Topical
Psalm 1:2–3

New Testament in a Year
Matthew 25:31–46

Entire Bible in a Year
Leviticus 8–10;
Matthew 25:31–46

DAY 7

Topical
2 Timothy 2:15

New Testament in a Year
Matthew 26:1–25

Entire Bible in a Year
Leviticus 11–12;
Matthew 26:1–25

5. What is a result of obeying the Bible? _____

_____

_____

_____

6. Why should you continue reading the Bible? _____

_____

_____

_____

7. What can help you meditate on God's Word? _____

_____

_____

_____

THE HOLY SPIRIT

REVIEW

Take a few moments to review together last week's study, memory verse, and the daily readings. You can use these questions to spark dialogue:

1. What truth or principle stood out to you most in last week's study and/or devotional readings?

2. Since we last met, have you had opportunity to apply or share a truth from the previous study?

3. Do you have any questions related to last week's devotional readings or assignment?

INTRODUCTION

At the moment of your salvation, God Himself came to live within you in the person of the Holy Spirit.

NOTES

EPHESIANS 1:13

In whom ye also trusted, after that ye heard the word of truth, the gospel of your salvation: in whom also after that ye believed, ye were sealed with that holy Spirit of promise,

But what does that mean for your life on a daily basis? How does the Holy Spirit work in your life? Is it mysterious and mystical? Or is it real and practical?

In this study, we will see how the Holy Spirit works in your life, how you can cooperate with Him, and what the result of His work will be.

—————— LESSON SEVEN ——————

The Holy Spirit Ministers to Your Heart

Shortly before Jesus was crucified, He explained to His disciples that He would soon be leaving them but that the Holy Spirit would take His place in their lives.

JOHN 14:16

And I will pray the Father, and he shall give you another Comforter, that he may abide with you for ever;

As we saw in Lesson 2, the Holy Spirit is God—He is part of the Trinity. And as we saw in Lesson 4, the Holy Spirit indwells our hearts the moment we trust Christ as our Saviour. From that point on, He begins ministering to our hearts in tender and significant ways.

He is the divine _____.

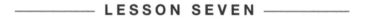

Jesus referred to the Holy Spirit as the "Comforter" four times in His discussion with His disciples before His crucifixion.

But the fruit of the Spirit is love, joy, peace, longsuffering, gentleness, goodness, faith, Meekness, temperance: against such there is no law.—Galatians 5:22–23

HOLY SPIRIT 139

JOHN 14:16

And I will pray the Father, and he shall give you another Comforter, that he may abide with you for ever;

▶ John 14:26

▶ John 15:26

▶ John 16:7

Christians deal with heartaches and trials just as unbelievers do. Sometimes Christians even have additional trouble *because* they are Christians.[1] Yet, the Holy Spirit is there to comfort us. He reminds us of God's promises and assures us by His very presence in our lives that God has not left us alone.

He guides you to _____.

Without the Holy Spirit's guidance in our lives, we would be left to navigate our way through life's daily decisions and concerns on our own. If we listen to the Holy Spirit, however, He will often bring Scriptures and biblical principles to mind that speak to the needs of our lives.

▶ John 14:26

▶ John 16:13

Part of His work in guiding us is to help us understand the Bible. Remember, the Holy Spirit inspired the Bible. So when you are confused about what the Bible means, remember to ask the Author—who is within you—to help you as you study.

NOTES

CONVERSATION STARTER

Have you ever been reading a book and wished you could ask the author a question? When you read the Bible you do have the Author with you. Ask Him to give you understanding before you read.

---

1. This was certainly a common experience of Christians in the first century. Often they would endure severe persecution because of their faith in Christ. Even then, however, God promised them His help, grace, and strength. See Acts 8:1, 11:19, 13:50, and Romans 8:35.

He strengthens you for _____.

In Lesson 10, you will discover that the Holy Spirit has specially and supernaturally equipped every believer to serve in the local church. But even with His equipping, we sometimes grow weary and faint. The Holy Spirit renews our hope and gives us energy from within.

▶ **Romans 15:13**

▶ **Ephesians 3:16**

He empowers your _____.

One of the earliest desires of a new Christian is to share the good news of salvation with others. But you cannot convince others by your own cleverness or persuasion to trust Jesus as their Saviour. The Holy Spirit uses your witness (telling others what Jesus did for you) and convicts those whom you talk to of their need for Him.

▶ **Acts 1:8**

▶ **Acts 5:32**

Every day, the Holy Spirit is with you to minister to your heart in ways you may not even be aware of. As you learn to recognize and rely on His work in your life, you will see how needful it is and learn to depend on it as you grow in your Christian life.

Being Filled with the Holy Spirit Makes the Christian Life Work

Have you ever considered how _____ the Christian life is? Truthfully, trying harder to be better in our own

But the fruit of the Spirit is love, joy, peace, longsuffering, gentleness, goodness, faith, Meekness, temperance: against such there is no law.—Galatians 5:22–23

HOLY SPIRIT ⟨141⟩

NOTES

strength is an exercise in futility. But the Holy Spirit empowers change in our lives from the _____ out. Let's see how God designed this to work:

Scripture instructs us to be _____ with the Spirit.

The fullness of the Holy Spirit is not to be confused with the indwelling of the Holy Spirit. As we've already seen, when we accepted Christ as our personal Saviour, the Holy Spirit began to dwell in us permanently.[2]

But now, He desires to fill us up—to _____ our actions and reactions.

▶ **Ephesians 5:18**

This verse gives us a picture of a person who is drunk. The inebriated person is not in control of themselves; they are under the influence of another substance. Even so, the Holy Spirit wants us to daily yield to Him so that we obey and allow Him to control us.

Scripture instructs us to _____ the Spirit.

Growth in the Christian life takes place in the daily choices—as day by day we make the decision to "walk in the Spirit."

▶ **Galatians 5:16, 25**

This is a matter of saying "no" to our fleshly impulses and saying "yes" to the Holy Spirit.

CONVERSATION STARTER

It has been wisely stated, "When we are filled with the Holy Spirit, it is not that we have more of Him but that He has more of us." Discuss together: are there areas in your life that you need to yield over to the Holy Spirit?

---

2. Ephesians 1:13–14

Scripture warns us not to _____ against the Spirit.

Christians can grieve and quench the work of the Holy Spirit in their lives.

_____ the Holy Spirit takes place when we willfully sin even when He convicts our hearts that we are doing wrong.

▶ **Ephesians 4:30–31**

_____ the Holy Spirit takes place when we continually ignore or resist His promptings. When we do this, after a time, we will cease to hear His voice.

▶ **1 Thessalonians 5:19**

There is nothing more frustrating than trying to live the Christian life in human strength. But God never asked us to do that. Instead, He comes alongside to guide us, invites us to surrender to Him, and fills us with His power to live godly lives.

The Fruit of the Spirit Is Evidence of His Transformation in Your Life

The incredible blessing of the Spirit-filled life is that as the Holy Spirit transforms your life from the inside, it begins to show in some very specific ways on the outside. His work shows up in many ways that are referenced throughout the New Testament, but in Galatians 5:22–23, we have a succinct list:

GALATIANS 5:22–23

But the fruit of the Spirit is love, joy, peace, longsuffering, gentleness, goodness, faith, Meekness, temperance: against such there is no law.

But the fruit of the Spirit is love, joy, peace, longsuffering, gentleness, goodness, faith, Meekness, temperance: against such there is no law.—Galatians 5:22–23

HOLY SPIRIT 143

As these qualities, known collectively as "the fruit of the Spirit," continue to develop in your life, they are evidence that the Holy Spirit is at work. Let's consider each of them briefly:

NOTES

The Holy Spirit produces _____.

▶ 1 Corinthians 13:4–7

The Holy Spirit produces _____.

▶ John 15:11

The Holy Spirit produces _____.

▶ John 16:33

The Holy Spirit produces _____.

Longsuffering is the ability to suffer long with other people or situations. It is patience or endurance.

▶ 2 Timothy 2:3

The Holy Spirit produces _____.

▶ 1 Thessalonians 2:7

The Holy Spirit produces _____.

▶ Galatians 6:10

The Holy Spirit produces _____.

▶ Luke 17:5

The Holy Spirit produces _____.

Meekness is not weakness. It is strength under God's control. It is yielding our way for God's glory.

▶ **Matthew 5:5**

▶ **Titus 3:2**

The Holy Spirit produces _____.

Temperance is the opposite of excess. It is self-control—a disciplined life.

▶ **1 Corinthians 9:23–24**

Take a moment and look back over the list above. You could work ten lifetimes and never perfect that list. Or you could yield to the Holy Spirit each day and let Him grow this fruit in you.

But the fruit of the Spirit is love, joy, peace, longsuffering, gentleness, goodness, faith, Meekness, temperance: against such there is no law.—Galatians 5:22–23

HOLY SPIRIT   145

APPLICATION

The work of the Holy Spirit in our lives is so significant that we will reference different aspects of it in every remaining lesson of this course. But His greatest work in your life hinges on your willingness to yield to Him.

There are three vital ways you should yield to the Holy Spirit:

Make a _____ commitment to yield every part of your life to Him. If you have not done so already, pray and tell the Lord that you are wholly willing for Him to work in your life in any and every way He will.

Daily _____ your commitment to yield to Him. Life has a way of undermining our commitment to live for God. As the pressures and struggles of life come, sometimes we forget who we belong to and who is right there beside us—the Holy Spirit! It is helpful to begin each day with a simple prayer, "Holy Spirit, I surrender to You today. I want to live for You and obey You. Help me to hear Your voice, and use me in the lives of others around me." It really is that simple.

Specifically _____ the Holy Spirit to develop the areas in your life that you see are lacking. Look again at the list of the fruit of the Spirit. What do you see lacking in your life? Ask the Holy Spirit to develop that in you, and be attentive to the means He uses—perhaps messages in church or conversations with Christian friends. Perhaps begin a Bible study on that topic of Christian growth. (Ask your mentor to help you get started.)

NOTES

THIS STUDY IN REVIEW

1. The Holy Spirit Ministers to Your Heart
2. Being Filled with the Holy Spirit Makes the Christian Life Work
3. The Fruit of the Spirit is Evidence of His Transformation in Your Life

NOTES

PREVIOUS MEMORY
VERSES

2 TIMOTHY 3:16
1 JOHN 5:7
1 JOHN 4:3
ROMANS 8:16
JEREMIAH 33:3
1 PETER 2:2

——— ASSIGNMENTS ———

Write Galatians 5:22–23 in the space below, and plan to memorize this verse so you can quote it to your discipler next week.

_____

_____

_____

_____

Read the five daily readings throughout this coming week, including answering the questions on day five. These questions are where you will pick up with your discipleship meeting next week.

DAY 1

A Resident Comforter

But when the Comforter is come, whom I will send unto you from the Father, even the Spirit of truth, which proceedeth from the Father, he shall testify of me: And ye also shall bear witness, because ye have been with me from the beginning. —**John 15:26–27**

[BIBLE READING]

Topical
John 14:16

New Testament in a Year
Matthew 26:26–50

Entire Bible in a Year
Leviticus 13;
Matthew 26:26–50

Bob Greene of the *Chicago Tribune* told the story of a fifteen-year-old boy in Missouri who was diagnosed with an advanced form of leukemia. He was told that his only hope was an aggressive series of chemotherapy treatments that would produce devastating side effects. As you can imagine the young man was discouraged. In an effort to help cheer him, his aunt ordered flowers to be sent to his hospital. When the floral arrangement arrived, there was a second note from a twenty-two-year-old clerk at the flower shop. She told the young man that she had experienced the same disease and treatment as a seven year old and survived. Greene concluded, "In a hospital filled with millions of dollars of the most sophisticated medical equipment…it was a salesclerk in a flower shop who gave Douglas hope and the will to carry on."

All of us face difficulties and challenges, and we need encouragement and comfort. However the reality is that sometimes those who could offer us hope do not. Yet even in those moments when it seems that there is no one who cares for us, we always have the Holy Spirit. He never leaves or forsakes us. The Greek word translated "Comforter" means someone who is called to help us.

When we are tired and discouraged, the Holy Spirit provides comfort. The primary means through which He works in our hearts and minds is through the Scriptures. Jesus said, "*But the Comforter, which is the Holy Ghost, whom the Father will send in*

NOTES

my name, he shall teach you all things, and bring all things to your remembrance, whatsoever I have said unto you" (John 14:26). If we do not have the Word of God being put into our hearts and minds through reading, studying, memorizing and meditating on the Scriptures, we are taking away His tools to work and limiting the comfort the Holy Spirit can bring to us.

The Lord does not abandon us in the hard times. Through the indwelling of the Holy Spirit, He is a constant presence in the life of every believer. He is God's promise of our eternal security and our abiding hope.

_____

_____

_____

_____

_____

DAY 2

Inside Out Renewal

For which cause we faint not; but though our outward man perish, yet the inward man is renewed day by day. For our light affliction, which is but for a moment, worketh for us a far more exceeding and eternal weight of glory; While we look not at the things which are seen, but at the things which are not seen: for the things which are seen are temporal; but the things which are not seen are eternal.
—**2 Corinthians 4:16–18**

[BIBLE READING]

Topical
John 16:7

New Testament in a Year
Matthew 26:51–75

Entire Bible in a Year
Leviticus 14;
Matthew 26:51–75

Life is more than we can manage on our own. Trying to live the Christian life apart from the power of God is a guaranteed path to frustration and despair. There are constant attacks from the devil as he seeks to discourage and defeat us. Just like a car needs to be filled with gas again and again to keep running, we need a source of strength and renewal, and that is one of the things that the Holy Spirit does for us.

There are sources of strength that are inward and spiritual that produce a positive physical effect on us as well. When Jesus finished witnessing to the woman at the well in Samaria, the disciples came to Him with food. He did not need physical food to be refreshed because His spirit had been blessed by seeing a lady come to faith in Him as the Messiah and then bring many people from her town to Him as well. *"But he said unto them, I have meat to eat that ye know not of"* (John 4:32).

The key for us to avoid being dragged down by the cares of the world is to stay in touch with the Holy Spirit. If we cut ourselves off from His influence by willful sin, embracing the world, or forsaking the fellowship of other Christians, we should not expect to receive His renewing power to meet our needs. We need the Comforter, and we must not reject His ministry. When we yield ourselves to His control, we receive the strength to face the world again.

During the 1992 Olympics, British runner Derek Redmond tore his hamstring in a 400-meter race. He attempted to finish under his own power, limping toward the finish line. Finally he collapsed on the track. Then a large man burst through the security lines and came to his aid. It was Derek's father, Jim Redmond. He put his son's arm across his shoulders and half carried him the rest of the way around the track. He renewed his son's strength to reach the finish line. This is a wonderful illustration of the work of renewal that the Holy Spirit performs in our lives.

_____

_____

_____

_____

_____

DAY 3

Filled for Service

As every man hath received the gift, even so minister the same one to another, as good stewards of the manifold grace of God. If any man speak, let him speak as the oracles of God; if any man minister, let him do it as of the ability which God giveth: that God in all things may be glorified through Jesus Christ, to whom be praise and dominion for ever and ever. Amen. —**1 Peter 4:10–11**

[BIBLE READING]

Topical
Romans 15:13

New Testament in a Year
Matthew 27:1–26

Entire Bible in a Year
Leviticus 15–16;
Matthew 27:1–26

The filling of the Holy Spirit and the power that He produces in our lives, our prayers, our preaching, our teaching, and our witnessing is for a specific purpose. God is not looking for people who desire to bring glory to themselves. He wants people who are willing to yield to His purposes and be used as He sees fit.

Picture a glove lying on a table. What does it do? Nothing. It stays exactly where it was left. It has no ability to accomplish anything on its own. It has no will of its own. However, when that glove is filled with a hand, it can move. It can throw a snowball or drive a car or swing a golf club or carry a package. What is the difference? The difference is the filling. It is the same way in our lives. When we are filled with the Holy Spirit, we become useful in God's service.

When we talk about being filled with the Holy Spirit, we are talking about being under His control. The Spirit-filled Christian does not go where *he* wants to go. He does not think what *he* wants to think. He does not do what *he* wants to do. Instead he does what *God* wants. There is a great struggle going on in the hearts of many believers for control. We know that God intends for us to be useful in His service. We know that He has good works He wants us to perform. Yet we are reluctant to yield to the direction and filling of the Holy Spirit.

NOTES

Some people have great natural talents and abilities. Yet human ability cannot accomplish God's work. Only a yielded believer who is filled with the Spirit can accomplish things of lasting value for the Lord. This is the calling of God on every Christian. Not all of us will be involved in ministry as a full time profession like pastors and other church workers. But all of us are to be witnesses and examples, sharing the gospel with those around us. The work of the church needs all of its members to be involved. This requires the fullness of the Holy Spirit on the part of each of us.

_____

_____

_____

_____

_____

DAY 4

Portrait of a Spirit-Filled Christian

But the fruit of the Spirit is love, joy, peace, longsuffering, gentleness, goodness, faith, Meekness, temperance: against such there is no law. And they that are Christ's have crucified the flesh with the affections and lusts. If we live in the Spirit, let us also walk in the Spirit. —**Galatians 5:22–25**

[BIBLE READING]

Topical
Acts 5:32

New Testament in a Year
Matthew 27:27–50

Entire Bible in a Year
Leviticus 17–18;
Matthew 27:27–50

In the early church, the apostles selected a group of men to serve the needs of the widows in the congregation. We call these men the first deacons, because of the role that they played in the church. The apostles did not just pick anyone. They looked for men with certain character traits that would make sure they were suited for the job. *"Wherefore, brethren, look ye out among you seven men of honest report, full of the Holy Ghost and wisdom, whom we may appoint over this business"* (Acts 6:3). One of the men they selected was Stephen.

We don't know anything about Stephen's background or training, but we do know that he was filled with the Holy Spirit. He was not a preacher—just a man in the church who could be trusted to take care of what needed to be done. His witnessing was so powerful that his enemies hired witnesses to lie about Stephen and brought him to trial. And in the fullness of the Spirit, Stephen preached one of the most powerful sermons ever recorded.

Most of Acts 7 is the message that Stephen delivered when he was brought before the Sanhedrin, the Jewish religious governing body. We've already seen the importance of the Word of God to the work of the Holy Spirit in our lives, and Stephen's sermon is filled with direct quotes and illustrations from the Old Testament. He revealed how again and again the nation of Israel had refused to obey God. That is no surprise because Jesus said of the Holy Spirit, *"And when he is come, he will reprove the world of sin, and of righteousness, and of judgment"* (John 16:8).

Being filled with the Holy Spirit gives us the courage and power to be effective in presenting the gospel, even to a hostile world that does not want to hear the message. The power of the Holy Spirit was so strong on Stephen's life that his enemies killed him so they wouldn't have to hear the truth any more. Though Stephen died for his faithful witness, he also saw a glimpse of Heaven and was received by Jesus standing up to meet him. *"But he, being full of the Holy Ghost, looked up stedfastly into heaven, and saw the glory of God, and Jesus standing on the right hand of God,"* (Acts 7:55).

_____

_____

_____

_____

_____

DAY 5

Review of Week Seven

The questions below cover the material we studied in this lesson and are given here to help you cement these truths in your mind and heart. Feel free to look back over previous pages as you answer these questions. When you begin the next lesson with your discipler, take a few minutes to discuss any questions you have from this week's material.

1. Give some examples of how the Holy Spirit ministers to our hearts. _____
   _____
   _____
   _____

2. Whose job is it to convict others to trust Jesus as their Saviour? _____
   _____
   _____
   _____

3. What does Scripture say about allowing the Holy Spirit to work in the Christian life? _____
   _____
   _____
   _____

4. What does it mean when the Holy Spirit desires to fill us? ____
   _____
   _____
   _____

[BIBLE READING]

Topical
Ephesians 5:18

New Testament in a Year
Matthew 27:51–66

Entire Bible in a Year
Leviticus 19–20;
Matthew 27:51–66

DAY 6

Topical
Ephesians 4:30–31

New Testament in a Year
Matthew 28

Entire Bible in a Year
Leviticus 21–22;
Matthew 28

DAY 7

Topical
1 Corinthians 9:23–24

New Testament in a Year
Mark 1:1–22

Entire Bible in a Year
Leviticus 23–24;
Mark 1:1–22

NOTES

5. What happens after we continually grieve and quench the Holy Spirit? _____

_____

_____

6. Where is a list of the fruit of the Spirit in the Bible, and what are the fruits of the Spirit? _____

_____

_____

_____

7. What are three ways you should yield to the Holy Spirit? _____

_____

_____

_____

THE LIFE OF A DISCIPLE

———— REVIEW ————

Take a few moments to review together last week's study, memory verse, and the daily readings. You can use these questions to spark dialogue:

1. What truth or principle stood out to you most in last week's study and/or devotional readings?

2. Since we last met, have you had opportunity to apply or share a truth from the previous study?

3. Do you have any questions related to last week's devotional readings or assignment?

———— INTRODUCTION ————

True discipleship is so much more than a course; it is a commitment to follow Christ unconditionally.

▶ **Matthew 16:24**

During Christ's ministry on earth, He had multitudes of people who followed Him and many people who believed on Him. But few people were willing to follow Him unconditionally.

LUKE 14:25–27, 33

And there went great multitudes with him: and he turned, and said unto them, If any man come to me, and hate not his father, and mother, and wife, and children, and brethren, and sisters, yea, and his own life also, he cannot be my disciple. And whosoever doth not bear his cross, and come after me, cannot be my disciple….So likewise, whosoever he be of you that forsaketh not all that he hath, he cannot be my disciple.

In this lesson, we will look at what the life of a disciple looks like. Being a true disciple is a process of surrendering daily, battling sin in our lives, and living a lifestyle that is pleasing to God.

What does it mean to fully follow Jesus? As someone once said, "Salvation is the miracle of a moment; discipleship is the process of a lifetime."

So what does the life of a disciple look like?

——————— **LESSON EIGHT** ———————

A Disciple Is Fully Surrendered to God

Full surrender to God is the beginning point of true discipleship.

▸ **Romans 12:1**

Notice three truths about surrender based on Romans 12:1.

It is _____ by God's mercy to us: *I beseech you therefore, brethren, by the mercies of God…*

There hath no temptation taken you but such as is common to man: but God is faithful, who will not suffer you to be tempted above that ye are able; but will with the temptation also make a way to escape, that ye may be able to bear it.—1 Corinthians 10:13

DISCIPLE 159

NOTES

It is the realization of the great mercy God has shown to us that compels us to surrender our lives back to Him.

It is _____: *...that ye present your bodies a living sacrifice, holy, acceptable unto God...*

First-century readers of this passage would have immediately connected the word "sacrifice" to the Old Testament animal sacrifices—a complete transaction. But for us, it is to be a *living* sacrifice. This means that we surrender *every* area of our lives to the Lord. This includes our relationships, activities, entertainment, money, possessions, goals, dreams, time—everything. Of course, this doesn't mean that we have no relationships, activities, entertainment, etc., but that we give God control over each of these areas and are surrendered to follow His direction in each.

It is _____: *...which is your reasonable service.*

Jesus gave His *life* for us. Giving ours back to Him is the least we could do.

Jesus made full surrender a clear condition of discipleship.

MATTHEW 10:37–38

He that loveth father or mother more than me is not worthy of me: and he that loveth son or daughter more than me is not worthy of me. And he that taketh not his cross, and followeth after me, is not worthy of me.

He is to have the first place in our lives—above every human relationship or commitment.

CONVERSATION STARTER

Is there someone to whom you feel you will be indebted for life? Perhaps they saved your life in a near-death experience, or they supported you during a difficult season, and you would do absolutely anything for them. That level of gratefulness is the idea expressed in Romans 12:1.

A Disciple Battles Sin and the Flesh

One of the most discouraging realizations for a new Christian is that they still sin. It would be nice if when we got saved, our ability to sin vanished, but that's simply not the case. As long as we are on this earth, we will battle sin.

Sin begins in the form of a temptation—a desire that draws us away from God.

▶ James 1:13–15

There are _____ main sources of temptation.

These three forces are constantly working against us.

The world—The world's systems, philosophies, and practices are directed against God.

1 JOHN 2:15–16
Love not the world, neither the things that are in the world. If any man love the world, the love of the Father is not in him. For all that is in the world, the lust of the flesh, and the lust of the eyes, and the pride of life, is not of the Father, but is of the world.

The flesh—Before you were saved, your mind, will, and emotions were trained to live apart from God. The old patterns of your mind, will, and emotions are at odds with the new patterns God wants to create in your life.

GALATIANS 5:17–24
For the flesh lusteth against the Spirit, and the Spirit against the flesh: and these are contrary the one to the other: so that ye cannot do the things that ye would. But if ye be led of the Spirit, ye are not under the law. Now the works of the flesh are manifest, which are these; Adultery,

There hath no temptation taken you but such as is common to man: but God is faithful, who will not suffer you to be tempted above that ye are able; but will with the temptation also make a way to escape, that ye may be able to bear it.—1 Corinthians 10:13

DISCIPLE (161)

fornication, uncleanness, lasciviousness, Idolatry, witchcraft, hatred, variance, emulations, wrath, strife, seditions, heresies, Envyings, murders, drunkenness, revellings, and such like: of the which I tell you before, as I have also told you in time past, that they which do such things shall not inherit the kingdom of God. But the fruit of the Spirit is love, joy, peace, longsuffering, gentleness, goodness, faith, Meekness, temperance: against such there is no law. And they that are Christ's have crucified the flesh with the affections and lusts.

The devil—Satan actively and persistently targets the child of God with temptation—so much so, that one of his names is even "the tempter."

MATTHEW 4:3
And when the tempter came to him, he said, If thou be the Son of God, command that these stones be made bread.

God has given us the _____ to overcome temptation.

Thankfully, although we are often tempted to sin, God has given us the power to overcome temptation. When Jesus died for us on the cross, He broke the power that sin has over us, setting us free to respond to His power in us.

▶ **Romans 6:6**

Note: The phrase "our old man" refers to our old nature that had no power to say "no" to sin.

Temptation itself is not sin. When we feel tempted, we have the power to resist the temptation.

▶ **1 Corinthians 10:13**

NOTES

What is the "way of escape" that God has given us? Notice these ways God has given us to overcome temptation:

_____ **the Word of God.** Even Jesus used the Word of God when He was tempted by the devil in the wilderness.[1] When you experience regular temptation or sin in a particular area, find several verses (perhaps ask your discipler to help you) that deal with that area. Then memorize those verses so you have them in your heart at the time of temptation.

PSALM 119:11
Thy word have I hid in mine heart, that I might not sin against thee.

_____ **you don't have to sin.** God's grace gives you the power to say "no" to sin.

TITUS 2:11–12
For the grace of God that bringeth salvation hath appeared to all men, Teaching us that, denying ungodliness and worldly lusts, we should live soberly, righteously, and godly, in this present world;

_____ **temptation when possible.** Sometimes we set ourselves up for temptation by making it easy to sin. The Bible calls this making "provision for the flesh."

ROMANS 13:14
But put ye on the Lord Jesus Christ, and make not provision for the flesh, to fulfil the lusts thereof.

Avoid ungodly _____. If there are particular people who lead you into a place of temptation, don't spend time with them.

---

1. You can read the full account in Matthew 4:1–11.

There hath no temptation taken you but such as is common to man: but God is faithful, who will not suffer you to be tempted above that ye are able; but will with the temptation also make a way to escape, that ye may be able to bear it.—1 Corinthians 10:13

DISCIPLE 163

1 Timothy 5:22

...neither be partaker of other men's sins: keep thyself pure.

_____ **for help.** If you are held bondage in habitual sin, ask a godly, mature Christian (perhaps your discipler, Bible class leader, or pastor) to pray with you and hold you accountable. In some cases, you may need biblical counsel to understand how God's Word can give you victory over the specific sin you are fighting.

James 5:16

Confess your faults one to another, and pray one for another, that ye may be healed. The effectual fervent prayer of a righteous man availeth much.

Keep short _____ **with God.** The moment the Holy Spirit convicts you of sin, confess it to God (agreeing with Him that it is sin) and ask for His forgiveness.

1 John 1:9

If we confess our sins, he is faithful and just to forgive us our sins, and to cleanse us from all unrighteousness.

_____ **to the Holy Spirit.** Begin each day in prayer, yielding yourself to the Holy Spirit.

Galatians 5:16

This I say then, Walk in the Spirit, and ye shall not fulfil the lust of the flesh.

Satan tries to wear us down by reminding us of our past sins and telling us that it is no use to keep fighting. A disciple of Jesus,

NOTES

however, refuses to believe that lie. A disciple keeps fighting sin to live a life pleasing to God.[2]

A Disciple Lives a Sanctified Life

The word *sanctified* simply means "_____." It refers to something that is distinguished or sacred. God instructs us to keep our lives pure of sin and to live in a way that is set apart to God. As we live a sanctified life, God can use us in His service.

▶ **2 Timothy 2:19–21**

We serve a _____ God.

The defining attribute of God is His holiness.

▶ **Isaiah 6:3**

God is not only free of sin, but He is exalted above all.

▶ **Exodus 15:11**

God calls us to _____ holy lives.

Because God is holy, He calls us, as His people, to live holy lives.

▶ **1 Peter 1:14–16**

CONVERSATION STARTER

Do you have a favorite mug? Before you drink from that mug, you make sure it is clean and prepared for you to use. Similarly, God chooses to use people who have set themselves apart from sin and for His use.

---

2. For further study on having victory over temptation, see *Escape: How to Have Victory over Temptation* by Stephen Chappell (Striving Together Publications, 2014).

There hath no temptation taken you but such as is common to man: but God is faithful, who will not suffer you to be tempted above that ye are able; but will with the temptation also make a way to escape, that ye may be able to bear it.—1 Corinthians 10:13

DISCIPLE 165

NOTES

In "all manner of conversation"—in our lifestyle—we are to be distinct as God's children. We should be distinct in our speech, in our relationships, in our philosophies and beliefs, in our family life, in our appearance—every aspect of our lives should show forth the holiness of God.

This truth is called the doctrine of *separation*—separating (not isolating) ourselves from the world and to God.

▶ **2 Corinthians 6:17**

One of the key areas of holiness is sexual purity.

▶ **1 Corinthians 6:15–20**

We live in a culture that glorifies immorality. Many new Christians have lived in sexual sin or wrestle with temptations that are of a sexual nature. If this is something that you struggle with, share that with your pastor or mentor to ask for counsel on breaking free from it and accountability for walking in victory.

The world wants to conform us to be like it. But God tells us instead to let His Word renew our minds so that we become like *Him*.

▶ **Romans 12:2**

God's _____ develops holiness.

You and I simply cannot sustain a life of holiness on our own. But God's grace develops it in us as we mature in our Christian walk.

▶ **Titus 2:11–12**

NOTES

The Christian life is a holy life, and it will manifest itself in separation from activities that are sinful or questionable—activities that would harm our testimony as we tell others about the Lord.

You should know that living a set apart life is not always easy, and not everyone will understand. Even Jesus Himself was ridiculed and persecuted.

▶ **Matthew 10:24–25**

Even as we seek to live in a way that honors God's holiness, we must allow His love to show through our lives. A lack of holiness will harm our witness, but it is our love that is the mark of a true disciple.

▶ **John 13:35**

There hath no temptation taken you but such as is common to man: but God is faithful, who will not suffer you to be tempted above that ye are able; but will with the temptation also make a way to escape, that ye may be able to bear it.—1 Corinthians 10:13

DISCIPLE 167

APPLICATION

There is a difference between a believer and a disciple. Following the Lord fully as a disciple isn't always easy, but it is rewarding! Here are three ways you can put the truths we've seen in this lesson into practice:

Make a definite _____ to fully surrender to God. Just as an Old Testament animal sacrifice would be a once-for-all sacrifice, make a once-for-all commitment to unreservedly follow the Lord. Record the date here and in your Bible.

In response to God's mercy to me, I choose today, once-for-all, to yield every part of my life as a living sacrifice to God: _____ (date)

Daily ask God to _____ your heart. One of the keys to victory over sin is to stay in close fellowship with God. Ask Him to reveal any sin in your life, and then ask Him to forgive you. Psalm 139:23–24 are verses you can pray to the Lord: *Search me, O God, and know my heart: try me, and know my thoughts: And see if there be any wicked way in me, and lead me in the way everlasting.*

_____ your life. Can other people see the distinction of God's holiness in you? Are there habits, activities, or associations that you need to change?

NOTES

THIS STUDY IN REVIEW

1. A Disciple Is Fully Surrendered to God
2. A Disciple Battles Sin and the Flesh
3. A Disciple Lives a Sanctified Life

NOTES

PREVIOUS MEMORY
VERSES

2 TIMOTHY 3:16
1 JOHN 5:7
1 JOHN 4:3
ROMANS 8:16
JEREMIAH 33:3
1 PETER 2:2
GALATIANS 5:22–23

ASSIGNMENTS

Write 1 Corinthians 10:13 in the space below, and plan to memorize this verse so you can quote it to your discipler next week.

_____

_____

_____

_____

Read the five daily readings throughout this coming week, including answering the questions on day five. These questions are where you will pick up with your discipleship meeting next week.

DAY 1

The Way of Escape

Wherefore let him that thinketh he standeth take heed lest he fall. There hath no temptation taken you but such as is common to man: but God is faithful, who will not suffer you to be tempted above that ye are able; but will with the temptation also make a way to escape, that ye may be able to bear it. —**1 Corinthians 10:12–13**

[BIBLE READING]

Topical
Matthew 16:24

New Testament in a Year
Mark 1:23–45

Entire Bible in a Year
Leviticus 25; Mark 1:23–45

It is important for us to understand that every Christian is tempted. There is no sin or shame in being tempted—the problem comes when we give in to the temptation. Martin Luther said, "You can't stop a bird from flying over your head, but you can stop him from building a nest on top of your head." We cannot keep temptation from coming. Even Jesus was tempted. The key to victory is in properly responding when we are tempted.

Satan came to Jesus with three specific temptations that he is still using against believers today. First, he tempted Jesus to meet a legitimate need, His hunger, in an illegitimate way. Using divine power to satisfy a temporal need and a selfish purpose would have been a sin. Second, he tempted Jesus to presume on God's protection by throwing Himself off the Temple and asking God to rescue Him from the consequences of His actions. Finally, he tempted Jesus to avoid the pain and suffering of the cross by bowing down and worshiping Satan rather than worshiping God.

In each temptation, Jesus responded with the Word of God. He said, "It is written" and quoted the Old Testament passage that opposed what Satan was asking Him to do. While Jesus was able, He did not overcome Satan through divine power. Instead, He responded in a way that gives us a pattern and example to follow.

NOTES

Each time we are tempted we have an opportunity to escape and avoid sin. Someone said the reason it is so hard to overcome temptation is that we don't want to discourage it completely. Yet instead of allowing the temptation to linger, which almost always leads to sin eventually, we should do as Jesus did and rebuke the temptation with the Word of God. This makes it very important for us to be familiar with what the Scripture says so that we can see through the lies of the enemy and overcome them with the truth. Though we will never achieve a state of sinlessness and perfection, we can have victory over any given temptation if we use the means of escape which God has promised to provide.

_____

_____

_____

_____

_____

DAY 2

The Divine Motivator

For the grace of God that bringeth salvation hath appeared to all men, Teaching us that, denying ungodliness and worldly lusts, we should live soberly, righteously, and godly, in this present world; Looking for that blessed hope, and the glorious appearing of the great God and our Saviour Jesus Christ; Who gave himself for us, that he might redeem us from all iniquity, and purify unto himself a peculiar people, zealous of good works. —**Titus 2:11–14**

[BIBLE READING]

Topical
Romans 12:1

New Testament in a Year
Mark 2

Entire Bible in a Year
Leviticus 26–27; Mark 2

A little girl was spending the afternoon with her mother when she began acting up and was sent to her room. Before she left, she asked her mother, "Why do we do bad things, Mom?" Her mother replied, "The devil tempts us and we listen." The little girl thought about it for a minute then said, "Then why doesn't God speak up?"

Have you ever found yourself wondering why you sin? If you're saved and have accepted Christ as your Saviour, then you have been forgiven of your sins, yet you still do wrong. You still struggle to obey certain of God's commands. Why is that? The mom in our story was right—Satan tempts us and we listen.

Additionally, we have our own flesh to deal with. We all have a history of selfish and sinful responses to the challenges and temptations of life that are ingrained into our minds and emotions. And we are very prone to fall back into those patterns even after we are saved.

And then we have the world around us enticing us toward sin. The world highlights the pleasures of sin while minimizing or hiding the consequences.

NOTES

But as Christians, we realize God has given us the victory over sin. He paid for it all the day He died on the cross. This is what grace is all about—God's forgiveness to free us from sin.

Does grace mean we have a free ticket to do as we desire? Not at all. Many people today view grace as a license or free pass to live however they want. They say, "Christ has paid for my sins, so whatever I do is already forgiven." Sadly, they miss the very essence of grace. God's grace gives us the power to say "no" to sin—to "deny ungodliness and worldly lusts."

Next time you are tempted to sin, remember God's grace. And remember that it gives you the power to say "no."

_____

_____

_____

_____

_____

DAY 3

Developing Bible-Based Convictions

Let not him that eateth despise him that eateth not; and let not him which eateth not judge him that eateth: for God hath received him. Who art thou that judgest another man's servant? to his own master he standeth or falleth. Yea, he shall be holden up: for God is able to make him stand. One man esteemeth one day above another: another esteemeth every day alike. Let every man be fully persuaded in his own mind. — **Romans 14:3–5**

[BIBLE READING]

Topical
Matthew 10:37–38

New Testament in a Year
Mark 3:1–19

Entire Bible in a Year
Numbers 1–2; Mark 3:1–19

There are some completely clear-cut commandments in the Bible. For instance, we always know that it is right to share the gospel with others and it is always wrong to steal. There are many areas with black and white instructions for us, and it is always a mistake for us to seek God's direction in such matters—He has already told us.

But in other cases there is no commandment, so we must apply the principles of Scripture to make a decision about whether something is acceptable or not. It is important for us to draw these principles and our way of living from the Word of God. Our opinions may be right or wrong, but God's Word is always right. If we have grounded our choices on a proper application of Scripture, they will not lead us astray. Here are seven questions you can ask to help make a decision about doubtful matters and be guided by the Bible:

Am I being brought under the power of something that should not be controlling my life (1 Corinthians 6:12)?

Am I edifying myself (my flesh) or others (1 Corinthians 10:23)?

NOTES

Can I ask God to bless it in good conscience (Colossians 3:17, Acts 24:16)?

If Christ returned at this very moment, would I be ashamed to meet Him (1 Corinthians 1:8, 1 Thessalonians 5:23)?

Would it cause another brother to stumble (Romans 14:13–15; 15:1–2)?

Would it cause a lost person to reject the gospel (1 Corinthians 10:31–33)?

Does my conscience condemn me (1 Peter 3:16, Hebrews 3:18, 1 Timothy 1:5)?

If our desire is to do right and honor God, we will make our choices not with an eye toward what we can get away with, but with an eye toward making sure that we are doing things that will please Him. Our hearts are not trustworthy guides to discern right and wrong. We can easily rationalize something that we really want to do. Ultimately all choices come down to a matter of the heart. Our prayer should be the prayer of David: *"Who can understand his errors? cleanse thou me from secret faults"* (Psalm 19:12).

_____

_____

_____

_____

_____

DAY 4

This Hope Within

Behold, what manner of love the Father hath bestowed upon us, that we should be called the sons of God: therefore the world knoweth us not, because it knew him not. Beloved, now are we the sons of God, and it doth not yet appear what we shall be: but we know that, when he shall appear, we shall be like him; for we shall see him as he is. And every man that hath this hope in him purifieth himself, even as he is pure. —**1 John 3:1–3**

[BIBLE READING]

Topical
James 1:13–15

New Testament in a Year
Mark 3:20–35

Entire Bible in a Year
Numbers 3–4;
Mark 3:20–35

When his expedition to Antarctica was stranded by ice, Sir Ernest Shackleton took a few of his men on a risky voyage across open ocean on a tiny boat. The rest of the crew stayed behind awaiting their rescue. When Shackleton finally reached inhabited land, he quickly returned with a rescue mission. But moving ice threatened to cut off the rescue. Finally an avenue in the ice opened up, and the ship rushed in. The stranded crew rushed aboard and made it back to open water just in time. The story goes that once they were safely away, Shackleton said, "It was fortunate you were all packed and ready to go!" They replied, "We never gave up hope. Whenever the sea was clear of ice, we rolled up our sleeping bags and reminded each other, 'The boss may come today.'"

The fact that Jesus could return at any moment is a powerful motivation for us to purify our lives. That is not something we can do through strength of will or determination. The process of sanctification is just as dependent on God's grace as our justification (salvation) is. Paul asked, *"Are ye so foolish? having begun in the Spirit, are ye now made perfect by the flesh?"* (Galatians 3:3). When we are focused on the return of the Lord, we seek God's grace to live in such a way that we will not be ashamed when we see Him.

NOTES

It is certain that the Lord will return, but none of us knows when that will take place. Though some try to set dates and claim a high level of certainty, Jesus declared that the knowledge of His coming was not revealed to men. *"But of that day and hour knoweth no man, no, not the angels of heaven, but my Father only"* (Matthew 24:36). Since the Lord could appear at any moment, we must be ready every moment. That means that we make our decisions and choices keeping in mind the truth that we could face the Lord today, and that helps us choose the things that are pleasing to God.

_____

_____

_____

_____

_____

DAY 5

Review of Week Eight

[BIBLE READING]

Topical
1 John 2:15–16

New Testament in a Year
Mark 4:1–20

Entire Bible in a Year
Numbers 5–6;
Mark 4:1–20

The questions below cover the material we studied in this lesson and are given here to help you cement these truths in your mind and heart. Feel free to look back over previous pages as you answer these questions. When you begin the next lesson with your discipler, take a few minutes to discuss any questions you have from this week's material.

1. What is true discipleship? _____
    _____
    _____
    _____

DAY 6

Topical
Romans 6:6

New Testament in a Year
Mark 4:21–41

Entire Bible in a Year
Numbers 7–8;
Mark 4:21–41

2. In what form does sin begin? _____
    _____
    _____
    _____

DAY 7

Topical
1 Corinthians 10:13

New Testament in a Year
Mark 5:1–20

Entire Bible in a Year
Numbers 9–11;
Mark 5:1–20

3. What are the three main sources of temptation? _____
    _____
    _____
    _____

4. How can we take advantage of the "way of escape" that God has given us? _____
    _____
    _____
    _____

NOTES

5. What does the phrase "making provision for the flesh" mean?

   _____

   _____

   _____

6. What does the word *sanctified* mean? _____

   _____

   _____

   _____

7. What develops holiness in us as we mature in our Christian walk? _____

   _____

   _____

   _____

9 THE LOCAL CHURCH

REVIEW

Take a few moments to review together last week's study, memory verse, and the daily readings. You can use these questions to spark dialogue:

1. What truth or principle stood out to you most in last week's study and/or devotional readings?

2. Since we last met, have you had opportunity to apply or share a truth from the previous study?

3. Do you have any questions related to last week's devotional readings or assignment?

INTRODUCTION

One of the best parts of the Christian life is being part of the local church. The church is an institution that Christ Himself established, and it is His vehicle in bringing the gospel to all the world. And you and I get to be part of it!

The word *church* can mean wildly different things to different people, so it's important to understand what the Bible teaches about the church. In this lesson, we'll see the importance of the church, what the church actually is, and how God uses the church in our lives.

————— LESSON NINE —————

The Church Is Precious

Christ loved the church so much that He gave Himself for it.

▶ **Ephesians 5:25**

Although church attendance does not save us or get us to Heaven[1], the church is very important to God and is a vital aspect of Christian growth.

Christ _____ the church.

To trace the beginning of the church, we need only to revisit the early moments of the ministry of Christ. For the church began with Jesus, and we see the first assembly forming as Jesus called His disciples.

▶ **Matthew 4:18–22**

Christ _____ the church.

No church belongs to a pastor or a person. We may talk about "my church," in the sense that we are a member of it, but the church belongs to Christ.

▶ **Acts 20:28**

CONVERSATION
STARTER

Who is the most precious person in your life? Would you be willing to die for them? Is there a cause that you are a part of that you would be willing to die for?

---

1. Ephesians 2:8–9

Not forsaking the assembling of ourselves together, as the manner of some is; but exhorting one another: and so much the more, as ye see the day approaching.—Hebrews 10:25

CHURCH 181

Christ _____ the church.

Before ascending to Heaven, Christ gave specific instructions to the church to reach the world with the gospel.

▶ Matthew 28:19–20

Christ is to have _____ in the church.

Although the church meets many needs in a Christian's life (we'll see these later in this lesson), the church does not exist for us. Ultimately, it exists to glorify Christ. He is to have first place.

▶ Colossians 1:18

The church isn't man's idea, and it isn't an optional part of the Christian life.

When a Christian says that they can worship God independently of the local church, they are disregarding *God's* love for and emphasis on the church. When they love and commit to the local church, they are showing their love and commitment for that which is precious to Christ.

The Church Is Distinct

The church is more than a building—it is a place where Christians meet together to grow in God's Word, to glorify God, and to build lasting friendship with other Christians.

The church is not simply a "universal" body of saved people. It is comprised of local assemblies that consist of saved, baptized believers.

Throughout the New Testament, emphasis is placed on the _____
church—individual bodies of believers who gather together as a
church and follow the New Testament patterns of church practices.

The book of Acts tells about the first church in Jerusalem.

ACTS 2:47
*Praising God, and having favour with all the people. And the Lord
added to the church daily such as should be saved.*

And then it describes how churches were established in other cities
as the gospel spread.

ACTS 9:31
*Then had the churches rest throughout all Judaea and Galilee and
Samaria, and were edified; and walking in the fear of the Lord, and in
the comfort of the Holy Ghost, were multiplied.*

ACTS 15:41
And he went through Syria and Cilicia, confirming the churches.

ACTS 16:5
*And so were the churches established in the faith, and increased in
number daily.*

The next nine New Testament books after Acts (Romans, 1 and
2 Corinthians, Galatians, Ephesians, Philippians, Colossians, and
1 and 2 Thessalonians) are epistles (letters) written to local churches.

1 CORINTHIANS 1:2
*Unto the church of God which is at Corinth, to them that are sanctified
in Christ Jesus, called to be saints, with all that in every place call
upon the name of Jesus Christ our Lord, both theirs and ours:*

The three epistles following these (1 and 2 Timothy and Titus) are
written to local church leaders. Thus, twelve of the New Testament

Not forsaking the assembling of ourselves together, as the manner of some is; but exhorting one another: and so much the more, as ye see the day approaching.—Hebrews 10:25

CHURCH 183

epistles specifically deal with the organization, operation, and relationships within the local church.

Just what is the local church? And how is it structured?

The local church is a _____ assembly.

Jesus first announced His church in Matthew 16 when He told Peter, "Upon this rock I will build my church; and the gates of hell shall not prevail against it."

▶ **Matthew 16:13–18**

Note: Although some have taught that Jesus in this passage was making Peter the first pope, reading the surrounding verses shows that when Jesus said "upon this rock" He was referring not to Peter himself, but to the declaration Peter had just made that Jesus was indeed the Son of God. Thus, Jesus stated He was building the church on Himself—that He is the founding rock, or cornerstone. (See also Ephesians 2:20 and 1 Peter 2:6.)

The word Jesus used for *church* is the Greek word *ekklesia,* and it means "a called out assembly." A local church is a group of people who are "called out" from the world in the sense that they have identified with Christ and are joined together for the purpose of forming a church as described in the New Testament.

The local church is _____ after New Testament churches.

Throughout the New Testament, we see a pattern for how a local church is organized, what it believes, and how it operates.

We'll look at this using an acrostic of the word *Baptists.* Although there are local churches in other denominations, our church is a

Baptist church because as a whole, this list sums up Baptist beliefs and practices for the church. (These are our Baptist distinctives—what sets Baptist churches apart from others.) We believe this list most accurately reflects the New Testament teaching of the church.

_____ **Authority in all matters of faith and practice:** We believe the Bible is inspired and infallible and is the final authority. It is from God's Word that we understand and teach the fundamental doctrines of our faith as well as pattern our church polity—or structure of governance.

2 Timothy 3:16

All scripture is given by inspiration of God, and is profitable for doctrine, for reproof, for correction, for instruction in righteousness:[2]

_____ **or self-governing power of the local church:** Because Christ is the head of the church, we believe that every local church should be independent of a hierarchical framework or outside governmental structure.

Colossians 1:18

And he is the head of the body, the church: who is the beginning, the firstborn from the dead; that in all things he might have the preeminence.[3]

Ephesians 1:22–23

And hath put all things under his feet, and gave him to be the head over all things to the church, Which is his body, the fullness of him that filleth all in all.

---

2. See also John 17:17, Acts 17:11, Hebrews 4:12, and 2 Peter 1:20–21.
3. See also, Acts 13–14 and Acts 20:19–30.

Not forsaking the assembling of ourselves together, as the manner of some is; but exhorting one another: and so much the more, as ye see the day approaching.—Hebrews 10:25

CHURCH 185

_____ **of believers:** God's Word assures believers that we have direct access to God through our relationship with Christ.

1 TIMOTHY 2:5–6

For there is one God, and one mediator between God and men, the man Christ Jesus; Who gave himself a ransom for all, to be testified in due time.[4]

_____ **within the church:** Scripture only mentions two church offices—pastor (also referred to as *elder* or *bishop*) and deacon. These two offices are to be filled by godly men of integrity in each local church. Scripture gives specific qualifications for these offices.[5]

PHILIPPIANS 1:1

Paul and Timotheus, the servants of Jesus Christ, to all the saints in Christ Jesus which are at Philippi, with the bishops and deacons:[6]

_____ **soul liberty:** We believe that each person must make a personal decision of repentance and faith in Christ. Parents do not make this decision for their children, and the government cannot make it for its people.[7] Additionally, each person is responsible before God in matters of holiness and conscience.[8]

ROMANS 10:13

For whosoever shall call upon the name of the Lord shall be saved.

---

4. See also Hebrews 4:14–16 and 1 Peter 2:5–10.
5. See 1 Timothy 3:1–13, Titus 1:6–9, and 1 Peter 5:1–4.
6. See also Acts 6:1–7.
7. See also Romans 10:9–17.
8. See also Romans 14.

_____ **of church and state:** Although Christians should be law-abiding citizens, the state should have no power to create a state religion or to intervene in the free expression of religious liberty.[9]

Acts 5:29–31

Then Peter and the other apostles answered and said, We ought to obey God rather than men. The God of our fathers raised up Jesus, whom ye slew and hanged on a tree. Him hath God exalted with his right hand to be a Prince and a Saviour, for to give repentance to Israel, and forgiveness of sins.

_____**—baptism and the Lord's Table:** These are ordinances—not sacraments. They have no part in salvation and only serve as pictures of what Christ did for us. Both of them should only be performed under the authority of a local church.

Matthew 28:19

Go ye therefore, and teach all nations, baptizing them in the name of the Father, and of the Son, and of the Holy Ghost:[10]

We looked at baptism at length in Lesson 4, so we won't review that here. But let's take a moment to understand the Lord's Table (sometimes called communion, referring to the closeness of our relationship to the Lord).[11]

Jesus Himself instituted the Lord's Table the night before He was crucified. He instructs us to regularly[12] observe it as a church, taking

---

9. See also Matthew 22:21 and Romans 13:1–4.
10. See also Acts 2:42 and Acts 8:36–38.
11. For a booklet that describes this ordinance in more detail, see *The Purpose of the Lord's Table* (Striving Together Publications, 2012).
12. Scripture does not tell us how often to observe the Lord's Table. Some churches serve it weekly, others monthly, others yearly, and others anywhere in between.

Not forsaking the assembling of ourselves together, as the manner of some is; but exhorting one another: and so much the more, as ye see the day approaching.—Hebrews 10:25

CHURCH 187

time to remember His sacrifice for us and to examine our lives for sin that would hinder our fellowship with Him.

1 Corinthians 11:23–26

For I have received of the Lord that which also I delivered unto you, That the Lord Jesus the same night in which he was betrayed took bread: And when he had given thanks, he brake it, and said, Take, eat: this is my body, which is broken for you: this do in remembrance of me. After the same manner also he took the cup, when he had supped, saying, This cup is the new testament in my blood: this do ye, as oft as ye drink it, in remembrance of me. For as often as ye eat this bread, and drink this cup, ye do shew the Lord's death till he come.

_____ **and personal holiness:** We believe that Christ's ultimate sacrifice demands our complete consecration, and we desire that our daily living would reflect the holiness of our great God. We believe that members of the church should live a life that is distinct from the world.

2 Corinthians 6:14

Be ye not unequally yoked together with unbelievers: for what fellowship hath righteousness with unrighteousness? and what communion hath light with darkness?

1 Peter 1:16

Because it is written, Be ye holy; for I am holy.

These eight beliefs are a top-end picture of the basic teaching and practices of churches in the New Testament. The church is not an organization as much as it is an organism—a living, functioning body of believers who are saved, baptized, and organized to fulfill the New Testament instructions for the church.

The Church Is Vital

The church is not simply an add-on to the Christian life. It is an essential part of Christian growth, and it is essential in God's plan for holding truth and reaching the world with the gospel.

It is the guardian of _____.

If the church won't hold and stand for the truth, who will?

The church is the pillar and ground of the truth.

1 TIMOTHY 3:15

But if I tarry long, that thou mayest know how thou oughtest to behave thyself in the house of God, which is the church of the living God, the pillar and ground of the truth.

Christians are to contend for the faith.

JUDE 3

Beloved, when I gave all diligence to write unto you of the common salvation, it was needful for me to write unto you, and exhort you that ye should earnestly contend for the faith which was once delivered unto the saints.

It is God's plan to _____ the world.

God has commanded us to bring the gospel to the entire world, and the local church is the vehicle by which this takes place—through personal outreach and worldwide missions.

MATTHEW 28:19–20

Go ye therefore, and teach all nations, baptizing them in the name of the Father, and of the Son, and of the Holy Ghost: Teaching them to observe all things whatsoever I have commanded you: and, lo, I am

Not forsaking the assembling of ourselves together, as the manner of some is; but exhorting one another: and so much the more, as ye see the day approaching.—Hebrews 10:25

CHURCH 189

NOTES

with you alway, even unto the end of the world. Amen. (We'll look at how this practically takes place in Lesson 12.)

It is God's place to _____ the Christian.

Notice these purposes for the local church that help you grow in your Christian walk:

To preach the Word of God: Bible preaching works in our hearts and helps us grow into spiritual maturity.

▶ **Acts 13:5**

▶ **Romans 10:17**

To provide fellowship: The local church is a place where we can meet people who desire to serve the Lord and live for Him. Christian friends are vital in helping us grow spiritually.

▶ **Acts 2:42**

To provide oversight: Christ is the Head of the church, but He has designated the pastor as an undershepherd who provides spiritual leadership. Your pastor is a gift, given to encourage, edify, and equip your life for spiritual growth and fruitfulness. A wise Christian will establish a strong relationship and maintain spiritual accountability with their pastor.

▶ **Hebrews 13:17**

To restore sinful members: The church is to be a place where we not only *receive* grace, but where we also *extend* it to others who have fallen into sin and want to be restored to fellowship with God and their church family.

▶ **Galatians 6:1**

NOTES

To disciple new believers: Through the services, Bible classes, and discipleship program of the church, Christians are taught how to live for Christ and serve Him on a day-to-day basis.

▸ **Ephesians 4:11–12**

To mature new Christians: Christian growth doesn't stop after we accept Christ as our Saviour. It is actually just beginning. At church, we learn how to grow to be more like our Saviour.

▸ **Ephesians 4:15**

To bring glory to God: God deserves our glory, honor, and praise. It pleases Him when Christians gather together to worship Him.

▸ **Ephesians 3:21**

All of this—and more!—is God's provision for your growth. And it all takes place through the local church.

No wonder Scripture instructs us to not forsake the assembling of ourselves at church!

▸ **Hebrews 10:25**

It is one of the most vital parts of your Christian life.

CONVERSATION STARTER

What do you most look forward to in coming to church? Share with one another two or three things you appreciate about your church.

Not forsaking the assembling of ourselves together, as the manner of some is; but exhorting one another: and so much the more, as ye see the day approaching.—Hebrews 10:25

CHURCH 191

APPLICATION

As we've seen in this lesson, the local church is an integral part of our Christian growth. This would be a good time to make a few key decisions regarding your involvement in the local church:

Decide to be _____ in your attendance. In the Christian life, there is no substitute for the church. Determine now that you are going to attend every regularly-scheduled church service that you can.

Decide to be _____ to leadership. Your pastor, Bible class teacher, and others who invest in your life through your church are there for your spiritual benefit. Be accountable with them in matters of your church attendance and personal growth. Be transparent in sharing when you're going through a difficult time or facing tough temptations. Ask them for counsel when you need to make major life decisions. They are there to help you, but to do so effectively, they need you to give them entrance into your life.

Decide to be _____ in your involvement. More then *attending* the church, be *involved* in your church. In our next lesson, we'll see specific opportunities for involvement as well as God's unique equipping for your involvement. But determine now that you want to be a part of God's work through your church.

NOTES

THIS STUDY IN REVIEW

1. The Church Is Precious
2. The Church Is Distinct
3. The Church Is Vital

NOTES

PREVIOUS MEMORY
VERSES

───────────

2 Timothy 3:16
1 John 5:7
1 John 4:3
Romans 8:16
Jeremiah 33:3
1 Peter 2:2
Galatians 5:22–23
1 Corinthians 10:13

───────────

─────── **ASSIGNMENTS** ───────

Write Hebrews 10:25 in the space below, and plan to memorize this verse so you can quote it to your discipler next week.

_____

_____

_____

_____

Read the five daily readings throughout this coming week, including answering the questions on day five. These questions are where you will pick up with your discipleship meeting next week.

DAY 1

My Church Doesn't Belong to Me

[BIBLE READING]

Topical
Acts 20:28

New Testament in a Year
Mark 5:21–43

Entire Bible in a Year
Numbers 12–14;
Mark 5:21–43

For by him were all things created, that are in heaven, and that are in earth, visible and invisible, whether they be thrones, or dominions, or principalities, or powers: all things were created by him, and for him: And he is before all things, and by him all things consist. And he is the head of the body, the church: who is the beginning, the firstborn from the dead; that in all things he might have the preeminence.
—**Colossians 1:16–18**

You've probably met people who *used* to go to church. In some cases, they stopped going because they never heard the truths of God's Word preached. They may have been in a church that never taught salvation through Jesus alone, and so they stopped going because they were not saved and did not have a personal relationship with God.

But other times, people stop going to church because they had expectations of how the church should relate to them, and it didn't happen. Surveys reveal that some of the most common reasons people stop going to church are life changes—job promotion, moving or marriage—a feeling that the church isn't loving; and disappointment with the church leadership. Some people simply see the church as an optional part of Christian growth. Scripture declares otherwise.

The Bible highlights the importance of regular, consistent fellowship with other believers to our Christian growth. Paul wrote, *"I thank my God upon every remembrance of you, Always in every prayer of mine for you all making request with joy, For your fellowship in the gospel from the first day until now"* (Philippians 1:3–5). Continued fellowship is a prerequisite to spiritual growth.

The reality is that the mindset of our self-centered culture has infected Christians. Many view church only through the lens of what they get. If the music isn't exactly to their preference or if the style of preaching isn't what they are used to, they drift away. If they don't get to sit in their favorite pew or if someone doesn't speak to them, they view that as a reason to leave. Church is not primarily about us. We come to church to worship God and to learn from His Word. A Christian who is looking for a church that will make him feel good is unlikely to remain in one church for very long. Worse, he is unlikely to grow to become a mature believer.

When you go to church, remember that the church doesn't belong to you—it belongs to Jesus! Attend faithfully to worship Him, learn from His Word, fellowship with other Christians, and honor the Lord who loves the church.

_____

_____

_____

_____

_____

DAY 2

Why So Many Churches?

And unto the angel of the church in Smyrna write; These things saith the first and the last, which was dead, and is alive; I know thy works, and tribulation, and poverty, (but thou art rich) and I know the blasphemy of them which say they are Jews, and are not, but are the synagogue of Satan. Fear none of those things which thou shalt suffer: behold, the devil shall cast some of you into prison, that ye may be tried; and ye shall have tribulation ten days: be thou faithful unto death, and I will give thee a crown of life. — **Revelation 2:8–10**

[BIBLE READING]

Topical
Colossians 1:18

New Testament in a Year
Mark 6:1–29

Entire Bible in a Year
Numbers 15–16;
Mark 6:1–29

According to the Center for Religion and Civic Culture, Los Angeles is the most religiously diverse city in the world. In this one city, there are dozens of different faiths and thousands of churches, mosques, synagogues, and other places of worship. Yet the reality is that the vast majority of those religious assemblies are teaching false doctrine. They are not faithfully proclaiming the Word of God or telling people how to be saved.

The fact that a group calls themselves a church does not mean that they are Christians or that they are teaching true doctrine. Throughout history, Satan has counterfeited God's work in order to deceive people. He makes things that look good on the surface, but underneath are filled with lies and snares. It is vital that we exercise discernment when it comes to recognizing if a church is faithfully preaching God's truth.

Here are three key questions that will help you identify whether a church or a Bible teacher is a true church or Bible teacher:

What do they teach about Jesus? Do they look to Him just as a good teacher and example, or do they worship Him as the Son of God and the Saviour of the world? First John 2:22–23 says, *"Who* *is a liar but he that denieth that Jesus is the Christ? He is antichrist, that denieth the Father and the Son. Whosoever denieth the Son, the same hath not the Father: (but) he that acknowledgeth the Son hath the Father also."*

What do they teach about salvation? Do they believe that man has a part in earning his salvation by what he does or does not do, or do they teach that faith in the finished work of Christ on the cross is all we need to be saved? Ephesians 2:8–9 says, *"For by grace are ye saved through faith; and that not of yourselves: it is the gift of God: Not of works, lest any man should boast."*

What do they teach about the Bible? Do they teach that there are mistakes in Scripture and we must interpret it in light of modern values, or do they hold a high view of the Word of God? Second Timothy 3:16 says, *"All scripture is given by inspiration of God, and is profitable for doctrine, for reproof, for correction, for instruction in righteousness."*

There are other important truths that Bible preaching churches teach and practice. But these three are key beliefs that distinguish between a counterfeit church and a church that believes the important doctrines of Christianity.

_____

_____

_____

_____

_____

DAY 3

Doctrine Matters

And with many other words did he testify and exhort, saying, Save yourselves from this untoward generation. Then they that gladly received his word were baptized: and the same day there were added unto them about three thousand souls. And they continued stedfastly in the apostles' doctrine and fellowship, and in breaking of bread, and in prayers. —**Acts 2:40–42**

[BIBLE READING]

Topical
1 Timothy 2:5–6

New Testament in a Year
Mark 6:30–56

Entire Bible in a Year
Numbers 17–19;
Mark 6:30–56

The model for what a church should look like is given to us in the New Testament. The more closely a church follows the Bible pattern in their doctrine, their philosophy and their practice, the stronger the church will be. As we saw in this week's study, the doctrines and beliefs of the New Testament are in line with Baptist faith and practice.

The young Christians saved on the day of Pentecost *"continued steadfastly in the apostle's doctrine…."* The early church cherished the doctrines of the faith, so much that they were willing to suffer for them rather than to compromise. Acts 5:27–29 records, *"And when they had brought them, they set them before the council: and the high priest asked them, Saying, Did not we straitly command you that ye should not teach in this name? and, behold, ye have filled Jerusalem with your doctrine, and intend to bring this man's blood upon us. Then Peter and the other apostles answered and said, We ought to obey God rather than men."*

Churches who place more value in drawing crowds than seeing lives changed are willing to water down doctrine with unscriptural, but socially pleasing, methods. These methods, however, can never replace the biblical model of sound biblical preaching seen in Scripture. A church that is built on the unchanging foundation of the Word of God has the basis to help believers grow and mature in the Lord.

We make the statement that the Scripture is our guide to both faith and practice. That means that what we believe and how we behave are based on the Bible. Opinions change and cultures shift, but God's Word abides. Jesus said, *"Therefore whosoever heareth these sayings of mine, and doeth them, I will liken him unto a wise man, which built his house upon a rock: And the rain descended, and the floods came, and the winds blew, and beat upon that house; and it fell not: for it was founded upon a rock"* (Matthew 7:24–25).

_____

_____

_____

_____

_____

DAY 4

You Need the Church

Let us hold fast the profession of our faith without wavering; (for he is faithful that promised;) And let us consider one another to provoke unto love and to good works: Not forsaking the assembling of ourselves together, as the manner of some is; but exhorting one another: and so much the more, as ye see the day approaching.
—**Hebrews 10:23–25**

[BIBLE READING]

Topical
1 Peter 1:16

New Testament in a Year
Mark 7:1–13

Entire Bible in a Year
Numbers 20–22;
Mark 7:1–13

Church attendance is not optional for the child of God. It is a vital, necessary component of our walk with the Lord. We need to hear the Word of God preached and taught. We need to sing and worship God in fellowship with other believers. We need to pray together and laugh together and weep together. We need to give our tithes and offerings as part of our worship of the Lord. Church is not a minor part of the Christian life—it is one of the most important parts.

Charles Spurgeon said, "There was a dear sister, now in Heaven, who attended this Tabernacle for years, though she was so deaf that she never heard a word that was spoken. The reasons she gave for being here were that, at any rate, she could join in the hymns, and that, had she stayed away, she would have felt as if she was disassociated from the people of God; and other people, perhaps, might not have known the reason for her absence, and it might, therefore, have been a bad example to them."

Church should be something we look forward to with joy, not something we regard as an obligation to dread. David wrote, *"I was glad when they said unto me, Let us go into the house of the LORD"* (Psalm 122:1). If we view church properly, understanding how important it is in God's plan for our lives, we will be excited about

NOTES

the opportunities that being with God's people in God's house present to us. There will always be someone you can encourage with a kind word—remember church is not all about us.

Church attendance should be a habit. If you wait until you wake up on Sunday morning to decide whether you will go to church, you are likely to find a reason to stay home. On the other hand, if the matter is already settled, it will simply be something that you do on a normal and regular basis. Jesus was in the habit of regular attendance for worship, and we should be as well. *"And he came to Nazareth, where he had been brought up: and, as his custom was, he went into the synagogue on the sabbath day, and stood up for to read"* (Luke 4:16).

_____

_____

_____

_____

_____

DAY 5

Review of Week Nine

The questions below cover the material we studied in this lesson and are given here to help you cement these truths in your mind and heart. Feel free to look back over previous pages as you answer these questions. When you begin the next lesson with your discipler, take a few minutes to discuss any questions you have from this week's material.

1. Who established the church and why does it exist? _____
   _____
   _____
   _____

2. What is a local church? _____
   _____
   _____
   _____

3. What does the word *ekklesia* (the Greek word for church) mean? _____
   _____
   _____
   _____

4. What is the purpose of observing the Lord's Table? _____
   _____
   _____
   _____

[BIBLE READING]

Topical
Jude 1:3

New Testament in a Year
Mark 7:14–37

Entire Bible in a Year
Numbers 23–25;
Mark 7:14–37

DAY 6

Topical
Matthew 28:19–20

New Testament in a Year
Mark 8

Entire Bible in a Year
Numbers 26–28; Mark 8

DAY 7

Topical
Matthew 19:26

New Testament in a Year
Mark 9:1–29

Entire Bible in a Year
Numbers 29–31;
Mark 9:1–29

NOTES

5. In what three ways is the church vital? _____

    _____

    _____

    _____

6. What are some of the purposes for the local church that help you grow in your Christian walk? _____

    _____

    _____

    _____

7. What are three decisions you can make regarding your involvement in the local church? _____

    _____

    _____

    _____

10 YOUR PLACE IN YOUR CHURCH FAMILY

REVIEW

Take a few moments to review together last week's study, memory verse, and the daily readings. You can use these questions to spark dialogue:

1. What truth or principle stood out to you most in last week's study and/or devotional readings?

2. Since we last met, have you had opportunity to apply or share a truth from the previous study?

3. Do you have any questions related to last week's devotional readings or assignment?

INTRODUCTION

In our last study, we saw some big-picture truths about the church. We saw what the church actually is, how it should operate, and the importance God places on it. But the church is more than a doctrine; it is a family—a place to grow with brothers and sisters in Christ.

So how do *you* fit into this family? In this lesson, we'll look at how you can be involved in the work of your church, the spiritual gifts God has given you to enable you for this work, and the relationships you have with others in your church family.

—————— **LESSON TEN** ——————

Join in the Work of the Ministry

You've heard the adage, "Many hands make light work." This is definitely true in relation to the work of the church.

God has entrusted the church with the _____ and the responsibility to take it to all the world.

▶ **Matthew 28:19–20**

He has also entrusted the church with the responsibility of encouraging and serving one another, and bringing others along in spiritual _____ and maturity.

▶ **Ephesians 4:15**

These responsibilities do not belong solely to the pastor or the church leadership—they belong to the church as a _____.
It is not the pastor's job to do the work of the entire church! Rather, it is his job (along with others who aid him) to equip church members to do the work.

▶ **Ephesians 4:11–12**

NOTES

The apostles and prophets were temporary roles in the early church before the writing of God's Word was complete.[1] The roles of evangelists and pastors and teachers, however, continue today.

God has given church leaders the job of equipping _____ to take part in the work of the ministry and edifying (building up) the body of Christ by reproducing new Christians who mature as disciples.

▶ **2 Timothy 2:2**

How, then, can *you* join in the work of the ministry? The good news is that God has especially equipped you for this very task.

Use Your Spiritual Gifts

The Holy Spirit provides every child of God with one or more spiritual gifts. These gifts are divine enablements given to us at salvation for the express purpose of serving God through the local church.

_____ **your gift.**

Even as the roles of the apostles and prophets were temporary, so there were some gifts, called "sign gifts" (miraculous gifts such as speaking in tongues, visions, healing, and prophesying) that were also temporary. God used these gifts to authenticate the work of the

---

1. Ephesians 2:20 explains that these roles were a foundation to the early church: "*And are built upon the foundation of the apostles and prophets, Jesus Christ himself being the chief corner stone.*"

apostles, and the need for them disappeared with the completion of the written Word of God.[2]

However, the Holy Spirit still gives gifts to Christians to equip us for ministry. These spiritual gifts are summarized in Romans 12.

▶ **Romans 12:6–8**

Let's briefly examine each of the spiritual gifts listed in these verses:

Prophecy: Before the Bible was complete, prophecy was two-fold —*foretelling* and *forthtelling*. Foretelling is what people often associate with prophecy—predicting future events based on God's revelation to the prophet. Forthtelling, however, is actually the main role of prophecy—declaring God's Word to others. Even in the Old Testament, the prophets' main ministry was to preach the truth. In some cases, they foretold future events as they preached. Today, we have the complete revelation of God to man recorded in the Bible, and the spiritual gift of prophecy is a call from God to declare His Word to others. People with the spiritual gift of prophecy are passionate to declare the Word of God.

Ministry: This spiritual gift is also known as the gift of *helps.*[3] It is a desire to serve and help people in a variety of ways—often volunteering service in unglamorous and unappreciated jobs. Never underestimate the importance of this spiritual gift. If you have a passion to serve behind the scenes, be faithful and diligent, knowing your service is vital.

Teaching: This is the ability and desire to teach God's truth and help people understand how His Word applies to their lives. This spiritual gift requires diligent study and sound interpretation of Scripture. It is a vital need for every local church.

2. See 1 Corinthians 13:8–10; 14:20–22.
3. See 1 Corinthians 12:28.

NOTES

Exhortation: This is the ability and desire to encourage others in the Christian life. These Christians love to lift up others with positive words and deeds, and they are especially concerned with the heart. Exhorters want to motivate others to love and serve God with whole-hearted passion.

Giving: This is the ability and desire to give to God's work and God's people. It is accompanied by the provision to give. These Christians are generous by nature and love to give to God's work. Those with the gift of giving have great delight in unobtrusively giving to meet the needs of others and further the work of God.

Ruling: Also called *administration,* this is the ability to lead and administrate part of God's work. It reveals itself through natural abilities to organize, think strategically, implement a plan, or coordinate teams of people. Christians with this gift have a God-given ability to manage and administrate, and they find great joy in seeing order and progress.

Mercy: This is the God-given ability to feel the pain of others and help them during times of difficulty. Those with the gift of mercy are naturally good at empathizing with those carrying heavy burdens. They know what to say (and when to be silent) and have a strong desire to lift loads and minister to those who are suffering.

God has given each Christian at least one of these gifts, and He desires for you to use your gift as you serve with others in the local church.

_____ **your gift.**

Like a physical body needs all of its parts, the body of Christ needs all of its people.

NOTES

CONVERSATION
STARTER

Discuss with your discipler ministry opportunities in your church that may be a good match for your spiritual gift. What steps do you need to take to get plugged into ministry? What group of people could you serve? Who could you serve with who would mentor you in service?

▶ **1 Corinthians 12:18–24**

You are vital to the health and strength of the rest of the church family, and you should use your spiritual gift.

Review the list of spiritual gifts again. What gift (or gifts) do you believe you have been given? How can you begin using your spiritual gift in service with your church family?

As important as it is to identify and use your spiritual gifts, it is also important to understand that just because you do not have a particular gift does not mean that you can't participate in something all Christians should do. (People without the spiritual gift of mercy can still visit and minister to someone in the hospital, and people without the spiritual gift of giving can and should still give to God's work.) It simply means that you will find some areas of ministry that come more naturally to you, and those would be good areas in which you should focus your ministry within the body of Christ.

Remain Committed to the Family

Being part of a local church carries similar commitments as being part of a family. As a church family, our lives are connected to one another in the body of Christ.

How do we demonstrate our commitment to the family?

_____ one another regularly.

Scripture gives many "one another" commands, regarding how we interact with our brothers and sisters in Christ. There are literally dozens of these, but let's notice just a few of the most common:

Love one another.

▶ John 15:12[4]

Serve one another.

▶ Galatians 5:13

Be gracious toward one another.

▶ Ephesians 4:2

Be like minded one toward another.

▶ Romans 15:5

Give preference to one another.

▶ Romans 12:10

As you can see, we are to value our relationships with one another and to invest in them with love, service, and kindness.

_____ differences biblically.

Every relationship of importance encounters conflict, and relationships with others in your church are no exception. How you resolve conflict, however, will either undermine or strengthen that relationship.

Forgive from your heart.

Some offenses can simply be forgiven without the need even for discussion. If you can forgive the other person from your heart without bringing it up to them, start there.

---

4. See also John 13:34–35, 15:12, 17; Romans 13:8; 1 Thessalonians 3:12, 4:9; 1 Peter 1:22; 1 John 3:11, 4:7, 11; 2 John 5.

▶ **Ephesians 4:32**

_____ *to the other person.*

Most differences between Christians could be resolved if both parties would simply talk to one another.

▶ **Matthew 18:15**

When we air our grievances with others, we add to the hurt involved and minimize the possibility of reconciliation. This is why Scripture tells us to simply go to the person who has offended us.

▶ **Proverbs 26:22**

Share with someone else who can be part of a _____.

If you try to go to the other person but they will not hear you, and if the matter is of a serious nature so that it would hurt others if it is not resolved, privately bring it to church leadership and ask for their help in seeking reconciliation.

▶ **Matthew 18:16–17**

In all of these steps, remember that the goal is not to prove who is right or who is wrong, but to bring about a _____

_____.

The relationships with our brothers and sisters in Christ are valuable. We should not treat them lightly nor discard them quickly. Be committed to love and serve one another in your church family and, when there is conflict, to tenaciously seek restoration to the relationship.

APPLICATION

The local church is one of God's greatest works on earth. And being part of it is one of God's great gifts to *you!* But it shouldn't end there. God wants to use you as a gift to your church! Here are a few ways that you can participate in the work of God through your church:

Take the spiritual gifts test. To best develop and use your spiritual gift, it is helpful to identify what that gift is. At strivingtogether.com/Free-Resources.html you will find a free, downloadable Spiritual Gifts Test that can help you discover your spiritual gift and identify the areas where God has gifted you for service.

Ask to be involved in ministry through your church. Remember, the work of the ministry is not just for the pastor; it is for the church family. Ask your pastor or class leader how you can roll up your sleeves and jump in where you are needed most. If you believe you know what your spiritual gift is, ask how you can be specifically trained for areas of ministry that would allow you to use your gift.

Invest in others. Look for opportunities to reach out to others around you in your church family. Develop relationships that are of a spiritual, encouraging nature. Look for ways to be a giver to others.

NOTES

THIS STUDY IN
REVIEW

1. Join in the Work
   of the Ministry
2. Use Your Spiritual
   Gifts
3. Remain Committed
   to the Family

NOTES

PREVIOUS MEMORY
VERSES

2 Timothy 3:16
1 John 5:7
1 John 4:3
Romans 8:16
Jeremiah 33:3
1 Peter 2:2
Galatians 5:22–23
1 Corinthians 10:13
Hebrews 10:25

——————— **ASSIGNMENTS** ———————

Write Ephesians 4:11–12 in the space below, and plan to memorize these verses so you can quote them to your discipler next week.

_____

_____

_____

_____

Read the five daily readings throughout this coming week, including answering the questions on day five. These questions are where you will pick up with your discipleship meeting next week.

DAY 1

The Value of Teamwork

And he gave some, apostles; and some, prophets; and some, evangelists; and some, pastors and teachers; For the perfecting of the saints, for the work of the ministry, for the edifying of the body of Christ: Till we all come in the unity of the faith, and of the knowledge of the Son of God, unto a perfect man, unto the measure of the stature of the fulness of Christ:—**Ephesians 4:11–13**

[BIBLE READING]

Topical
Matthew 28:19–20

New Testament in a Year
Mark 9:30–50

Entire Bible in a Year
Numbers 32–34;
Mark 9:30–50

The work of the church is not a work which can be accomplished by one individual or by a few. It requires the labor of all of the members to accomplish the tasks that God has given to the church. Sometimes people make the mistake of thinking that the pastor and staff are the ones who are to do the work of the church. Yet in truth, every Christian is called to be a worker for God. One of the main purposes of pastors and teachers is to equip each of the saints to do the work of the ministry.

As we read the New Testament we see again and again that ordinary people—laymen and women who were not in full time ministry—do the work of the church. They witness to the lost, they give to the needs of others, they teach and encourage and instruct new converts. Paul wrote, *"Now he that planteth and he that watereth are one: and every man shall receive his own reward according to his own labour. For we are labourers together with God: ye are God's husbandry, ye are God's building"* (1 Corinthians 3:8–9).

We are not meant to go to church to watch a show put on by others. We are participants rather than spectators. A Christian who is doing no work for God is a disobedient Christian. God has given each of us different spiritual gifts to use to build His church. While some of these gifts are used in a more public or visible way than others, all of them are vitally important. The work that is done behind the scenes is just as important as the work that is done on the platform.

If each member of the team is not pulling his or her weight, then the entire team suffers. This is true in business and sports, and it is true in the Christian realm as well. *"From whom the whole body fitly joined together and compacted by that which every joint supplieth, according to the effectual working in the measure of every part, maketh increase of the body unto the edifying of itself in love"* (Ephesians 4:16). God has work for you to do that no one else is as well qualified or gifted to perform. Be part of the team and get involved.

_____

_____

_____

_____

_____

DAY 2

Gifted to Give

That there should be no schism in the body; but that the members should have the same care one for another. And whether one member suffer, all the members suffer with it; or one member be honoured, all the members rejoice with it. Now ye are the body of Christ, and members in particular. And God hath set some in the church, first apostles, secondarily prophets, thirdly teachers, after that miracles, then gifts of healings, helps, governments, diversities of tongues. —**1 Corinthians 12:25–28**

[BIBLE READING]

Topical
Ephesians 4:11–12

New Testament in a Year
Mark 10:1–31

Entire Bible in a Year
Numbers 35–36;
Mark 10:1–31

It is said that once the great Italian conductor Sir Michael Costa was leading the rehearsal of a combined orchestra and choral group in preparation for a performance. As the many musicians played and sang, each contributed something to the overall sound he was seeking. According to the story at one point one of the piccolo players stopped playing. Immediately Costa stopped everything. "What happened to the piccolo?" he asked. It seemed like a small thing for one instrument to be missing, but to the conductor, it made a noticeable difference.

Each one of us play an important role in the body of Christ, and each of us has been given spiritual gifts to be used, not for our own benefit and glory, but for the good of the cause of Christ. When we are selfish and worried about what we can get rather than what we can give, we are robbing the church of our gifts, but we are also robbing ourselves of the blessing that comes from generously using our resources for God's kingdom work. Paul said, *"I have shewed you all things, how that so labouring ye ought to support the weak, and to remember the words of the Lord Jesus, how he said, It is more blessed to give than to receive"* (Acts 20:35).

The gifts that we have been given may not seem to be important. We may wish that we had other gifts instead. Yet that is the wrong attitude and approach. God knows exactly how we fit into His plan for the church. Our job is not to complain and wish for better or different gifts, but to use whatever we have been given in whatever ways we can. *"For, brethren, ye have been called unto liberty; only use not liberty for an occasion to the flesh, but by love serve one another"* (Galatians 5:13).

In the final analysis, it is our love for God and for others that motivates us to use our gifts to build the church. When our love is properly placed, then it will be easy for us to make whatever sacrifices are required for the good of others.

_____

_____

_____

_____

_____

DAY 3

One Another

Brethren, if a man be overtaken in a fault, ye which are spiritual, restore such an one in the spirit of meekness; considering thyself, lest thou also be tempted. Bear ye one another's burdens, and so fulfil the law of Christ. For if a man think himself to be something, when he is nothing, he deceiveth himself. —**Galatians 6:1–3**

[BIBLE READING]

Topical
2 Timothy 2:2

New Testament in a Year
Mark 10:32–52

Entire Bible in a Year
Deuteronomy 1–3;
Mark 10:32–52

There are dozens and dozens of "one another" verses in the Word of God. Each of them is there to encourage us to not just focus on ourselves but to genuinely care for the needs of others. There are lots of repetition of this instruction because it goes against the grain of our selfish natures. The greatest challenge to building strong and healthy relationships within the body of Christ is that we become too focused on ourselves to make the investments in helping and meeting the needs of others. Here are just a few of the things God calls each of us to do.

Live peaceably. It is not right for Christians to constantly be fighting with each other when the Prince of Peace is supposed to be ruling in our hearts. *"Salt is good: but if the salt have lost his saltness, wherewith will ye season it? Have salt in yourselves, and have peace one with another"* (Mark 9:50).

Share the same mind. When we are thinking like Jesus thinks, we find it easy to be in agreement with each other. *"Now the God of patience and consolation grant you to be likeminded one toward another according to Christ Jesus"* (Romans 15:5).

Don't tear each other down. Words are extremely powerful and we can use our words to either build up or tear down the other members of the body of Christ. "*But if ye bite and devour one another, take heed that ye be not consumed one of another*" (Galatians 5:15).

Forgive. Everyone has hurts and wounds. It is essential that we do not hold onto them, but rather let go of the past and forgive those who hurt us. "*And be ye kind one to another, tenderhearted, forgiving one another, even as God for Christ's sake hath forgiven you*" (Ephesians 4:32).

Speak good things. There are always things we could criticize, but instead we should focus on what will encourage others and never harm their reputation or testimony. "*Speak not evil one of another, brethren. He that speaketh evil of his brother, and judgeth his brother, speaketh evil of the law, and judgeth the law: but if thou judge the law, thou art not a doer of the law, but a judge*" (James 4:11).

Love. Above all else, our relationships in the body of Christ should be characterized by genuine, sacrificial love for each other. "*A new commandment I give unto you, That ye love one another; as I have loved you, that ye also love one another*" (John 13:34).

_____

_____

_____

_____

_____

DAY 4

The Value of Relationships

Moreover if thy brother shall trespass against thee, go and tell him his fault between thee and him alone: if he shall hear thee, thou hast gained thy brother. But if he will not hear thee, then take with thee one or two more, that in the mouth of two or three witnesses every word may be established. —**Matthew 18:15–16**

[BIBLE READING]

Topical
Romans 12:6–8

New Testament in a Year
Mark 11:1–18

Entire Bible in a Year
Deuteronomy 4–6;
Mark 11:1–18

Because relationships are between fallible people with sin natures, even within the church, there will be times when things happen that threaten to break them apart. Jesus warned, *"It is impossible but that offences will come"* (Luke 17:1), and that principle is true in each of our lives. The question is not whether things will happen that cause problems—the question is how we will respond. The Bible places the responsibility for restoring broken relationships on us, whether we are the one who has done wrong, or whether we have been wronged. In either case, we should take the initiative to fix things. Peter wrote, *"Let him eschew evil, and do good; let him seek peace, and ensue [follow] it"* (1 Peter 3:11).

If we sit back and wait on the other person to take the first step, the broken relationship may never be restored. Even if the other person is at fault, we can go to them and explain how we have been hurt and find out if there is anything that can be done to solve the problem. It is important for us to be careful not to automatically assume that we are completely right and have no responsibility in fixing the situation. In most cases, there is at least some fault on both sides of a disagreement.

Elizabeth Barrett was one of twelve children in a highly artistic family. Her parents encouraged the use of her talents, and she became one of the best known female poets in England. But

NOTES

while her parents promoted her writing, they did not encourage romance—in fact, her father forbade all of his children to marry under threat of being cut off completely from the family if they did. Despite that prohibition, Elizabeth began a secret romance via correspondence with the poet Robert Browning who had written to express his admiration for her work.

When she was forty years old, she eloped with him, and the couple moved to Italy. For the next ten years, she wrote her parents a letter each week. When her father died, all the letters Elizabeth had sent were returned to her unopened. That bitter man robbed both himself and his daughter of what could and should have been a wonderful relationship because he would not forgive.

Don't make the mistake of undervaluing Christian relationships. Invest in them with time and encouragement along the way, and when friction arises, do anything and everything you can to make things right.

_____

_____

_____

_____

_____

DAY 5

Review of Week Ten

The questions below cover the material we studied in this lesson and are given here to help you cement these truths in your mind and heart. Feel free to look back over previous pages as you answer these questions. When you begin the next lesson with your discipler, take a few minutes to discuss any questions you have from this week's material.

1. Why does the Holy Spirit give a Christian spiritual gifts? _____
    _____
    _____
    _____

2. With what has God entrusted the church? _____
    _____
    _____
    _____

3. What are the spiritual gifts listed in Romans 12? _____
    _____
    _____
    _____

4. What are some of the most common ways regarding how we should act with other Christians? _____
    _____
    _____
    _____

[BIBLE READING]

Topical
Ephesians 4:32

New Testament in a Year
Mark 11:19–33

Entire Bible in a Year
Deuteronomy 7–9;
Mark 11:19–33

DAY 6

Topical
Matthew 18:15

New Testament in a Year
Mark 12:1–27

Entire Bible in a Year
Deuteronomy 10–12;
Mark 12:1–27

DAY 7

Topical
John 15:12

New Testament in a Year
Mark 12:28–44

Entire Bible in a Year
Deuteronomy 13–15;
Mark 12:28–44

5. What is one way to resolve most differences between Christians?

    _____

    _____

    _____

6. What should the goal be regarding resolving conflict amongst others? _____

    _____

    _____

    _____

7. What are a few ways you can participate in the work of God through your church? _____

    _____

    _____

    _____

11 FINANCIAL STEWARDSHIP

REVIEW

Take a few moments to review together last week's study, memory verse, and the daily readings. You can use these questions to spark dialogue:

1. What truth or principle stood out to you most in last week's study and/or devotional readings?

2. Since we last met, have you had opportunity to apply or share a truth from the previous study?

3. Do you have any questions related to last week's devotional readings or assignment?

INTRODUCTION

One of the most significant areas of life is our finances. Regardless of whether we have a lot or a little, our financial decisions impact our lives every day.

God's Word has much to say in the area of finances—and especially about God's provision for His children. In this lesson, we'll see

God's ownership and provision, His instructions on giving, and His promises to reward our gifts.

CONVERSATION STARTER

Have you ever taken care of a friend or neighbor's house or pet while they were out of town? What would their reaction have been if you had decided to permanently move into their house or bring their pet to your house? You were not the owner, but the manager of their belongings. Another example: Are you in a manager position in your job? If so, you have resources (material and personnel) to manage in order to reach your boss' objectives, but you are not free to use these resources for personal profit.

LESSON ELEVEN

God Provides Everything We Have

Every good gift in our lives comes from the hand of God.

▶ **James 1:17**

This leads us to three truths that are absolutely crucial for understanding how a Christian should view their finances:

God is the _____ of all.

As the Creator, God is also the owner of everything. What we have comes from Him.

▶ **Psalm 24:1**

It is God who provides for our needs.

▶ **Psalm 145:15–16**

We are the _____ of His blessings.

A steward is a manager. Strictly speaking, we don't *own* the resources at our disposal; we *manage* them.

▶ **1 Corinthians 4:2**

We will give an _____ of our stewardship.

The way in which we manage God's resources is important, because we will give an account to the Lord.

▶ **Romans 14:10–12**

All three of these truths are seen in a parable Jesus told. A parable is a fictional story to illustrate spiritual truth. As you read the following verses, understand who the various characters and objects in the story represent:

The nobleman: Jesus

The servants: Christians

A pound: an amount of Roman money, at least several days' wages

▶ **Luke 19:12–27**

Through this parable we see that Christ has entrusted us with His resources, but He wants us to use them for Him. One day, He will return and will call us to give an account of how we managed His blessings.

God's Word Instructs Us to Give

There are many principles all throughout God's Word regarding making wise financial decisions. (We'll look at a few of these in days 3–4 of the devotional readings this week.) But in this lesson, we will focus primarily on scriptural principles regarding giving to God's work.

Both through direct instruction and the examples of first-century Christians, we see three specific ways to give:

Give _____.

NOTES

Early in the Bible, God's people recognized the importance of giving a tithe—a tenth—of what God had given them back to God.

The example of Abraham: When God blessed Abraham with a great victory, he gave a tithe of the spoils.

▶ **Genesis 14:20**

The promise of Jacob: Jacob promised God that he would give one tenth of all God gave to him.

▶ **Genesis 28:22**

The command of God: God commanded his people in the Old Testament to give a tithe. The tithe is so important that not giving it is literally robbing God, and God promises a direct blessing in proportion to our obedience.

▶ **Malachi 3:8–10**

The instruction to early Christians: Paul instructed first-century Christians to give regularly and to give in proportion to God's blessing on them. They were not to give just "whenever they felt like it," but they gave each Sunday as God gave to them.

▶ **1 Corinthians 16:2**

Give _____.

One of the most moving examples of giving in the Bible is that of the Macedonian Christians. The Apostle Paul wrote of their generous sacrifice in 2 Corinthians 8, using their example to encourage others to likewise give to God's work—even when it requires sacrifice. Notice especially, how it is God's grace at work in a person's heart that brings them to a point of giving sacrificially.

▶ **2 Corinthians 8:1–4**

Give _____.

Biblical giving is not rooted in guilt, but in grace. It is the glad response of a heart who recognizes God's goodness in giving to us. Thus, biblical giving comes from a willing heart.

▶ **2 Corinthians 9:7**

God Rewards Our Giving

Giving begins with what God has already given to us, but it doesn't end with our gifts. It ends with the incredible promises of God.

God will meet our _____.

Although some people teach that if you give to God, you will become wealthy, this is not promised in God's Word. In fact, as we saw in the testimony of the Macedonian Christians who gave out of their poverty, it is scripturally inaccurate.

From those same Macedonian Christians, however, we see another promise—that God promises to meet our needs as we give to Him.

In Philippians 4, Paul wrote directly to these Christians, thanking them for their generous giving.

▶ **Philippians 4:19**

Jesus also promised that our Heavenly Father—who knows every need in our lives—will take care of us. Because of His care, we

NOTES

should not worry about our needs as we respond to His grace by investing in His kingdom.

▶ **Matthew 6:25–33**

God will _____ our gifts.

Although God does not promise the blessings of health and wealth to every Christian who gives, He does promise to bless us in proportion to our giving.

▶ **Luke 6:38**

God has given to us, and He instructs us to give to His work and to those in need. As we give, He gives again to us. One Christian described the process this way: "God shovels in, and I shovel out, but God has a bigger shovel." These blessings are not always monetary, but they are real, and they make a difference in our lives.

God will multiply _____ to our account.

The greatest reason to give to God's work is that it is an opportunity to invest in eternity.

As Paul thanked the Macedonian Christians at Philippi, he told them that the work he was able to do in leading others to the Lord through their gifts became spiritual fruit to their account.

▶ **Philippians 4:15–18**

When you give to the local church, you are not so much giving *to* the church as you are giving *through* the church. As your gift is used to reach people with the gospel through the ministries and the

missions of your church, the souls that are saved are fruit to *your* eternal account. What an opportunity!

APPLICATION

We've seen that God is the giver of every resource, that He instructs us to give, and that He rewards our gifts. These truths are significantly different from the worldly philosophies of gaining all you can and/or spending what you have simply to bring yourself pleasure.

How can you shift your thinking and your financial habits to the truths we've seen in this lesson? Here are three practical ways to put these truths to practice!

Take God up on the tithing challenge. God not only tells us to tithe, but He invites us to prove His faithfulness by it: *"Bring ye all the tithes into the storehouse, that there may be meat in mine house, and prove me now herewith, saith the* Lord *of hosts, if I will not open you the windows of heaven, and pour you out a blessing, that there shall not be room enough to receive it"* (Malachi 3:10). Take God up on this challenge, and begin tithing.

Give by grace. Anyone can give offerings of their excess, but it takes the grace of God in a heart to give sacrificially. In this lesson, we saw that first-century Christians gave even out of their poverty. So give sacrificially to God's work.

Share God's goodness with others. As you experience God's blessings in response to your giving, tell others of God's faithfulness in your life!

NOTES

THIS STUDY IN REVIEW

1. God Provides Everything We Have
2. God's Word Instructs Us to Give
3. God Rewards Our Giving

NOTES

PREVIOUS MEMORY
VERSES

2 TIMOTHY 3:16
1 JOHN 5:7
1 JOHN 4:3
ROMANS 8:16
JEREMIAH 33:3
1 PETER 2:2
GALATIANS 5:22–23
1 CORINTHIANS 10:13
HEBREWS 10:25
EPHESIANS 4:11–12

——— ASSIGNMENTS ———

Write Philippians 4:19 in the space below, and plan to memorize
this verse so you can quote it to your discipler next week.

_____

_____

_____

_____

Read the five daily readings throughout this coming week, including
answering the questions on day five. These questions are where you
will pick up with your discipleship meeting next week.

DAY 1

Take No Thought

Wherefore, if God so clothe the grass of the field, which to day is, and to morrow is cast into the oven, shall he not much more clothe you, O ye of little faith? Therefore take no thought, saying, What shall we eat? or, What shall we drink? or, Wherewithal shall we be clothed? (For after all these things do the Gentiles seek:) for your heavenly Father knoweth that ye have need of all these things.
—Matthew 6:30–32

[BIBLE READING]

Topical
James 1:17

New Testament in a Year
Mark 13:1–20

Entire Bible in a Year
Deuteronomy 16–18;
Mark 13:1–20

During World War I, Eddie Rickenbacker became a national hero and received the Medal of Honor for shooting down twenty-six enemy aircraft. He remained popular, and during World War II, he was sent on numerous missions to support the troops. While flying over the Pacific in 1942 Rickenbacker's plane ran out of fuel and was forced to land in the ocean. For more than three weeks, the seven survivors drifted in a raft with almost no food or water before they were finally rescued. Later Rickenbacker said, "Let the moment come when nothing is left but life, and you will find that you do not hesitate over the fate of material possessions."

Most of the people around us are driven by a constant desire to accumulate more and more stuff, mistakenly believing that contentment and security can be obtained by possessions. As a result, their thoughts are filled with how to make more and get more and keep more. This path leads to frustration, as Jesus warned us: *"And he said unto them, Take heed, and beware of covetousness: for a man's life consisteth not in the abundance of the things which he possesseth"* (Luke 12:15).

Focusing our thoughts on possessions and trying to get enough to ensure our needs are met is an approach that is doomed to failure.

NOTES

Solomon, who was rich beyond understanding and had all power as an absolute ruler, understood this principle well. In Ecclesiastes 5:10 he wrote, *"He that loveth silver shall not be satisfied with silver; nor he that loveth abundance with increase: this is also vanity."* Instead we need to build our faith and trust in God to meet our needs. He never suffers an economic downturn or a financial setback. He always has more than enough to meet every need that we face.

People who think constantly about material things will never truly be content. Paul wrote, *"But godliness with contentment is great gain. For we brought nothing into this world, and it is certain we can carry nothing out. And having food and raiment let us be therewith content"* (1 Timothy 6:6–8). Only the person who relies on God and is content with what he has can truly be at peace.

_____

_____

_____

_____

_____

DAY 2

Being a Faithful Steward

Let a man so account of us, as of the ministers of Christ, and stewards of the mysteries of God. Moreover it is required in stewards, that a man be found faithful. But with me it is a very small thing that I should be judged of you, or of man's judgment: yea, I judge not mine own self. —**1 Corinthians 4:1–3**

[BIBLE READING]

Topical
Psalm 24:1

New Testament in a Year
Mark 13:21–37

Entire Bible in a Year
Deuteronomy 19–21;
Mark 13:21–37

A steward is someone who is entrusted to care for something that belongs to another. Perhaps giving, like no other area, reveals our sense of accountability and stewardship. When we give to the Lord, we acknowledge that we are God's servants and that we delight in furthering His cause. George Müller, who cared for thousands of children at his orphanages in England, wrote, "Let us walk as stewards and not act as owners, keeping for ourselves the means with which the Lord has entrusted us. He has not blessed us that we may gratify our own carnal mind, but for the sake of using our money in His service and to His praise."

Although everything we have comes from God and already belongs to God, we are prone to forget that truth and act as if we got our possessions and resources on our own and we have the right to do with them however we see fit. Making a conscious choice to acknowledge God as the owner of our material possessions reminds us that He is our generous provider. When we mentally retain the ownership of our resources, we end up eternally bankrupt—if not financially bankrupt. The sooner we purposefully turn it all over to God and enlist ourselves as His stewards, the better.

Stewardship is a two-sided discipline that requires both contentment and discernment. On one hand, we recognize that being caught up in the proverbial competition with the Joneses or having our spending determined by our own insatiable appetites is not worth the price. The old adage "a penny saved is a penny earned" is true, but it can be lived only by those who possess the godly trait of contentment. Efficient stewardship requires that we learn to live within our means.

In addition to contentment, we need wise discernment in our budgeting. There are people who are struggling to purchase groceries and pay their electric bill while still maintaining a cable television subscription. Sometimes we need to step back and evaluate our financial priorities. Does our spending reflect the reality that everything we have belongs to God and that we will give an account for how we use the resources He has entrusted to us? Are we using our money as a tool, or is our money controlling us and changing our behavior?

_____

_____

_____

_____

_____

DAY 3

Handling Money Wisely

He that is faithful in that which is least is faithful also in much: and he that is unjust in the least is unjust also in much. If therefore ye have not been faithful in the unrighteous mammon, who will commit to your trust the true riches? And if ye have not been faithful in that which is another man's, who shall give you that which is your own?
—**Luke 16:10–12**

[BIBLE READING]

Topical
1 Corinthians 4:2

New Testament in a Year
Mark 14:1–26

Entire Bible in a Year
Deuteronomy 22–24;
Mark 14:1–26

There are very few things that reveal more about a person's character than the way that they handle money. How we use our resources reveals more about what we truly value than what we say matters most to us reveals. Money is a good tool but a very bad master, and we need to use wisdom as we deal with it. Here are three basic Bible principles that will help us properly manage our money:

Work diligently. God blesses hard work. Diligence is a character trait, not a gift. Although God has gifted some people with sharp business intuition or a natural ability to make wise investments, all of us can develop diligence. Money and possessions that come to us as a result of diligence are more appreciated because we understand what was involved in getting them. Diligence is not hinged on a location or position. "*He becometh poor that dealeth with a slack hand: but the hand of the diligent maketh rich*" (Proverbs 10:4).

Give generously. Giving is not a matter of *can* or *can't*, but of *will* or *won't*. In other words, we will be faithful to give based on our willingness, not on our prosperity. This is how the Christians Paul mentioned in 2 Corinthians 8:3 were able to give "*beyond their power.*" They were so willing, so desirous to have part in God's work that they chose to give even at the point of extreme sacrifice. Someone once said, "The more passionate our faith, the

NOTES

more consistent our giving." Our willingness to give to the Lord is a tangible measure of our love for Him.

Save regularly. Some Christians struggle with the idea of saving, because they feel it shows greed or selfishness. But the Bible teaches that it is important to keep part of what we earn. *"A gracious woman retaineth honour: and strong men retain riches"* (Proverbs 11:16). Maintain your savings account with an open hand, ready to use that blessing to honor the Lord in whatever way He directs you.

_____

_____

_____

_____

_____

DAY 4

Making Eternal Investments

Lay not up for yourselves treasures upon earth, where moth and rust doth corrupt, and where thieves break through and steal: But lay up for yourselves treasures in heaven, where neither moth nor rust doth corrupt, and where thieves do not break through nor steal: For where your treasure is, there will your heart be also.
—**Matthew 6:19–21**

[BIBLE READING]

Topical
Romans 14:10–12

New Testament in a Year
Mark 14:27–53

Entire Bible in a Year
Deuteronomy 25–27;
Mark 14:27–53

We have seen some principles for managing our money wisely, but the most important principle to keep in mind is the difference between the temporal and the eternal. Everything that we see around us will one day be destroyed. *"But the day of the Lord will come as a thief in the night; in the which the heavens shall pass away with a great noise, and the elements shall melt with fervent heat, the earth also and the works that are therein shall be burned up"* (2 Peter 3:10).

The only way to have anything that truly lasts is to make eternal investments—to put our resources into God's kingdom. When we give to the Lord's work, there are earthly blessings, but the greatest and most important benefits will come after our lives here on earth have ended. Paul wrote to the generous church at Philippi to thank them for their support of his ministry and said, *"For even in Thessalonica ye sent once and again unto my necessity. Not because I desire a gift: but I desire fruit that may abound to your account"* (Philippians 4:16–17). One day many of us will have the wonderful experience of meeting people in Heaven who are there, in part, because of the giving that we did for the sake of the gospel.

The truth is that we never know what will result from the investments we make in God's work. In the late 1800s, a little girl

NOTES

named Hattie Mae Wiatt couldn't attend Sunday school every week at Grace Baptist Church in Philadelphia because it was too crowded. She died in 1886 and her grieving mother gave the pastor 57 cents which she had saved to help purchase a larger building. When the pastor told that story, the members of the church were moved to action and quickly donated the money that purchased the first of the buildings that would become the Temple Baptist Church, Temple University, and Temple Hospital.

Anything that we give to God can be multiplied by His power to accomplish eternal purposes. We do not have to wait until we can do great things to give. If we simply give what we have, we can trust God to do the rest…and we may be part of something far greater than we can imagine.

_____

_____

_____

_____

_____

DAY 5

Review of Week Eleven

The questions below cover the material we studied in this lesson and are given here to help you cement these truths in your mind and heart. Feel free to look back over previous pages as you answer these questions. When you begin the next lesson with your discipler, take a few minutes to discuss any questions you have from this week's material.

1. What three truths are absolutely crucial for understanding how a Christian should view their finances? _____

    _____

    _____

    _____

2. As a steward of God, what is our job? _____

    _____

    _____

    _____

3. How much is a tithe? _____

    _____

    _____

    _____

4. How did Paul instruct the first-century Christians on giving?

    _____

    _____

    _____

[BIBLE READING]

Topical
2 Corinthians 9:7

New Testament in a Year
Mark 14:54–72

Entire Bible in a Year
Deuteronomy 28–29;
Mark 14:54–72

DAY 6

Topical
Philippians 4:19

New Testament in a Year
Mark 15:1–25

Entire Bible in a Year
Deuteronomy 30–31;
Mark 15:1–25

DAY 7

Topical
Luke 6:38

New Testament in a Year
Mark 15:26–47

Entire Bible in a Year
Deuteronomy 32–34;
Mark 15:26–47

NOTES

5. Giving to God does not make you become wealthy, but rather what has God promised to do if you give? _____

    _____

    _____

    _____

6. What are some of the ways that God will reward our giving?

    _____

    _____

    _____

7. What is the greatest reason to give to God's work? _____

    _____

    _____

    _____

12 GO AND TELL THE GOOD NEWS

---------- **REVIEW** ----------

Take a few moments to review together last week's study, memory verse, and the daily readings. You can use these questions to spark dialogue:

1. What truth or principle stood out to you most in last week's study and/or devotional readings?

2. Since we last met, have you had opportunity to apply or share a truth from the previous study?

3. Do you have any questions related to last week's devotional readings or assignment?

---------- **INTRODUCTION** ----------

The greatest news in the entire world is the message of salvation—that Jesus died to pay for our sins, that He rose from the dead, and that He offers forgiveness to all who will trust Him as their Saviour. This is called the _____, which means the "good news."

▶ **1 Corinthians 15:1, 3–4**

NOTES

God used someone to bring this message to you, and it is now your privilege to bring it to others.

In today's study, we discover God's plan for getting this message to the entire world, your part in that plan, and how the Holy Spirit empowers you for the job.

———— **LESSON TWELVE** ————

We Are Commanded to Spread the Gospel

When Jesus came to earth, His mission was to seek and to save the lost.

▶ **Luke 19:10**

When Jesus saw people lost in sin, His heart was moved with compassion for them.

▶ **Matthew 9:36**

And it was for this mission that Christ gave His life.

▶ **Matthew 20:28**

Spreading the gospel is the responsibility of the _____.

After Jesus was resurrected and before He ascended to Heaven, He gave His disciples instructions to reach the entire world with the gospel. We call this the "Great Commission."

▶ **Matthew 28:18–20**

Simply put, spreading the gospel and teaching new believers are the _____ of the local church. Other

For God so loved the world, that he gave his only begotten Son, that whosoever believeth in him should not perish, but have everlasting life.—John 3:16

GOSPEL 243

ministries and activities are encouraging and helpful, but they are not the church's main purpose.

Spreading the gospel is accomplished through _____ and _____.

God has given us a plan to be able to spread the gospel in our own communities and around the world simultaneously.

▶ **Acts 1:8**

When we share the gospel personally, we often call that "soulwinning" because we are using our witness to tell others how their souls can be saved.

▶ **Proverbs 14:25**

▶ **Proverbs 11:30**

Additionally, as a church, we support people who go to countries around the world bringing the message of salvation. This is called "missions," and it is God's plan to reach the world with the gospel.

The first missionaries were sent out from the church in Antioch.

▶ **Acts 13:1–3**

As you read through the rest of the book of Acts, you'll find that these missionaries went to city after city preaching the gospel and then organizing a church with the new believers in each city. This is still God's plan for missions today, and it is our privilege to support missionaries with prayer and financial gifts and thus have part in spreading the gospel in places we may never go.

We Are Instructed to Witness

Spreading the gospel is not just "the church's job." It is the _____ of every Christian. Remember, the local church is comprised of _____ people.

God has entrusted us with the gospel, and we must be faithful to give it to others.

▶ **1 Timothy 1:11**

So, how do we do this?

Know the gospel and _____ to share it.

God made salvation simple and easy to share. It is so simple, in fact, that there are just five main points you need to remember as you are sharing the gospel with someone else:

God loves you.
JOHN 3:16
For God so loved the world, that he gave his only begotten Son, that whosoever believeth in him should not perish, but have everlasting life.

Everyone is a sinner.
ROMANS 3:23
For all have sinned, and come short of the glory of God;

Sin has a price that must be paid.
ROMANS 6:23
For the wages of sin is death; but the gift of God is eternal life through Jesus Christ our Lord.

For God so loved the world, that he gave his only begotten Son, that whosoever believeth in him should not perish, but have everlasting life.—John 3:16

GOSPEL 245

Jesus Christ died to pay for your sin.

ROMANS 5:8

But God commendeth his love toward us, in that, while we were yet sinners, Christ died for us.

You can ask Jesus Christ to be your Saviour.

ROMANS 10:13

For whosoever shall call upon the name of the Lord shall be saved.

These streamlined points are the main truths of the gospel. If you learn this outline and the verses that go with it, you will be well on your way to being able to tell others how they can be saved.

The very best way to learn how to be a personal soulwinner is to go with an experienced soulwinner and to listen to him or her share the gospel several times.[1]

Be _____ to share your faith.

God has made us His ambassadors of the gospel message.

▶ **2 Corinthians 5:20**

This means that you want to be ready at all times to share your faith—whether an unexpected opportunity arises or you have specially created an opportunity. Always be ready to share with others what God has done in your life.

▶ **1 Peter 3:15**

Here are some practical tips:

---

1. An additional resource for learning to share your faith is the book *Take It Personally* by Paul Chappell (Striving Together Publications, 2016).

NOTES

CONVERSATION STARTER

As a mentor, walk through the main points above, as if you are presenting the gospel to the person you are discipling. Demonstrate how you share these truths in a conversation.

CONVERSATION STARTER

Discuss the opportunities in your church to be part of soulwinning and to learn from an experienced soulwinner.

NOTES

**CONVERSATION
STARTER**

Practice giving a
gospel tract to one
another, role playing
as if the other
is unsaved.

**CONVERSATION
STARTER**

Discuss the organized
soulwinning times
available at your
church. These
are often great
opportunities to
be partnered with
an experienced
soulwinner who can
teach you to share
the gospel.

Carry gospel _____ wherever you go. Put several tracts or outreach cards in your pocket, wallet, purse, car door, backpack— whatever place will be handy for you to be prepared to give them out. Gospel tracts are great to be able to leave with someone if you only have a minute with them (such as a store cashier), and they are often a helpful conversation starter with a co-worker or neighbor.

See every relationship in your life as an _____ to be God's ambassador. Doubtless, you know unsaved people —family members, friends, co-workers, neighbors, people with whom you do business, etc. Who knows but that God may have placed you in their lives to bring them the gospel? Look for opportunities to share with them the wonderful news of salvation.

Schedule a _____ to go soulwinning. Although we should be soulwinners everywhere we go, our busy lives often crowd out this God-given assignment. What gets scheduled gets done, so schedule a regular time to purposefully share the gospel.

We Are Enabled by the Holy Spirit

Does the prospect of sharing your faith with someone else scare you? If so, there is good news! You have a divine Helper—God Himself!

The Holy Spirit _____ us.

As Christ commissioned the disciples to take the gospel into all the world, He assured them of His presence.

▶ **Matthew 28:20**

Jesus promised His disciples that the Holy Spirit would enable them to witness for Him.

For God so loved the world, that he gave his only begotten Son, that whosoever believeth in him should not perish, but have everlasting life.—John 3:16

GOSPEL 247

NOTES

▶ **Acts 1:8**

The Holy Spirit works in _____.

Not only does the Holy Spirit help *us* as we share His message, but He helps the *listener* understand His truth.

As we are obedient to share the message of the gospel, it is actually the Holy Spirit who works in the heart of our hearers to convict them of their need for Christ and to convince them to place their faith in Him.

Notice these words Jesus spoke to His disciples, assuring them of the reality of the Holy Spirit's presence in their lives:

▶ **John 16:7–9**

We could say that the Holy Spirit is the real Soulwinner. We are simply the witnesses that He uses.

What a privilege it is to *know* the gospel. And now, it is your privilege to *share* the gospel!

—————— **APPLICATION** ——————

Getting to share the good news of salvation with another person is one of the greatest joys of the Christian life—topped only by the joy of getting to see someone trust Christ as their Saviour.

Here are a few ways you can prepare to share the gospel with others:

1. Begin praying for opportunities to share the gospel. Whom do you know personally that you should share the gospel with? Add that person's name to your daily prayer list, and ask the Lord to give you an opportunity. You might even ask your mentor to go with you to present the gospel to this person.

THIS STUDY IN REVIEW

1. We Are Commanded to Spread the Gospel
2. We Are Instructed to Witness
3. We Are Enabled by the Holy Spirit

NOTES

2. Ask someone to train you, and schedule a regular time to witness together. Whom do you know who already knows how to share the gospel clearly with others? Take the initiative and ask that person if you can go with them several times as they are witnessing so you can learn from them. (If you're a man, it's always better to ask a man; likewise if you're a lady, to ask a lady.)

3. Practice, practice, practice! Learn the five main points with their verses, and practice leading an imaginary person through them aloud. Practice over and over. This will help you listen to yourself and know if you're explaining clearly. It will also help you become more familiar with the basic message so you can share it with real people who need the Lord.

PREVIOUS MEMORY VERSES

2 TIMOTHY 3:16
1 JOHN 5:7
1 JOHN 4:3
ROMANS 8:16
JEREMIAH 33:3
1 PETER 2:2
GALATIANS 5:22–23
1 CORINTHIANS 10:13
HEBREWS 10:25
EPHESIANS 4:11–12
PHILIPPIANS 4:19

——————— **ASSIGNMENTS** ———————

Memorize these five verses so you will easily be able to share them with others:

- John 3:16
- Romans 3:23
- Romans 6:23
- Romans 5:8
- Romans 10:13

Read the five daily readings throughout this coming week, including answering the questions on day five. These questions are where you will pick up with your discipleship meeting next week.

DAY 1

Convictions of a Soulwinner

Be it known unto you all, and to all the people of Israel, that by the name of Jesus Christ of Nazareth, whom ye crucified, whom God raised from the dead, even by him doth this man stand here before you whole. This is the stone which was set at nought of you builders, which is become the head of the corner. Neither is there salvation in any other: for there is none other name under heaven given among men, whereby we must be saved. —**Acts 4:10–12**

[BIBLE READING]

Topical
Luke 19:10

New Testament in a Year
Mark 16

Entire Bible in a Year
Joshua 1–3; Mark 16

Every believer has a responsibility to be a witness of the gospel that brought them salvation. Soulwinning is not a special gifting reserved for only a few believers. It is the obligation and privilege of every individual Christian to tell others about Jesus. The message of salvation is the most important thing that we can ever share with anyone. It is a tragedy for people to die and go to Hell because no one is willing to tell them about Jesus. Winning souls is not the pastor's job or the deacons' job or the Sunday school teachers' job alone—it is the job of every child of God. Here are three convictions that every effective soulwinner shares:

Hell is real. Every man, woman, and child that we meet has an eternal soul, and there are only two destinations they can reach. There is a place of eternal damnation, torment and separation from God which is where all those who die without placing their faith in Jesus Christ alone as Saviour will go when their lives end. Jesus spoke of the reality of Hell: *"And if thine eye offend thee, pluck it out: it is better for thee to enter into the kingdom of God with one eye, than having two eyes to be cast into hell fire: Where their worm dieth not, and the fire is not quenched"* (Mark 9:47–48).

NOTES

Heaven is real. The place where God's throne rests is also a real place—just as real as any city here on earth. But unlike the places we live, Heaven is perfect. Nothing evil will ever enter that perfect place, and as a result, it will be a place of complete peace and satisfaction. *"And God shall wipe away all tears from their eyes; and there shall be no more death, neither sorrow, nor crying, neither shall there be any more pain: for the former things are passed away"* (Revelation 21:4).

Jesus is the only way of salvation. Though some teach that there are many paths to Heaven and that all religions are just different ways of reaching God, the Bible tells of a single, exclusive plan of salvation. God has only provided one means of entering Heaven, and no matter how sincere someone may be in following another path, it will only lead to Hell. *"Jesus saith unto him, I am the way, the truth, and the life: no man cometh unto the Father, but by me"* (John 14:6).

_____

_____

_____

_____

_____

DAY 2

Compassion of a Soulwinner

But when he saw the multitudes, he was moved with compassion on them, because they fainted, and were scattered abroad, as sheep having no shepherd. Then saith he unto his disciples, The harvest truly is plenteous, but the labourers are few; Pray ye therefore the Lord of the harvest, that he will send forth labourers into his harvest. — **Matthew 9:36–38**

[BIBLE READING]

Topical
Matthew 9:36

New Testament in a Year
Luke 1:1–20

Entire Bible in a Year
Joshua 4–6; Luke 1:1–20

It is impossible for us to truly love God as we should without demonstrating a love for others. Every person we meet will spend eternity either in Heaven or Hell—and God has commanded us to tell them of the only hope of Heaven through salvation in Jesus Christ. There is no greater demonstration of God's love than sharing it with others, and there is no greater indication of our compassion and love for others than to take the time to tell them how they can go to Heaven. This is the most important thing we can do with our lives because it has an eternal impact.

Born in Connecticut in 1718, David Brainerd was orphaned as a teenager. A local pastor took him into his home, and when he was twenty-one, Brainerd went to Yale as a student. He had been convinced that he could gain God's favor on his own, but he came under conviction during a revival and realized that salvation was only of God's grace. When Brainerd finished his education, he determined to become a missionary to the American Indians. He declined the call to pastor a large and wealthy church in New York to live in poverty among the Indians.

He began works in Massachusetts, Pennsylvania, and New Jersey, traveling long miles and often sleeping outside in bad weather. Brainerd said, "I care not where I go or how I live or what I endure so that I may save souls. When I sleep, I dream of them; when I awake, they are first in my thoughts." Never strong in body, Brainerd contracted pulmonary consumption, and died in the home of Jonathan Edwards at the age of twenty-nine. Though he did not see as many converts as he hoped during his lifetime, his story became a great challenge that was used to call many to enter missionary work.

The church today needs a great host of people who will care more about reaching the lost than about success in the business world, getting a bigger house, or the win-loss record of a sports team. Our passion demonstrates what we truly love, and it is only when we have a real passion for the lost that we will be effective in reaching them.

_____

_____

_____

_____

_____

DAY 3

Being Prepared with your Message

And all things are of God, who hath reconciled us to himself by Jesus Christ, and hath given to us the ministry of reconciliation; To wit, that God was in Christ, reconciling the world unto himself, not imputing their trespasses unto them; and hath committed unto us the word of reconciliation. Now then we are ambassadors for Christ, as though God did beseech you by us: we pray you in Christ's stead, be ye reconciled to God. —**2 Corinthians 5:18–20**

[BIBLE READING]

Topical
1 Peter 3:15

New Testament in a Year
Luke 1:21–38

Entire Bible in a Year
Joshua 7–9; Luke 1:21–38

After serving in the Union Army during the Civil War, Major D. W. Whittle returned home to a successful business career with the Elgin Clock Company. It would not be long before his association with D. L. Moody persuaded him to give up that career for full time evangelistic work. Whittle wrote a number of hymns, including "Showers of Blessing" and "I Know Whom I Have Believed." Whittle became a greatly used personal soulwinner as well, but that was not always the case.

Whittle told a friend named Howard Pope that at one point while he was still in his business career but had started preaching and singing, a lady came to his office and said, "Major Whittle, my husband was greatly impressed with the services last night, and he promised me that he would come down and see you this morning." Whittle told her, "He just asked the price of brass, and talked around a little." "That was just an excuse for his coming," she told him. Whittle responded, "I am sorry to say that all I talked about was just brass too." In recounting the story later Whittle said, "That was a mistake I never forgot."

NOTES

Having specific times scheduled for sharing the gospel with others is good because having a schedule helps us in being faithful to fulfill this important obligation. But there are many other times when an opportunity may arise, and we need to be alert and prepared to take advantage of each one of those.

It is important to take the time to learn how to effectively present the gospel. Ask an experienced soulwinner to show you how to go through key verses in order. Learn effective ways that you can respond to some of the most common objectives people raise when they hear the gospel. Make it a habit to go soulwinning on a regular basis. Most importantly, seek to live in such a way that you can experience the power of the Holy Spirit on your life as you witness.

_____

_____

_____

_____

DAY 4

The Real Soulwinner

And he said unto them, It is not for you to know the times or the seasons, which the Father hath put in his own power. But ye shall receive power, after that the Holy Ghost is come upon you: and ye shall be witnesses unto me both in Jerusalem, and in all Judaea, and in Samaria, and unto the uttermost part of the earth.
—**Acts 1:7–8**

[BIBLE READING]

Topical
Matthew 28:20

New Testament in a Year
Luke 1:39–56

Entire Bible in a Year
Joshua 10–12; Luke 1:39–56

We've seen that every Christian has a responsibility to be a witness of the gospel to the lost, but it is important for us to remember that while we do the witnessing, it is really the Holy Spirit who touches the heart of the listener and brings conviction and salvation to those who believe. This power was the key to the success of the early church when they saw so many people become Christians in such a short period of time. *"And with great power gave the apostles witness of the resurrection of the Lord Jesus: and great grace was upon them all"* (Acts 4:33).

If we try to "win" souls through sales techniques, we may be able to talk someone into saying a prayer, but that is not the same thing as seeing someone genuinely converted. Our job is not to win people because that is beyond the power of any individual. Our job is to take the gospel to others and present it to them clearly and carefully with compassion, and trust God to produce the results.

It is the Holy Spirit who does the work of drawing men and women to accept the message of salvation and come to Jesus. Dr. John R. Rice said, "Pray for God to guide you where to go and what to say. Pray particularly for the power of the Holy Spirit upon you. Remember, soulwinning is a supernatural business and no one can do it without supernatural help."

NOTES

It is essential for anyone who desires to be a soulwinner to be walking continually in the fullness and power of the Holy Spirit. Since we never know when we will have an opportunity to present the gospel, we need to always have His guiding hand on our lives. Knowing that God wants people to be saved, we do not have to convince Him to participate in soulwinning—we simply have to be clean vessels so that we can be filled and used for His purpose.

_____

_____

_____

_____

_____

DAY 5

Review of Week Twelve

The questions below cover the material we studied in this lesson and are given here to help you cement these truths in your mind and heart. Feel free to look back over previous pages as you answer these questions. When you begin the next lesson with your discipler, take a few minutes to discuss any questions you have from this week's material.

1. What is the greatest news in the entire world? _____

    _____

    _____

    _____

2. What was Jesus' mission while He was here on earth? _____

    _____

    _____

    _____

3. What are two of the primary responsibilities of the church?

    _____

    _____

    _____

4. What do we call Jesus' command to reach the entire world with the gospel? _____

    _____

    _____

    _____

[BIBLE READING]

Topical
Acts 1:8

New Testament in a Year
Luke 1:57–80

Entire Bible in a Year
Joshua 13–15; Luke 1:57–80

DAY 6

Topical
2 Corinthians 5:20

New Testament in a Year
Luke 2:1–24

Entire Bible in a Year
Joshua 16–18; Luke 2:1–24

DAY 7

Topical
1 Corinthians 15:3–4

New Testament in a Year
Luke 2:25–52

Entire Bible in a Year
Joshua 19–21; Luke 2:25–52

NOTES

5. What are the five main points you need to remember as you are sharing the gospel with others? _____

    _____

    _____

    _____

6. What is the best way to learn how to be a personal soulwinner?

    _____

    _____

    _____

7. How does the Holy Spirit work through our witness? _____

    _____

    _____

    _____

13 LIVING IN LIGHT OF ETERNITY

REVIEW

Take a few moments to review together last week's study, memory verse, and the daily readings. You can use these questions to spark dialogue:

1. What truth or principle stood out to you most in last week's study and/or devotional readings?

2. Since we last met, have you had opportunity to apply or share a truth from the previous study?

3. Do you have any questions related to last week's devotional readings or assignment?

INTRODUCTION

Some of the most encouraging truths for a believer relate to the realities of eternity. The glorious truth is that the difficulties and burdens of this life won't last forever. We will spend eternity in the immediate presence of God.

Perhaps you've wondered how the events at the end of the world will take place and what our response should be to the future. In this study, we see what the Bible says about the spiritual battle surrounding us, the events the Bible prophesies, and how we can live with an eternal perspective.

—— LESSON THIRTEEN ——

A Daily Battle Rages

Scripture is clear that there are unseen spiritual forces in the world that actively oppose God and the people of God.

▶ **Ephesians 6:11–12**

Satan is at _____ against God.

Satan's original name was Lucifer, and God created him as a beautiful and powerful angel.

▶ **Ezekiel 28:12–15**

But he rebelled against God, wanting to be as God, and God expelled him from Heaven.

▶ **Isaiah 14:12–15**

Today, Satan actively resists God, God's work, and God's people.

He deceives.
REVELATION 12:9
And the great dragon was cast out, that old serpent, called the Devil, and Satan, which deceiveth the whole world: he was cast out into the earth, and his angels were cast out with him.

Henceforth there is laid up for me a crown of righteousness, which the Lord, the righteous judge, shall give me at that day...—2 Timothy 4:8

ETERNITY 261

He tempts.

MATTHEW 4:3

And when the tempter came to him, he said, If thou be the Son of God, command that these stones be made bread.

He accuses.

REVELATION 12:10

And I heard a loud voice saying in heaven, Now is come salvation, and strength, and the kingdom of our God, and the power of his Christ: for the accuser of our brethren is cast down, which accused them before our God day and night.

He perverts God's Word.

GENESIS 3:1–4

Now the serpent was more subtil than any beast of the field which the LORD God had made. And he said unto the woman, Yea, hath God said, Ye shall not eat of every tree of the garden? And the woman said unto the serpent, We may eat of the fruit of the trees of the garden: But of the fruit of the tree which is in the midst of the garden, God hath said, Ye shall not eat of it, neither shall ye touch it, lest ye die. And the serpent said unto the woman, Ye shall not surely die:

He hinder's God's servants.

1 THESSALONIANS 2:17–18

But we, brethren, being taken from you for a short time in presence, not in heart, endeavoured the more abundantly to see your face with great desire. Wherefore we would have come unto you, even I Paul, once and again; but Satan hindered us.

NOTES

God has equipped us for the _____.

One of the most common misunderstandings regarding this spiritual battle is the assumption that both forces are equally matched. This couldn't be further from the truth. God is infinitely greater than Satan.

1 JOHN 4:4
Ye are of God, little children, and have overcome them: because greater is he that is in you, than he that is in the world.

And God gives us everything we need to overcome Satan in what is called the "armor of God."

▶ **Ephesians 6:13–18**

Notice the elements of this armor:

Belt of truth— Believing in God's truth to protect us from deception and lies; having honesty and integrity about our lives

Breastplate of righteousness—Doing right

Shoes of the preparation of the gospel of peace—Being conscious of our testimony, ready to witness and bringing the gospel to others

Shield of faith—Trusting God

Helmet of salvation—Remembering God's grace that saved you and being assured of His promise

Sword of the Spirit—The Word of God

Prayer—Praying for others

As we choose to use this armor God has provided, we can be victorious in the daily spiritual battle we face.

Henceforth there is laid up for me a crown of righteousness, which the Lord, the righteous judge, shall give me at that day…—2 Timothy 4:8

ETERNITY  263

NOTES

Future Victory Is Certain

Through the pages of Scripture, God peels back the curtain of time and reveals key end time events.[1] The order in which they will take place chronologically, can be charted like this:

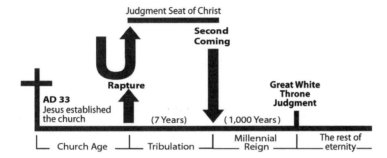

Let's look at each of these events:

We are living in the "_____ age."

As we discovered in Lesson 10, Christ purchased the church with His blood (Acts 20:28). From the moment Christ established the church, what we call the "church age" began. Our commission from Christ right now is to spread the good news of the gospel to everyone.

MARK 16:15

And he said unto them, Go ye into all the world, and preach the gospel to every creature.

During this time, the world will get worse and worse.

▶ **2 Timothy 3:1–4**

---

1. For a book-length treatment of these events, see *Understanding the Times* by Paul Chappell (Striving Together Publications, 2010).

NOTES

We will be caught up in the _____.

At any moment, Christ will take all believers to Heaven. This is called the "rapture." The word *rapture* means "to be caught up."

▶ **1 Thessalonians 4:16–17**

The Bible refers to the rapture as the "blessed hope" of believers.

▶ **Titus 2:13**

We will stand before the Judgment _____.

We'll look at this in detail at the end of this lesson. We just mention it for chronological order now.

God will judge the world during the _____.

For seven years following the Rapture, there will be a time of great trouble on earth as God judges those who reject Him.

▶ **Matthew 24:21**

Incredibly, even during God's judgment, men will still curse and reject God and refuse to repent.

▶ **Revelation 16:9, 11**

During this time, God will leave two witnesses to preach the gospel, and many (primarily of the Jews) will be saved. The majority of people, however, will continue to reject God.

Revelation 11:3
And I will give power unto my two witnesses, and they shall prophesy a thousand two hundred and threescore days, clothed in sackcloth.

Henceforth there is laid up for me a crown of righteousness, which the Lord, the righteous judge, shall give me at that day…—2 Timothy 4:8

ETERNITY 265

ChristT will return to earth at the _____.

During the Tribulation, the world will unite into a one-world government and one-world religion. When Jesus returns to earth, these forces will initiate war with Him at the Battle of Armageddon. Christ will return to earth (and those who have been in Heaven with Him) and will easily defeat these forces.

▸ **Revelation 19:11–16, 19–21**

Christ will rule over earth during the _____ _____.

For one thousand glorious years, Jesus will personally and physically reign as King over all the earth.

REVELATION 20:4

…and they lived and reigned with Christ a thousand years.

ISAIAH 65:25

The wolf and the lamb shall feed together, and the lion shall eat straw like the bullock: and dust shall be the serpent's meat. They shall not hurt nor destroy in all my holy mountain, saith the LORD.

Unbelievers will be judged at the _____ _____ Judgment.

At the end of the Millennial Reign, those who rejected Christ as their Saviour will be formally judged at the Great White Throne Judgment. (This judgment is only for the unsaved, not for those who have received Christ's atonement for their sin.)

▸ **Revelation 20:11–15**

NOTES

At this point, Satan will also be forever banished to eternal torment in Hell.

▶ **Revelation 20:10**

God will create a _____ heaven and a _____ earth.

God will replace the sin-cursed and fallen world with a new heaven and a new earth.

▶ **Revelation 21:1**

And we will worship, love, and praise God for the rest of a glorious, never-ending, eternity.

▶ **Revelation 22:1–5**

We Should Live Today in Light of Eternity

Knowing what God has revealed about the end times should cause us to live now with eternity in view. How specifically can we do that?

Share the _____ regularly.

In Lesson 12 we learned how to share the gospel with others. In light of eternity, it is vital that we make time to obey Christ's Great Commission on a regular basis. Indeed, our time is limited.

As one missionary wrote, "We shall have all eternity to celebrate the victories, but we have only the few hours before sunset in which to win them."[2]

---

2. Amy Carmichael, *Things as They Are* (Young People's Missionary Movement, 1906), 158.

Henceforth there is laid up for me a crown of righteousness, which the Lord, the righteous judge, shall give me at that day…—2 Timothy 4:8

ETERNITY   267

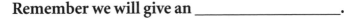

▶ **Mark 16:15–16**

Remember we will give an _____.

During the Tribulation on earth, we will stand before the Judgment Seat of Christ.

▶ **2 Corinthians 5:10**

This judgment is not the same as the Great White Throne Judgment.

It is not to determine if we are going to Heaven or Hell. Jesus' blood has already cleansed us from all our sin.[3]

It is not to judge us for every wicked thing we have done. Again, those sins were already judged at the cross.

Just as a competitor in an athletic competition would stand before the ancient bema seat to receive his reward, so we will stand before our Lord to be rewarded for faithful service.

The Judgment Seat of Christ is to *reward* us for the works we did for God out of pure motives.

▶ **1 Corinthians 3:12–15**

Scripture mentions at least five rewards—crowns—that we can win. Every child of God should have a goal to win each of these. Why? We will have the opportunity to cast them at Jesus' feet, giving honor to Him who enabled us to serve Him.

The Crown of Righteousness: This crown is given to those who look forward to the return of Christ.

---

3.   1 John 2:2

NOTES

CONVERSATION STARTER

Have you ever received a ribbon or trophy after you competed in an event? You were rewarded for the skill you did develop, but the moments you could have been training but didn't or the moments you spent in a counter-productive way to your training weren't revealed during the giving of the awards. Those moments were simply wasted—the only "punishment" being a loss of a higher reward.

2 Timothy 4:8

Henceforth there is laid up for me a crown of righteousness, which the Lord, the righteous judge, shall give me at that day: and not to me only, but unto all them also that love his appearing.

The Crown of Life: This is the martyr's crown, but it is also given to those who overcome temptation (James 1:12).

Revelation 2:10

Fear none of those things which thou shalt suffer: behold, the devil shall cast some of you into prison, that ye may be tried; and ye shall have tribulation ten days: be thou faithful unto death, and I will give thee a crown of life.

The Incorruptible Crown: This is given to those who exhibit temperance or moderation in their lives. It is the result of yielding to the Holy Spirit and being a testimony to those around us.

1 Corinthians 9:25

And every man that striveth for the mastery is temperate in all things. Now they do it to obtain a corruptible crown; but we an incorruptible.

The Crown of Rejoicing: This crown is given to those who have given their lives to reach people for Christ. The reason it is called a crown of rejoicing is because there is no greater joy than being used to win someone to Christ.

1 Thessalonians 2:19

For what is our hope, or joy, or crown of rejoicing? Are not even ye in the presence of our Lord Jesus Christ at his coming?

The Crown of Glory: This crown is given to those who faithfully help lead people in the Word of God. It is not reserved only for pastors. Every child of God should be actively involved in teaching someone else.

Henceforth there is laid up for me a crown of righteousness, which the Lord, the righteous judge, shall give me at that day…—2 Timothy 4:8

ETERNITY 269

NOTES

1 Peter 5:4

And when the chief Shepherd shall appear, ye shall receive a crown of glory that fadeth not away.

The most exciting moment of the Judgment Seat of Christ is what we have the privilege to do with these rewards—cast them at Jesus' feet in grateful worship.

▶ **Revelation 4:10–11**

APPLICATION

THIS STUDY IN REVIEW

1. A Daily Battle Rages
2. Future Victory Is Certain
3. We Should Live Today in Light of Eternity

Every day, you are in the middle of a spiritual battle. Satan actively works to resist you and to resist your efforts to live for God. Always remember, however, that God is greater and that He has given you the resources to live in daily victory.

Here are a few practical ways you can live in light of eternity:

"Put on" the armor of God. Every day, think through the various pieces of the armor of God, and make a decision to "wear" each piece.

Tell others about Christ, and invest in their spiritual growth. The most important way we can prepare for eternal rewards to cast at Jesus' feet is to lead others to Christ and to invest in their spiritual growth. We'll visit this topic in more detail in our final study.

Live every day looking forward to Jesus' return. Like a bride anticipating her wedding day, remember Christ's coming. This thought brings both joy and diligence!

NOTES

PREVIOUS MEMORY
VERSES

2 Timothy 3:16
1 John 5:7
1 John 4:3
Romans 8:16
Jeremiah 33:3
1 Peter 2:2
Galatians 5:22–23
1 Corinthians 10:13
Hebrews 10:25
Ephesians 4:11–12
Philippians 4:19
John 3:16
Romans 3:23
Romans 6:23
Romans 5:8
Romans 10:13

ASSIGNMENTS

Write 2 Timothy 4:7–8 in the space below, and plan to memorize these verses so you can quote them to your discipler next week.

_____

_____

_____

_____

Read the five daily readings throughout this coming week, including answering the questions on day five. These questions are where you will pick up with your discipleship meeting next week.

DAY 1

Complete Protection

Put on the whole armour of God, that ye may be able to stand against the wiles of the devil. For we wrestle not against flesh and blood, but against principalities, against powers, against the rulers of the darkness of this world, against spiritual wickedness in high places. Wherefore take unto you the whole armour of God, that ye may be able to withstand in the evil day, and having done all, to stand. —**Ephesians 6:11–13**

[BIBLE READING]

Topical
Ephesians 6:11–12

New Testament in a Year
Luke 3

Entire Bible in a Year
Joshua 22–24; Luke 3

The Bible frequently uses military metaphors to describe the Christian life. Every day, until we reach Heaven, we face attacks from the enemy who hopes to knock us off course and make us ineffective in our witness and work for God. Knowing the reality of the threats that we face, we need to be constantly on guard. Just as a soldier would not think of going out on to the battlefield without his protective gear, we should never go out into the world without wearing all of the pieces of the armor of God for they offer us complete protection.

Ephesians 6 lists the "armour of God," but each of these areas of armor are also mentioned other places in Scripture:

"Loins girt about with truth." The belt that holds the armor in place is the truth. *"Sanctify them through thy truth: thy word is truth"* (John 17:17).

"Breastplate of righteousness." The covering of the middle of our body is righteousness. *"The fear of the LORD is clean, enduring for ever: the judgments of the LORD are true and righteous altogether"* (Psalm 19:9).

"Preparation of the gospel of peace." Our feet are covered with readiness to witness. *"How beautiful upon the mountains are the feet of him that bringeth good tidings, that publisheth peace; that bringeth good tidings of good, that publisheth salvation; that saith unto Zion, Thy God reigneth!"* (Isaiah 52:7).

"Shield of faith." Our protection from the attacks of the enemy is faith. *"So then faith cometh by hearing, and hearing by the word of God"* (Romans 10:17).

"Helmet of salvation". Our heads are guarded by God's salvation. *"For unto us was the gospel preached, as well as unto them: but the word preached did not profit them, not being mixed with faith in them that heard it"* (Hebrews 4:2).

"Sword of the Spirit." Our only offensive weapon against the enemy is the Scriptures. *"Yet Michael the archangel, when contending with the devil he disputed about the body of Moses, durst not bring against him a railing accusation, but said, The Lord rebuke thee"* (Jude 9).

If our hearts and minds are guarded by the armor God has provided to us, we do not need to fear any attack that the enemy can bring against us.

_____

_____

_____

_____

_____

DAY 2

The Test of Fire

[BIBLE READING]

Topical
1 John 4:4

New Testament in a Year
Luke 4:1–30

Entire Bible in a Year
Judges 1–3; Luke 4:1–30

Now if any man build upon this foundation gold, silver, precious stones, wood, hay, stubble; Every man's work shall be made manifest: for the day shall declare it, because it shall be revealed by fire; and the fire shall try every man's work of what sort it is. If any man's work abide which he hath built thereupon, he shall receive a reward. If any man's work shall be burned, he shall suffer loss: but he himself shall be saved; yet so as by fire. —**1 Corinthians 3:12–15**

In the days of William Booth, few churches had any interest in reaching the outcasts of society who lived in poverty or on the streets. After the Salvation Army was founded and began to see many saved and lives transformed, Booth became a well-known figure in both England and America. At one point he was invited to meet with Queen Victoria. As they talked, she asked him what the secret of his success was. Booth replied, "Your Majesty, some men have a passion for money. Some people have a passion for things. I have a passion for people."

Every one of us gets the same amount of time each day. Though we do not know how long we will live, we do know that we have today. The question is how we will use the gift of time that we have been given. Will we spend the most precious resource that we have on the temporal or on the eternal? Works that are burned up at the Judgment Seat will not produce rewards. Only if we spend our time and resources on what matters to God will we hear Him say, "Well done."

The key to a life that is worthy of reward—a life that is invested in gold, silver and precious stones—is to spend each day on the things that are eternal. This cannot be something that we are going to get around to after life settles down and the kids are a little older. Instead it is something we must do right now, using each day wisely for maximum result. Moses wrote, *"So teach us to number our days, that we may apply our hearts unto wisdom"* (Psalm 90:12).

In everything that we do, each opportunity to invest the time, talent, and treasure that God has entrusted to us, we need to choose in light of the coming test. While we may be able to convince others that our work has value, God's fire will put it to the ultimate test. Only those things that meet His exacting standards and are done with motives that are proper will produce a lasting reward.

_____

_____

_____

_____

_____

DAY 3

God Knows What I Am Doing

For God is not unrighteous to forget your work and labour of love, which ye have shewed toward his name, in that ye have ministered to the saints, and do minister. And we desire that every one of you do shew the same diligence to the full assurance of hope unto the end: That ye be not slothful, but followers of them who through faith and patience inherit the promises. —**Hebrews 6:10–12**

[BIBLE READING]

Topical
Ephesians 6:13–18

New Testament in a Year
Luke 4:31–44

Entire Bible in a Year
Judges 4–6; Luke 4:31–44

In October of 1941 during the dark days of World War II, Winston Churchill went to speak at the Harrow School, where he had attended as a boy. To the assembled students he spoke of the challenges that England was facing and the challenges they would face in their lives. He offered them this guidance: "Never give in. Never give in. Never, never, never, never—in nothing, great or small, large or petty—never give in, except to convictions of honour and good sense. Never yield to force. Never yield to the apparently overwhelming might of the enemy."

All of us face challenges and difficulties. The secret of successful people in any field is not the absence of problems but the courage and hope to overcome them. Those who lose hope are already almost defeated. Paul wrote, *"And let us not be weary in well doing: for in due season we shall reap, if we faint not"* (Galatians 6:9). One of the tactics Satan uses very effectively is to tell us the lie that because the harvest has not yet come, it is not coming at all.

God's Word paints a different picture—the harvest comes "in due season." The principle we need to remember is that hope allows us to overcome obstacles. Dr. Bob Jones, Sr. said, "The test of your character is what it takes to stop you." Difficulty and even temporary defeat are not the end unless we allow them to be. Rather than looking at our problems, we should look to Christ in hope and follow the example He set for us of enduring to win the victory.

There is never a challenge that you face which comes as a surprise to God. He never forgets us, and He always knows not only what we are dealing with in the present but what is coming next. If we are faithful to continue, He will provide the power and strength and renewal that we need to keep going on the right path. Peter wrote, *"Wherefore gird up the loins of your mind, be sober, and hope to the end for the grace that is to be brought unto you at the revelation of Jesus Christ;"* (1 Peter 1:13).

_____

_____

_____

_____

_____

DAY 4

Forever Morning

And there shall be no more curse: but the throne of God and of the Lamb shall be in it; and his servants shall serve him: And they shall see his face; and his name shall be in their foreheads. And there shall be no night there; and they need no candle, neither light of the sun; for the Lord God giveth them light: and they shall reign for ever and ever. —**Revelation 22:3–5**

There are so many wonderful things about Heaven that all of the books in the world could not contain them, and even if they were written down, our finite minds could not grasp the infinite wonder that awaits us in eternity. When sin is banished forever and there are no more effects from the fall and the curse, life will be filled with joy, and there will no longer be any night. But the greatest glory of Heaven is not a golden street or gates carved from pearls or foundations made of precious stones. Instead it is the wonderful presence of the Son of God.

Charles Spurgeon said, "Beloved, if we were allowed to look within the veil which parts us from the world of spirits, we should see, first of all, the person of our Lord Jesus. If now we could go where the immortal spirits day without night circle the throne rejoicing, we should see each of them with their faces turned in one direction; and if we should step up to one of the blessed spirits, and say, 'O bright immortal, why are thine eyes fixed? What is it that absorbs thee quite, and wraps thee up in vision?' He, without deigning to give an answer, would simply point to the centre of the sacred circle, and lo, we should see a Lamb in the midst of the throne. They have not yet ceased to admire his beauty, and marvel at his wonders and adore his person."

[BIBLE READING]

Topical
1 Thessalonians 4:16–17

New Testament in a Year
Luke 5:1–16

Entire Bible in a Year
Judges 7–8; Luke 5:1–16

The central glory of Heaven will be that we will be eternally where God is. There will be no leaving and no parting—and no time so that we will never have to leave. John saw a great angel who announced the end of time. *"And sware by him that liveth for ever and ever, who created heaven, and the things that therein are, and the earth, and the things that therein are, and the sea, and the things which are therein, that there should be time no longer:"* (Revelation 10:6). This is the ultimate destination toward which we are heading. There will be days of defeat and discouragement, and trials and tribulations. But there is no defeat for the child of God. The worst that this life threatens—death—is merely the beginning of a new morning that will never end.

_____

_____

_____

_____

_____

DAY 5

Review of Week Thirteen

The questions below cover the material we studied in this lesson and are given here to help you cement these truths in your mind and heart. Feel free to look back over previous pages as you answer these questions. When you begin the next lesson with your discipler, take a few minutes to discuss any questions you have from this week's material.

1. What is one of the most common misunderstandings regarding the spiritual battle? _____
    _____
    _____
    _____

2. What does the word *rapture* mean? _____
    _____
    _____
    _____

3. What are the seven years of great trouble on earth following the Rapture called? _____
    _____
    _____
    _____

4. How many years will Christ personally and physically reign as King over all the earth? _____
    _____
    _____
    _____

[BIBLE READING]

Topical
Revelation 19:11–16

New Testament in a Year
Luke 5:17–39

Entire Bible in a Year
Judges 9–10; Luke 5:17–39

DAY 6

Topical
Mark 16:15–16

New Testament in a Year
Luke 6:1–26

Entire Bible in a Year
Judges 11–12; Luke 6:1–26

DAY 7

Topical
2 Timothy 4:8

New Testament in a Year
Luke 6:27–49

Entire Bible in a Year
Judges 13–15; Luke 6:27–49

NOTES

5. Where will unbelievers be judged? _____

_____

_____

_____

6. Where will the believers give an account of their lives? _____

_____

_____

_____

7. What are the five rewards—crowns—that we can be rewarded with? _____

_____

_____

_____

(14) CONTINUE

--- **REVIEW** ---

Take a few moments to review together last week's study, memory verse, and the daily readings. You can use these questions to spark dialogue:

1. What truth or principle stood out to you most in last week's study and/or devotional readings?

2. Since we last met, have you had opportunity to apply or share a truth from the previous study?

3. Do you have any questions related to last week's devotional readings or assignment?

--- **INTRODUCTION** ---

Congratulations! You are on the homestretch of the *Continue* discipleship course. We've come a long way in the past thirteen studies!

In this final study, we'll see the importance of not just *beginning* but *finishing* your Christian life with faithfulness.

Like the Apostle Paul, we want to finish our life still faithful and looking forward to meeting the Lord:

2 TIMOTHY 4:6–8
For I am now ready to be offered, and the time of my departure is at hand. I have fought a good fight, I have finished my course, I have kept the faith: Henceforth there is laid up for me a crown of righteousness, which the Lord, the righteous judge, shall give me at that day: and not to me only, but unto all them also that love his appearing.

The Christian life is not just a journey of knowing facts; it is a journey of knowing, loving, and serving God—for a lifetime!

In this study, we'll see three vital areas in which you must *continue:*

——— LESSON FOURTEEN ———

Continue in the Word

The baseline for being a disciple of Christ is continuing in His Word.

JOHN 8:31
Then said Jesus to those Jews which believed on him, If ye continue in my word, then are ye my disciples indeed;

Walking through this discipleship program with a mentor has hopefully given you a good foundation in understanding God's Word and applying it to your life. But don't stop now! This is just the beginning of a life-long journey of continuing in the Word of God.

_____ the Word

Maintain a spirit that is teachable and receptive to the Word of God. Receive it with a ready mind, and search it with a hungry heart.

Then said Jesus to those Jews which believed on him, If ye continue in my word, then are ye my disciples indeed;—John 8:31

CONTINUE 283

▶ **Acts 17:11**

When you hear God's Word preached or taught, remember to look past the "messenger" to the authority of God's Word itself. Approach God's Word with a willingness to receive and obey even before you hear a specific message from it.

▶ **1 Thessalonians 2:13**

_____ the Word

Be a student of Scripture.

▶ **2 Timothy 2:15**

Read it daily so you can apply it faithfully. Remember to make Bible reading, memory, and study part of the regular routines of your life.

Bible reading: If you have been using the topical reading plan, now would be a great time to switch over to the New Testament in a year plan. If you have been using the New Testament or whole Bible in a year plan, continue using it to daily read God's Word, even without the accountability of meeting each week with your mentor. (See Appendix E for New Testament and whole Bible in a year schedules.)

Bible memory: If you haven't done so already, visit Appendix C which provides many Scripture verses arranged under topics. Set specific goals for how many verses you want to memorize each week, month, year, and choose a topic that relates to needs in your life. Consistent Bible memory can change your life!

Bible study: In Lesson 7 we looked at how to study the Bible. As you finish this discipleship course, this would be a great time to choose a specific topic you would like to study on your own.

NOTES

CONVERSATION
STARTER

Take a few minutes to reflect on how your life has changed over the past few months in response to what you have learned in *Continue* discipleship. In what ways have you seen God bless your life as you've obeyed His Word by faith?

_____ the Word

As we've seen throughout this course, our goal is not simply to *know* God's Word; it is to *obey* God's Word.

The ultimate way we continue in God's Word is if after reading or hearing it, we move forward into applying it.

▶ **James 1:22–25**

Our goal in understanding God's Word should always be that we might obey it. So continue in the Word of God, and it will continue to change your life for the better!

Continue Following Jesus

Remember, discipleship isn't a course; it is a lifestyle. It is the process of unreservedly following Jesus—not just for a few months, but for a lifetime.

LUKE 9:23
And he said to them all, If any man will come after me, let him deny himself, and take up his cross daily, and follow me.

What does that mean on an ongoing basis?

Be fully _____.

Let there be no area of your life that you are holding back from the Lord.

▶ **Matthew 10:37–39**

▶ **Romans 12:1–2**

Then said Jesus to those Jews which believed
on him, If ye continue in my word, then are ye
my disciples indeed;—John 8:31

CONTINUE  285

Someone once said, "If Jesus is not Lord *of* all your life, He is not Lord *at* all in your life." In other words, disciples don't pick and choose what to obey and what to disregard. They simply surrender.

▸ **Luke 6:46**

Never think, though, of following Christ as a sacrifice. We may make some sacrifices—yielding activities or relationships or things—to follow the Lord. But in so doing, we gain in ways greater than what we "give up."

▸ **John 6:66–69**

As the missionary Jim Elliot said, "He is no fool who gives what he cannot keep to gain what he cannot lose."

Living a surrendered life is the best way to experience the joy of the Christian life.

▸ **John 15:10–11**

Be fully _____.

As you know, Satan actively works against the surrendered Christian.

▸ **Ephesians 6:11–13**

The Bible warns us to be vigilant to his attacks and temptations.

▸ **1 Peter 5:8**

Sometimes Satan uses direct persecution in his attacks.

▸ **2 Timothy 3:12**

Additionally, the trials of life will test your commitment to the Lord.

NOTES

**CONVERSATION
STARTER**

Has the Lord been convicting you of an area in your life that you haven't surrendered to Him? Or maybe of an area that you once surrendered but have been taking back? Share with each other to ask for prayer and accountability.

▶ **Acts 20:24**

Whatever the test may be, we are instructed to be committed—to remain strong in God's grace.

2 TIMOTHY 2:1
Thou therefore, my son, be strong in the grace that is in Christ Jesus.

2 TIMOTHY 2:3
Thou therefore endure hardness, as a good soldier of Jesus Christ.

Salvation is the miracle of a moment, but discipleship is the process of a lifetime. Keep following the Lord as a personal disciple.

Continue Mentoring Others

Discipleship does not end with one disciple. It is the process of *multiplying* disciples.

One good way to think of this is the difference between addition and multiplication.

When you share the gospel with another person and they trust Christ as their Saviour, that is addition—someone has been added to God's family.

But when you then take a new Christian under your wing and teach them how to follow the Lord as a disciple themselves and to share their faith with others, that is multiplication!

This is the full Great Commission Jesus gave to the church—not to just lead people to salvation, but to follow through in leading them to follow Christ in baptism (and being added to the church) and in becoming a personal disciple.

Then said Jesus to those Jews which believed on him, If ye continue in my word, then are ye my disciples indeed;—John 8:31

CONTINUE (287)

MATTHEW 28:19–20

Go ye therefore, and teach all nations, baptizing them in the name of the Father, and of the Son, and of the Holy Ghost: Teaching them to observe all things whatsoever I have commanded you: and, lo, I am with you alway, even unto the end of the world. Amen.

We see the progression from addition to multiplication in the book of Acts.

First, people were added to the church.

ACTS 2:41

Then they that gladly received his word were baptized: and the same day there were added unto them about three thousand souls.

ACTS 2:47

Praising God, and having favour with all the people. And the Lord added to the church daily such as should be saved.

ACTS 5:14

And believers were the more added to the Lord, multitudes both of men and women.)

Then, as these new believers became grounded in God's Word through the instruction of the local church, they *multiplied.*

ACTS 6:1

And in those days, when the number of the disciples was multiplied, there arose a murmuring of the Grecians against the Hebrews, because their widows were neglected in the daily ministration.

ACTS 6:7

And the word of God increased; and the number of the disciples multiplied in Jerusalem greatly; and a great company of the priests were obedient to the faith.

NOTES

ACTS 9:31

Then had the churches rest throughout all Judaea and Galilee and Samaria, and were edified; and walking in the fear of the Lord, and in the comfort of the Holy Ghost, were multiplied.

How can you be part of this process of multiplication?

Lead by your _____.

If you are going to help young Christians develop a personal walk with God and a commitment to Him, it is vital that you have a strong Christian testimony.

▶ **2 Timothy 3:10–11**

A preacher of yesteryear, H. A. Ironside, wisely said, "If lips and life do not agree, the testimony will not amount to much."

Do unbelievers around you know that you are a Christian? Does your lifestyle show a commitment to Christ? Would following your example lead a young Christian closer to the Lord?

▶ **1 Corinthians 11:1**

CONVERSATION
STARTER

What mature Christian in your life has motivated you to grow in your walk with God? God desires to use you to do that for someone else!

Invest _____.

Mentoring another Christian in discipleship is an investment. It is a commitment to love, pray for, and lead another Christian in spiritual growth. It is a willingness to take the truths you've been given and pass them on to others, teaching them to do the same… and the process continues.

▶ **2 Timothy 2:2**

Then said Jesus to those Jews which believed on him, If ye continue in my word, then are ye my disciples indeed;—John 8:31

CONTINUE 289

This process is the Bible pattern, and it is the goal of the discipleship ministry at our church.

Remember, above all, to continue following the Lord personally and sincerely. This will bring blessing in your life and will enable you to continue investing in the lives of others.

▶ **Ephesians 5:1**

APPLICATION

What an exciting journey *Continue* has been! As you complete this course, consider these ways you can be sure you are continuing as a disciple:

1. Stay in touch with your mentor. Although the official "discipleship program" has ended, you need continuing spiritual friendships and accountability. Your mentor is also your friend. Stay in touch, and remain open to spiritual input from your mentor.

2. Be a faithful witness of the gospel. Make it a serious prayer request and goal to personally lead someone to the Lord. Multiplying disciples begins with someone trusting Christ as their Saviour! Ask the Lord to let you see someone saved through your sharing the gospel with them.

3. Continue. Continue in God's Word. Continue following the Lord wholeheartedly. And continue witnessing and discipling others.

Congratulations! You've completed the course!

Only you're not finished…continue on!

NOTES

CONVERSATION STARTER

Do you feel you are ready to begin mentoring someone else? You will need approval from your church leadership. Discuss with your mentor if he/she believes you are ready or has any recommendations for you to help you become ready to take this next step.

THIS STUDY IN REVIEW

1. Continue in the Word
2. Continue Following Jesus
3. Continue Mentoring Others

ANSWER KEY FOR FILL-IN-THE-BLANKS

Week One—**The Word of God**

process	66	is	evidence
committed follower	2	God-breathed	translated
Scripture	before	Word of God	guides
God	New	40	true
Prayer	subjects	1,500	church
Living	author	3	life
Church	Revelation	3	growth
Financial	Inspiration	promised	promises
Witnessing	Scripture	process	temptation
discipler	written	write	change
grounded	humans	copy	obey
every	recorded	church	plainly revealed
attendance	author	truth	regular part
assignments	inspiration	church	
Bible	not	teach	

Week Two—**Knowing God**

revealed	God	resemble	Infinite
creation	Scriptures	likeness	in
origins	Son	greater	lives
faith	one	attributes	fruit
Creator	trinity	unique	everything
chance	persons	Holy	more
please	Father	Omnipresent	wants
history	Son	Omnipotent	comes
Eden	Spirit	Omniscient	measured
Noah's	same	Immutable	
conscience	image	Sovereign	

Week Three—**Who is Jesus?**

deity	is	sinned	obedience
false	liar	died	information
gospel	lunatic	saves	application
follow	Lord	resurrection	denies
names	us	ten	others
works	with	500	with
worship	450	church	
attributes	experience	lives	

Week Four—**Your Salvation**

moment	reality	work	immersion
lose	assurance	chastening	soon
possible	promises	corrects	after
gift	shall	confidence	refuses
relationship	cannot	obedience	testimony
security	presence	glad	
sealed	love	identification	
No	nothing	every	

Week Five—**Developing A Prayer Life**

talking	faith	earnestly	Disregard
asking	motives	plan	fellowship
When	God's	relationship	time
If	Jesus'	hindrances	list
regularly	Christians	Unconfessed	
continually	privately	Unforgiveness	

Week Six—**Your Relationship with God's Word**

profitable	Meditate	obey	Understanding
growth	memorizing	inside out	Obeying
Read	Study	renewed	Continued use
Hear	Apply	thinking	transformation

All scripture is given by inspiration of God, and is profitable for doctrine, for reproof, for correction, for instruction in righteousness:—2 Timothy 3:16

APPENDIX A 293

Week Seven—**The Holy Spirit**

Comforter	filled	love	faith
truth	control	joy	meekness
service	walk in	peace	temperance
witness	sin	longsuffering	definite
impossible	Grieving	gentleness	reaffirm
inside	Quenching	goodness	ask

Week Eight—**The Life of a Disciple**

motivated	Use	accounts	grace
complete	Remember	Yield	decision
reasonable	Avoid	set apart	search
three	friends	holy	Examine
power	Ask	live	

Week Nine—**The Local Church**

called out	patterned	Separation	faithful
purchased	Biblical	Two ordinances	accountable
commissioned	Autonomy	Separation	committed
preeminence	Priesthood	truth	
local	Two offices	reach	
called out	Individual	nurture	

Week Ten—**Your Place in Your Church Family**

gospel	you	Remember	solution
growth	Discover	Resolve	reconciled relationship
whole	Use	Go	

Week Eleven—**Financial Stewardship**

owner	regularly	needs
stewards	by grace	bless
account	willingly	fruit

Week Twelve—**Go and Tell the Good News**

gospel	missions	prepared	empowers
church	personal responsibility	tracts	hearts
primary responsibilities	individual	opportunity	
soulwinning	how	time	

Week Thirteen—**Living in Light of Eternity**

war	Seat of Christ	Great White Throne	account
battle	Tribulation	new	
church	Second Coming	new	
Rapture	Millennial Reign	gospel	

Week Fourteen—**Continue**

Receive	Apply	committed	personally
Study	surrendered	example	

(B) ANSWERS FOR LESSON REVIEW QUESTIONS

Week One—**The Word of God**

1. What is a disciple?
   A disciple is a committed follower of Jesus Christ.

2. What is the clearest way that God has revealed Himself?
   Through the pages of Scripture

3. Who is the author of the Bible?
   God

4. What does the word *inspiration* mean in the Bible
   "God-breathed"

5. How do we know that the Bible is preserved for us?
   God promised to preserve His Word.
   God tells us the process by which He has preserved His Word.
   God has preserved His Word historically.

6. What are some ways that the Word of God has power in our lives today?
   The Holy Spirit guides us.
   The Bible tells us what is true.
   It tells us how the church should operate.
   It instructs us in every area of life.

7. What is our responsibility as disciples concerning God's Word?
To read, study, and obey the Bible

Week Two—**Knowing God**

1. Believing that God created the world is a matter of what?
Faith

2. What are the two times in world history when the entire world knew the revealed truth of who God is?
The Garden of Eden
In Noah's day

3. What does the word *trinity* mean? What are the three Persons in the Godhead that make up the Trinity?
Tri-unity, or one in three.
God the Father
God the Son
God the Holy Spirit

4. Give some examples of God's many attributes. What are some that you want to see God develop in your life?
Holy
Omnipresent
Omnipotent
Omniscient
Immutable
Sovereign
Infinite

5. Everything God allows in our lives He uses for the purpose of molding us to what?
To the image of Jesus Christ

All scripture is given by inspiration of God, and is profitable for doctrine, for reproof, for correction, for instruction in righteousness:—2 Timothy 3:16

APPENDIX B 297

6. Why has God revealed Himself to us?

Because He wants a relationship with us

7. How is growth in our Christian life measured?

It is measured by becoming more like Christ.

Week Three—**Who is Jesus?**

1. Why is it vital that we believe in the deity of Christ—that Jesus is God?

Knowing who Jesus is guards us against false teachers, helps us in sharing the gospel with others, and allows us to know and follow Him.

2. What does the name Emmanuel mean?

God with us.

3. What verse tells us that Jesus understands our feelings, needs, and temptations not only by omniscient knowledge, but also by experience?

Hebrews 4:15

4. How did God prove His love for us?

By coming to earth and paying our penalty for sin

5. Why is it important in relation to Jesus' death for our sin that He actually is God?

If Jesus were not God, He could not have paid for the sins of the world; He would have been paying for His own sin.

6. There are many evidences in Scripture for Jesus' deity, but what is the most spectacular?

His bodily resurrection from the dead

7. What is one of the ways we know someone is a false teacher and that we should reject their teaching?
If they deny or question Jesus' deity

Week Four—**Your Salvation**

1. What are some of the metaphors the Bible uses to describe the time you trusted Jesus as your Saviour?
You passed from darkness to light.
You were born again.
You have been redeemed—brought back.
You are adopted into God's family.

2. Why is it impossible to ever lose your salvation?
God's gift is forever
Our relationship is sure
We have a "security deposit" (the Holy Spirit will never leave you)

3. How can we have assurance of our salvation?
We have assurance because of God's:
Promises
Presence
Love
Work in our lives
Chastening

4. Who assures our hearts of our relationship with God?
The Holy Spirit

5. What are the evidences of salvation in a Christian's life?
Hunger for the Word of God
Growing obedience to God's commandments
Love for other Christians

All scripture is given by inspiration of God, and is profitable for doctrine, for reproof, for correction, for instruction in righteousness:—2 Timothy 3:16

APPENDIX B 299

NOTES

6. What is the first way we can demonstrate that we want to obey our Lord's commands?
   Baptism

7. What are three important reasons to be baptized?
   Christ commands it.
   Christ was our example.
   Believers in the Bible practiced it.

Week Five—**Developing A Prayer Life**

1. What can we talk to God about in prayer?
   We can ask for needs and talk about our troubles.

2. When should we pray?
   We can pray at any time, and we should pray regularly. Prayer is not something we run to only in times of emergency. It is to be our regular communication with God.

3. Where should we pray?
   We can (and should) pray at any time and any place. God is available to us whenever and wherever.

4. What is one way of strengthening our faith and our boldness in prayer?
   Praying with other Christians

5. What are some of the things that can be a hindrance to our prayers?
   Unconfessed sin, unforgiveness, and disregard for the Bible

6. How do we get rid of these hindrances?
   We confess our sin through prayer and ask the Lord to forgive us.

NOTES

7. What are a few ways you can begin developing a meaningful prayer life?
    Plan a regular prayer time and begin a prayer list.

Week Six—**Your Relationship with God's Word**

1. As listed in 2 Timothy 3:16, what are the four areas that are vital for Christians who wants to build their life upon a foundation of truth?
    Doctrine, reproof, correction, and instruction

2. What are some ways you can include the Bible in your routine?
    Read the Bible daily, hear teaching and preaching of the Bible at church, think on or memorize verses from the Bible, study God's Word, and apply it to your life.

3. What is God's plan for our transformation as Christians?
    That as we meditate and think on the truths of the Bible, those truths would impact our actions and change our lives

4. What are three ways that God's Word can transform our lives?
    Understanding the Bible, obeying the Bible, and reading the Bible continually can transform our lives.

5. What is a result of obeying the Bible?
    Obeying the Bible allows the Holy Spirit to transform your life to become more and more like Jesus.

6. Why should you continue reading the Bible?
    Reading the Bible will allow you to apply God's Word to your life and will aid you in discerning right from wrong.

7. What can help you meditate on God's Word?
    Memorizing verses

All scripture is given by inspiration of God, and is profitable for doctrine, for reproof, for correction, for instruction in righteousness:—2 Timothy 3:16

APPENDIX B 301

NOTES

Week Seven—**The Holy Spirit**

1. Give some examples of how the Holy Spirit ministers to our hearts.
   The Holy Spirit:
   > *is the divine Comforter*
   > *guides you to truth*
   > *strengthens you for service*
   > *empowers your witness*

2. Whose job is it to convict others to trust Jesus as their Saviour?
   The Holy Spirit

3. What does Scripture say about allowing the Holy Spirit to work in the Christian life?
   Scripture instructs us to be filled with the Spirit.
   Scripture warns us not to sin against the Spirit.

4. What does it mean when the Holy Spirit desires to fill us?
   He wants to control our actions and reactions—He wants us to daily yield to Him so that we obey and allow Him to control us.

5. What happens after we continually grieve and quench the Holy Spirit?
   We cease to hear the Holy Spirit's voice.

6. Where is a list of the fruit of the Spirit in the Bible and what are the fruits of the Spirit?
   Galatians 5:22–23; love, joy, peace, longsuffering, gentleness, goodness, faith, meekness, and temperance

7. What are three ways you should yield to the Holy Spirit?
   Make a definite commitment to yield every part of your life to Him.
   Daily reaffirm your commitment to yield to Him.

NOTES

Specifically ask the Holy Spirit to develop the areas in your life that you see are lacking.

Week Eight—**The Life of a Disciple**

1. What is true discipleship?
   True discipleship is a commitment to follow Christ unconditionally.

2. In what form does sin begin?
   Sin begins in the form of a temptation—a desire that draws us away from God.

3. What are the three main sources of temptation?
   The world, the flesh, and the devil

4. How can we take advantage of the "way of escape" that God has given us?
   Use the Word of God.
   Remember you don't have to sin.
   Avoid temptation when possible.
   Avoid ungodly friends.
   Ask for help.
   Keep short accounts with God.
   Yield to the Holy Spirit.

5. What does the phrase "making provision for the flesh" mean?
   Setting ourselves up for temptation by making it easy to sin.

6. What does the word *sanctified* mean?
   "set apart"

7. What develops holiness in us as we mature in our Christian walk?
   God's grace

All scripture is given by inspiration of God, and is profitable for doctrine, for reproof, for correction, for instruction in righteousness:—2 Timothy 3:16

APPENDIX B ⓷⓪③

Week Nine—**The Local Church**

1. Who established the church and why does it exist?
    Jesus Christ established it, and it exists to glorify Him.

2. What is a local church?
    Individual bodies of believers (or a called out assembly of believers) who gather together as a church and follow the New Testament patterns of church practices.

3. What does the word *ekklesia* (the Greek word for church) mean?
    "a called out assembly"

4. What is the purpose of observing the Lord's Table?
    To remember Jesus' sacrifice for us and to examine our lives for sin that would hinder our fellowship with Him

5. In what three ways is the church vital?
    It is the guardian of truth.
    It is God's plan to reach the world.
    It is God's place to nurture the Christian.

6. What are some of the purposes for the local church that help you grow in your Christian walk?
    To preach the Word of God
    To provide fellowship
    To provide oversight
    To restore sinful members
    To disciple new believers
    To mature new Christians
    To bring glory to God

7. What are three decisions you can make regarding your involvement in the local church?
    Be faithful in your attendance

Be accountable to leadership
Be committed in your involvement

Week Ten—**Your Place in Your Church Family**

1. Why does the Holy Spirit give a Christian spiritual gifts?
   These gifts are given to better serve God through the local church.

2. With what has God entrusted the church?
   The gospel and the responsibility of to take the gospel to all the world.

3. What are the spiritual gifts listed in Romans 12?
   Prophecy
   Ministry
   Teaching
   Exhortation
   Giving
   Ruling
   Mercy

4. What are some of the most common ways regarding how we should act with other Christians?
   Love others, serve others, be kind to others

5. What is one way to resolve most differences between Christians?
   Most differences could be solved if both parties would simply talk to one another.

6. What should the goal be regarding resolving conflict amongst others?
   Bringing about a reconciled relationship, not proving who is right or who is wrong

All scripture is given by inspiration of God, and is profitable for doctrine, for reproof, for correction, for instruction in righteousness:—2 Timothy 3:16

APPENDIX B 305

7. What are a few ways you can participate in the work of God through your church?

    Take a spiritual gifts test

    Ask to be involved in ministry through your church

    Invest in others

Week Eleven—**Financial Stewardship**

1. What three truths are absolutely crucial for understanding how a Christian should view their finances?

    God is the owner of all.

    We are the stewards of His blessings.

    We will give an account of our stewardship.

2. As a steward of God, what is our job?

    A steward of God manages everything God gives him. We don't own whatever God gives us; we just manage it.

3. How much is a tithe?

    A tithe is a tenth.

4. How did Paul instruct the first-century Christians on giving?

    Paul instructed the Christians to give regularly and to give in proportion to God's blessing on them.

5. Giving to God does not make you become wealthy, but rather what has God promised to do if you give?

    God has promised to meet your needs as you give to Him.

6. What are some of the ways that God will reward our giving?

    God will meet our needs; He will bless our gifts; and He will multiply fruit to our account.

7. What is the greatest reason to give to God's work?
By giving to God's work, we have an opportunity to invest in eternity.

Week Twelve—Go and Tell the Good News

1. What is the greatest news in the entire world?
The message of salvation

2. What was Jesus' mission while He was here on earth?
To seek and to save the lost

3. What are two of the primary responsibilities of the church?
The two primary responsibilities of the church are to spread the gospel and teach new believers.

4. What do we call Jesus' command to reach the entire world with the gospel?
The "Great Commission"

5. What are the five main points you need to remember as you are sharing the gospel with others?
God loves you.
Everyone is a sinner.
Sin has a price that must be paid.
Jesus Christ died to pay for your sin.
You can ask Jesus Christ to be your Saviour.

6. What is the best way to learn how to be a personal soulwinner?
Go with an experienced soulwinner and listen to him or her share the gospel several times.

7. How does the Holy Spirit work through our witness?
The Holy Spirit empowers us and works in the hearts of those to whom we are witnessing.

All scripture is given by inspiration of God, and is profitable for doctrine, for reproof, for correction, for instruction in righteousness:—2 Timothy 3:16

APPENDIX B (307)

Week Thirteen—**Living in Light of Eternity**

1. What is one of the most common misunderstandings regarding the spiritual battle?

   One of the most common misunderstandings regarding the spiritual battle is the assumption that both forces (God vs. Satan) are equally matched.

2. What does the word *rapture* mean?

   "to be caught up"

3. What are the seven years of great trouble on earth following the Rapture called?

   The Tribulation

4. How many years will Christ personally and physically reign as King over all the earth?

   For one thousand years (the Millennial Reign)

5. Where will unbelievers be judged?

   The Great White Throne Judgment

6. Where will the believers give an account of their lives?

   The Judgment Seat of Christ

7. What are the five rewards—crowns—that we can be rewarded with?

   The Crown of Righteousness
   The Crown of Life
   The Incorruptible Crown
   The Crown of Rejoicing
   The Crown of Glory

TOPICAL VERSES FOR BIBLE MEMORY

Addictions

Proverbs 20:1; Isaiah 61:1; John 8:32; Romans 6:14–16; 8:2;
1 Corinthians 6:9–11; 9:26–27; Galatians 5:1

Anger

Psalm 37:8; Proverbs 14:17,29; 15:1; 16:32; 19:11; 22:24–25;
Ecclesiastes 7:9; Ephesians 4:26, 31; Colossians 3:8; James 1:19–20

Apathy

Romans 12:11; 1 Corinthians 10:31; Philippians 2:5; Colossians 3:23;
Revelation 3:15–16

Assurance

John 1:12; 10:27–28; Romans 4:20–21; 8:16–17; 8:38–39; 10:13;
Philippians 1:6; 2 Timothy 1:12; Hebrews 12:6–8; 1 Peter 1:4–5;
1 John 3:20–21; 4:13–16; 5:13

Authority

Romans 13:1–4; Hebrews 13:17; 1 Peter 2:18

NOTES

Parents

Exodus 20:12; Proverbs 20:20; 30:17; Ephesians 6:1; Colossians 3:20

Bitterness

Proverbs 26:24–26; Matthew 5:23–24; Luke 23:34; Ephesians 4:31; Hebrews 12:15; James 3:14–15; 1 John 2:9–11; 3:15

Boldness

Proverbs 28:1; Matthew 5:14–15; Romans 8:31; 2 Timothy 3:12; Hebrews 13:6

Complaining

Numbers 11:1; Psalm 34:1; Philippians 2:14; Hebrews 13:5

Contentment

Exodus 20:17; Proverbs 23:4–5; Matthew 6:19–24; Luke 12:15; Ephesians 5:3; Philippians 2:21; 4:11; Colossians 3:5–6; 1 Timothy 6:6–8; Hebrews 13:5

Cursing

Exodus 20:7; Psalm 19:14; Matthew 12:34–37; Ephesians 4:29; 5:3–4; James 3

Dating

Romans 13:14; 1 Corinthians 6:19; 2 Corinthians 6:14; Ephesians 6:1; 1 Thessalonians 4:3–7; 5:22; 2 Timothy 2:22

Dedication

Romans 12:1–2; Philippians 1:20–21

All scripture is given by inspiration of God, and is profitable for doctrine, for reproof, for correction, for instruction in righteousness:—2 Timothy 3:16

APPENDIX C (311)

Depression

Psalm 32:1–7, 42:5, 43:5; Isaiah 40:27–31; Matthew 6:34; 11:28–30; Luke 12:22–32; Romans 4:20–21; 2 Corinthians 4:8–9; Philippians 2:2, 21; 1 Peter 5:6–7

Devotions

Joshua 1:8; Psalm 1:1–2; 19:14; 63:1; 119:9–11; Proverbs 8:17; Jeremiah 29:13–14a; Acts 17:11; 2 Corinthians 3:18; Ephesians 4:22–24; 2 Timothy 2:15; James 1:21–25

Divorce

Matthew 5:31–32; 19:2–9; Luke 16:18; 1 Corinthians 7:10–15

Drinking

Proverbs 20:1; 23:31–32; Habakkuk 2:15; Romans 6:14,16; 8:2; 1 Corinthians 6:9–11; 9:26–27; Galatians 5:1; Ephesians 5:15–18

Envy

Proverbs 14:30; 23:17; 24:1; 1 Corinthians 13:4; Galatians 5:26; James 3:14–16; 5:9; 1 Peter 2:1–3

Forgiveness (God Forgives Me)

Psalm 32:1–5; 51:17; 103:12; 130:3–4; Isaiah 1:18; 55:6–7; Ephesians 4:32; Colossians 1:13–14; Hebrews 10:17; 1 John 1:9

Forgiveness (I Forgive Others)

Matthew 6:14–15; 18:21–25; Mark 11:25; 2 Corinthians 2:7–8; Ephesians 4:31–32

Friends (Good)

Psalm 119:63; Proverbs 13:20; 17:17; 18:24; 27:17

Friends (Bad)

Psalm 1:1; Proverbs 13:20; 22:24–25; 24:21; 1 Corinthians 5:11; 2 Corinthians 6:14; Ephesians 5:11

God's Will

Psalm 40:8; 85:13; 130:5; Proverbs 3:5–6; Matthew 6:33; 2 Timothy 3:15–17

Gossip

Psalm 101:5; Proverbs 4:24; 10:18; 11:11,13; 17:9; 20:19; 21:23; Romans 1:28–29,32; Ephesians 4:29

Gratefulness

Psalm 95:2; Luke 2:38; Ephesians 5:20; Colossians 3:15; 2 Thessalonians 1:3

Homesickness

Deuteronomy 31:6; Psalm 37:39–40; Isaiah 41:10; Philippians 2:3–5; 2 Timothy 1:7; 1 John 4:18

Homosexuality

Leviticus 18:22; Matthew 19:4–5; Romans 1:26–27,32; 1 Corinthians 6:9–11; Jude 7–8

Laziness

Proverbs 6:6–11; 15:19; 19:15; 24:30–34; Colossians 3:23; 1 Corinthians 10:31

Lustful Thinking

Proverbs 6:24–25; Matthew 5:27–28; Romans 13:14; 1 Corinthians 9:27; 10:6; Galatians 5:16; Ephesians 4:22; 2 Timothy 2:22; Titus 2:11–12; James 1:14; 1 Peter 1:14–16

All scripture is given by inspiration of God, and is profitable for doctrine, for reproof, for correction, for instruction in righteousness:—2 Timothy 3:16

APPENDIX C 313

Lying

Exodus 20:16; Psalm 52:1–4; Proverbs 6:16–19; 12:19,22; John 8:44; Ephesians 4:25; Colossians 3:9

Music

Psalm 40:3; 66:1–2; Romans 1:29–32; Ephesians 5:19; Philippians 4:8; Colossians 3:16; 1 John 2:15

Peer Pressure

Exodus 23:2; Proverbs 1:10; 13:20; Daniel 1:8; 3:12,16–18; 6:10

Pride

Proverbs 6:16–18; 8:13; 11:2; 16:5,18; Daniel 4:37; Luke 18:14; Romans 12:3; 2 Corinthians 10:5; Galatians 6:3; James 1:17; 4:6; 1 Peter 5:6

Secret Sins

Psalm 90:8; 101:3–7; Proverbs 4:23; 15:3; Ecclesiastes 12:14; Luke 8:17

Selfishness

Matthew 22:36–40; 1 Corinthians 13:4–8; Philippians 2:3–4; 2:21; 2 Timothy 3:2–5; Hebrews 3:13

Television (movies)

Proverbs 14:9; Romans 1:29–32; 2 Corinthians 11:3; Ephesians 5:16; Philippians 4:8

Thought Life

Psalm 19:14; 101:3; Isaiah 26:3; Ezekiel 11:5; Matthew 5:27–30; 2 Corinthians 10:5; Philippians 4:8; 2 Timothy 2:22

Tongue

Psalm 39:1; Ephesians 4:29; 5:3–4; Colossians 4:6

Trusting God

Deuteronomy 32:4; Psalm 20:7; 56:3; 62:8; 118:8; Proverbs 3:5–6; Isaiah 26:3–4; 41:10; 50:10; Jeremiah 29:11; Lamentations 3:22–23; Daniel 2:21

Witnessing

Psalm 126:5–6; Proverbs 11:30; Matthew 28:19–20; Mark 16:15; Acts 1:8; Romans 1:16; 10:13–15

Worry

Deuteronomy 33:27; Psalm 55:22; Isaiah 41:10; Matthew 6:34; Luke 12:22–32; Romans 4:20–21; Philippians 4:6; 2 Timothy 1:7; 1 Peter 5:7; 1 John 4:18

UNDERSTANDING BIBLE TRANSLATIONS

In Lesson 1 we saw that Scripture is not only divinely inspired—literally, God-breathed—but it is also divinely preserved. We looked specifically at several of God's promises to preserve His Word.

You may have wondered, then, why there are so many different translations of the Bible in English and why at our church we use the King James Version. This is a detailed and technical topic, but it boils down to a few specific considerations—the text from which a version is translated, the theology behind the text, and the technique used to translate.

Let's look at each of these briefly:

The Text

There are two primary families of manuscripts from which the Bible is translated—the Byzantine Text and the Alexandrian Text. These are named for the cities near where they were compiled or used. (The Byzantine Text family includes or is sometimes referred to as the Textus Receptus, Received Text, Antiochian Text, Majority Text, as well as a few other names. The Alexandrian Text family is sometimes called the Critical Text, Westcott/Hort Text, Nestle-Aland Text, and a few others.)

The Byzantine Text is from a closer location to where the New Testament was written, and its distribution has been in great abundance in Bible-believing churches through the centuries.

This table shows a few basic facts that highlight the differences these texts:

Byzantine	Alexandrian
Longer	Shorter
Physical copies of manuscripts are newer	Physical copies of manuscripts are older
Greater quantity of manuscripts	Smaller quantity of manuscripts
Widely distributed	Relatively localized
Record of use continual since the first century	Been used primarily only in the last 150 years

These facts are agreed upon by all scholars. The difference is in how the facts are interpreted. For the most part, these interpretations relate to God's promise to preserve His Word.

If one sees preservation as a *human* endeavor, he looks to the oldest physical copies of a manuscript. But if he believes God's Word has been *divinely* preserved, then the sheer volume of manuscripts testifies to God being at work.

Our belief is that since God has promised to preserve His Word for every generation (Psalm 12:7), the Byzantine manuscript reflects

All scripture is given by inspiration of God, and is profitable for doctrine, for reproof, for correction, for instruction in righteousness:—2 Timothy 3:16

APPENDIX D (317)

this providential preservation by God through careful copies of the text through the centuries. The King James Version in English was translated from the Byzantine manuscripts.

The Theology

In addition to the historical implications of the Byzantine or Alexandrian manuscripts, there are theological implications of these manuscripts that are reflected in the English versions into which they are translated.

There are verses throughout the Alexandrian manuscripts where theological truth has been diluted by omission. Below are a few verses that explain where some of these omissions or changes occur as well as their doctrinal significance. These verses can be used to test a modern version's origin.

Matthew 4:4—the words *"but by every word that proceedeth out of the mouth of God"* should be present. (This phrase speaks to the authority and sufficiency of God's Word. Without it, the verse could mean that any type of intellectual or spiritual sustenance is enough and that they are all the same.)

John 1:18—the words "begotten Son" should be present. (Everyone who is saved is a "son" or "daughter of God." The significance of Jesus being the *"begotten* Son" is that when He came to earth He was conceived of the Holy Spirit rather than of Joseph. The word *begotten* supports the deity of Christ.)

Acts 8:35–38—Verse 37 should be included. (Some Bibles delete or footnote verse 37, giving a false impression that baptism can save someone.)

1 Timothy 3:16—some Bibles read, "He was manifest in the flesh…." Those translated from a correct text would read, "God was manifest in the flesh…." (Of course *Jesus* was manifest in the flesh. The point of this verse is that *God* was manifest in the flesh—that Jesus is God.)

Many more verses could be cited (and have been given in more thorough treatments of this subject). The point here is that the difference between modern translations is not as simple as ease of use. There are real theological differences that are inherent in the texts from which they are translated.

The Technique

In addition to the textual and theological differences between the two manuscripts, many of today's translations have been handled with different translation techniques than the King James Version.

In many translations, rather than the translators trying to carefully translate each word or phrase into the equivalent English word or phrase, they have attempted to translate each thought into a reworded English thought. This inevitably leads to not just *translation,* but also *interpretation.*

Notice, for instance, the difference between these two approaches in Zechariah 13:6.

King James Version

And one shall say unto him, What are these wounds in thine hands? Then he shall answer, Those with which I was wounded in the house of my friends.

All scripture is given by inspiration of God, and is profitable for doctrine, for reproof, for correction, for instruction in righteousness:—2 Timothy 3:16

APPENDIX D ⬤319

The Message

And if someone says, "And so where did you get that black eye?" they'll say, "I ran into a door at a friend's house."

The contrast between these two translations shows the difference in *translating* God's Word versus *interpreting* God's Word. In the process of interpreting, many rich theological truths as well as vital cross references are lost.

We believe that every word of the Bible is inspired by God, not just the underlying thoughts.

PROVERBS 30:5

Every word of God is pure: he is a shield unto them that put their trust in him.

MATTHEW 4:4

But he answered and said, It is written, Man shall not live by bread alone, but by every word that proceedeth out of the mouth of God.

2 TIMOTHY 3:16

All scripture is given by inspiration of God, and is profitable for doctrine, for reproof, for correction, for instruction in righteousness:

So, when it comes to understanding and choosing a translation of the Bible, it is vital to remember these three areas of consideration:

1. **Look at the text from which it is translated.** Is it the text that has been used and endorsed by Bible-believing churches since the first century? Does it reflect God's supernatural preservation over the centuries?

2. **Look at the theology behind the text.** Is it theologically accurate and God-honoring? Does it weaken the doctrines of Scripture? Is it non-contradicting?

3.   Look at the technique behind the translation. Did the translators approach their work with a commitment to accurately translate God's Word, or did they attempt to translate and interpret broader thoughts?

Once again, this is a brief treatment of a detailed subject. For a book-length answer to the question of why we use the King James Version, we recommend *A More Sure Word* by Dr. R.B. Ouellette.

But even without understanding every technicality behind a translation, we can rejoice in the truth that God has promised to preserve His Word and that as we read it and apply it to our lives, He transforms our lives through His inspired Word.

— ONE-YEAR NEW TESTAMENT READING SCHEDULE —

January

- **1** Matthew 1
- **2** Matthew 2
- **3** Matthew 3
- **4** Matthew 4
- **5** Matthew 5:1–26
- **6** Matthew 5:27–48
- **7** Matthew 6:1–18
- **8** Matthew 6:19–34
- **9** Matthew 7
- **10** Matthew 8:1–17
- **11** Matthew 8:18–34
- **12** Matthew 9:1–17
- **13** Matthew 9:18–38
- **14** Matthew 10:1–20
- **15** Matthew 10:21–42
- **16** Matthew 11
- **17** Matthew 12:1–23
- **18** Matthew 12:24–50
- **19** Matthew 13:1–30
- **20** Matthew 13:31–58
- **21** Matthew 14:1–21
- **22** Matthew 14:22–36
- **23** Matthew 15:1–20
- **24** Matthew 15:21–39
- **25** Matthew 16
- **26** Matthew 17
- **27** Matthew 18:1–20
- **28** Matthew 18:21–35
- **29** Matthew 19
- **30** Matthew 20:1–16
- **31** Matthew 20:17–34

February

- **1** Matthew 21:1–22
- **2** Matthew 21:23–46
- **3** Matthew 22:1–22
- **4** Matthew 22:23–46
- **5** Matthew 23:1–22
- **6** Matthew 23:23–39
- **7** Matthew 24:1–28
- **8** Matthew 24:29–51
- **9** Matthew 25:1–30
- **10** Matthew 25:31–46
- **11** Matthew 26:1–25
- **12** Matthew 26:26–50
- **13** Matthew 26:51–75
- **14** Matthew 27:1–26
- **15** Matthew 27:27–50
- **16** Matthew 27:51–66
- **17** Matthew 28
- **18** Mark 1:1–22
- **19** Mark 1:23–45
- **20** Mark 2
- **21** Mark 3:1–19
- **22** Mark 3:20–35
- **23** Mark 4:1–20
- **24** Mark 4:21–41
- **25** Mark 5:1–20
- **26** Mark 5:21–43
- **27** Mark 6:1–29
- **28** Mark 6:30–56

March

- **1** Mark 7:1–13
- **2** Mark 7:14–37
- **3** Mark 8
- **4** Mark 9:1–29
- **5** Mark 9:30–50
- **6** Mark 10:1–31
- **7** Mark 10:32–52
- **8** Mark 11:1–18
- **9** Mark 11:19–33
- **10** Mark 12:1–27
- **11** Mark 12:28–44
- **12** Mark 13:1–20
- **13** Mark 13:21–37
- **14** Mark 14:1–26
- **15** Mark 14:27–53
- **16** Mark 14:54–72
- **17** Mark 15:1–25
- **18** Mark 15:26–47
- **19** Mark 16
- **20** Luke 1:1–20
- **21** Luke 1:21–38
- **22** Luke 1:39–56
- **23** Luke 1:57–80
- **24** Luke 2:1–24
- **25** Luke 2:25–52
- **26** Luke 3
- **27** Luke 4:1–30
- **28** Luke 4:31–44
- **29** Luke 5:1–16
- **30** Luke 5:17–39
- **31** Luke 6:1–26

April

- **1** Luke 6:27–49
- **2** Luke 7:1–30
- **3** Luke 7:31–50
- **4** Luke 8:1–25
- **5** Luke 8:26–56
- **6** Luke 9:1–17
- **7** Luke 9:18–36
- **8** Luke 9:37–62
- **9** Luke 10:1–24
- **10** Luke 10:25–42
- **11** Luke 11:1–28
- **12** Luke 11:29–54
- **13** Luke 12:1–31
- **14** Luke 12:32–59
- **15** Luke 13:1–22
- **16** Luke 13:23–35
- **17** Luke 14:1–24
- **18** Luke 14:25–35
- **19** Luke 15:1–10
- **20** Luke 15:11–32
- **21** Luke 16
- **22** Luke 17:1–19
- **23** Luke 17:20–37
- **24** Luke 18:1–23
- **25** Luke 18:24–43
- **26** Luke 19:1–27
- **27** Luke 19:28–48
- **28** Luke 20:1–26
- **29** Luke 20:27–47
- **30** Luke 21:1–19

May

- **1** Luke 21:20–38
- **2** Luke 22:1–30
- **3** Luke 22:31–46
- **4** Luke 22:47–71
- **5** Luke 23:1–25
- **6** Luke 23:26–56
- **7** Luke 24:1–35
- **8** Luke 24:36–53
- **9** John 1:1–28
- **10** John 1:29–51
- **11** John 2
- **12** John 3:1–18
- **13** John 3:19–36
- **14** John 4:1–30
- **15** John 4:31–54
- **16** John 5:1–24
- **17** John 5:25–47
- **18** John 6:1–21
- **19** John 6:22–44
- **20** John 6:45–71
- **21** John 7:1–27
- **22** John 7:28–53
- **23** John 8:1–27
- **24** John 8:28–59
- **25** John 9:1–23
- **26** John 9:24–41
- **27** John 10:1–23
- **28** John 10:24–42
- **29** John 11:1–29
- **30** John 11:30–57
- **31** John 12:1–26

— ONE-YEAR NEW TESTAMENT READING SCHEDULE —

June

- ☐ **1** John 12:27–50
- ☐ **2** John 13:1–20
- ☐ **3** John 13:21–38
- ☐ **4** John 14
- ☐ **5** John 15
- ☐ **6** John 16
- ☐ **7** John 17
- ☐ **8** John 18:1–18
- ☐ **9** John 18:19–40
- ☐ **10** John 19:1–22
- ☐ **11** John 19:23–42
- ☐ **12** John 20
- ☐ **13** John 21
- ☐ **14** Acts 1
- ☐ **15** Acts 2:1–21
- ☐ **16** Acts 2:22–47
- ☐ **17** Acts 3
- ☐ **18** Acts 4:1–22
- ☐ **19** Acts 4:23–37
- ☐ **20** Acts 5:1–21
- ☐ **21** Acts 5:22–42
- ☐ **22** Acts 6
- ☐ **23** Acts 7:1–21
- ☐ **24** Acts 7:22–43
- ☐ **25** Acts 7:44–60
- ☐ **26** Acts 8:1–25
- ☐ **27** Acts 8:26–40
- ☐ **28** Acts 9:1–21
- ☐ **29** Acts 9:22–43
- ☐ **30** Acts 10:1–23

July

- ☐ **1** Acts 10:24–48
- ☐ **2** Acts 11
- ☐ **3** Acts 12
- ☐ **4** Acts 13:1–25
- ☐ **5** Acts 13:26–52
- ☐ **6** Acts 14
- ☐ **7** Acts 15:1–21
- ☐ **8** Acts 15:22–41
- ☐ **9** Acts 16:1–21
- ☐ **10** Acts 16:22–40
- ☐ **11** Acts 17:1–15
- ☐ **12** Acts 17:16–34
- ☐ **13** Acts 18
- ☐ **14** Acts 19:1–20
- ☐ **15** Acts 19:21–41
- ☐ **16** Acts 20:1–16
- ☐ **17** Acts 20:17–38
- ☐ **18** Acts 21:1–17
- ☐ **19** Acts 21:18–40
- ☐ **20** Acts 22
- ☐ **21** Acts 23:1–15
- ☐ **22** Acts 23:16–35
- ☐ **23** Acts 24
- ☐ **24** Acts 25
- ☐ **25** Acts 26
- ☐ **26** Acts 27:1–26
- ☐ **27** Acts 27:27–44
- ☐ **28** Acts 28
- ☐ **29** Romans 1
- ☐ **30** Romans 2
- ☐ **31** Romans 3

August

- ☐ **1** Romans 4
- ☐ **2** Romans 5
- ☐ **3** Romans 6
- ☐ **4** Romans 7
- ☐ **5** Romans 8:1–21
- ☐ **6** Romans 8:22–39
- ☐ **7** Romans 9:1–15
- ☐ **8** Romans 9:16–33
- ☐ **9** Romans 10
- ☐ **10** Romans 11:1–18
- ☐ **11** Romans 11:19–36
- ☐ **12** Romans 12
- ☐ **13** Romans 13
- ☐ **14** Romans 14
- ☐ **15** Romans 15:1–13
- ☐ **16** Romans 15:14–33
- ☐ **17** Romans 16
- ☐ **18** 1 Corinthians 1
- ☐ **19** 1 Corinthians 2
- ☐ **20** 1 Corinthians 3
- ☐ **21** 1 Corinthians 4
- ☐ **22** 1 Corinthians 5
- ☐ **23** 1 Corinthians 6
- ☐ **24** 1 Corinthians 7:1–19
- ☐ **25** 1 Corinthians 7:20–40
- ☐ **26** 1 Corinthians 8
- ☐ **27** 1 Corinthians 9
- ☐ **28** 1 Corinthians 10:1–18
- ☐ **29** 1 Corinthians 10:19–33
- ☐ **30** 1 Corinthians 11:1–16
- ☐ **31** 1 Corinthians 11:17–34

September

- ☐ **1** 1 Corinthians 12
- ☐ **2** 1 Corinthians 13
- ☐ **3** 1 Corinthians 14:1–20
- ☐ **4** 1 Corinthians 14:21–40
- ☐ **5** 1 Corinthians 15:1–28
- ☐ **6** 1 Corinthians 15:29–58
- ☐ **7** 1 Corinthians 16
- ☐ **8** 2 Corinthians 1
- ☐ **9** 2 Corinthians 2
- ☐ **10** 2 Corinthians 3
- ☐ **11** 2 Corinthians 4
- ☐ **12** 2 Corinthians 5
- ☐ **13** 2 Corinthians 6
- ☐ **14** 2 Corinthians 7
- ☐ **15** 2 Corinthians 8
- ☐ **16** 2 Corinthians 9
- ☐ **17** 2 Corinthians 10
- ☐ **18** 2 Corinthians 11:1–15
- ☐ **19** 2 Corinthians 11:16–33
- ☐ **20** 2 Corinthians 12
- ☐ **21** 2 Corinthians 13
- ☐ **22** Galatians 1
- ☐ **23** Galatians 2
- ☐ **24** Galatians 3
- ☐ **25** Galatians 4
- ☐ **26** Galatians 5
- ☐ **27** Galatians 6
- ☐ **28** Ephesians 1
- ☐ **29** Ephesians 2
- ☐ **30** Ephesians 3

October

- ☐ **1** Ephesians 4
- ☐ **2** Ephesians 5:1–16
- ☐ **3** Ephesians 5:17–33
- ☐ **4** Ephesians 6
- ☐ **5** Philippians 1
- ☐ **6** Philippians 2
- ☐ **7** Philippians 3
- ☐ **8** Philippians 4
- ☐ **9** Colossians 1
- ☐ **10** Colossians 2
- ☐ **11** Colossians 3
- ☐ **12** Colossians 4
- ☐ **13** 1 Thessalonians 1
- ☐ **14** 1 Thessalonians 2
- ☐ **15** 1 Thessalonians 3
- ☐ **16** 1 Thessalonians 4
- ☐ **17** 1 Thessalonians 5
- ☐ **18** 2 Thessalonians 1
- ☐ **19** 2 Thessalonians 2
- ☐ **20** 2 Thessalonians 3
- ☐ **21** 1 Timothy 1
- ☐ **22** 1 Timothy 2
- ☐ **23** 1 Timothy 3
- ☐ **24** 1 Timothy 4
- ☐ **25** 1 Timothy 5
- ☐ **26** 1 Timothy 6
- ☐ **27** 2 Timothy 1
- ☐ **28** 2 Timothy 2
- ☐ **29** 2 Timothy 3
- ☐ **30** 2 Timothy 4
- ☐ **31** Titus 1

November

- ☐ **1** Titus 2
- ☐ **2** Titus 3
- ☐ **3** Philemon
- ☐ **4** Hebrews 1
- ☐ **5** Hebrews 2
- ☐ **6** Hebrews 3
- ☐ **7** Hebrews 4
- ☐ **8** Hebrews 5
- ☐ **9** Hebrews 6
- ☐ **10** Hebrews 7
- ☐ **11** Hebrews 8
- ☐ **12** Hebrews 9
- ☐ **13** Hebrews 10:1–18
- ☐ **14** Hebrews 10:19–39
- ☐ **15** Hebrews 11:1–19
- ☐ **16** Hebrews 11:20–40
- ☐ **17** Hebrews 12
- ☐ **18** Hebrews 13
- ☐ **19** James 1
- ☐ **20** James 2
- ☐ **21** James 3
- ☐ **22** James 4
- ☐ **23** James 5
- ☐ **24** 1 Peter 1
- ☐ **25** 1 Peter 2
- ☐ **26** 1 Peter 3
- ☐ **27** 1 Peter 4
- ☐ **28** 1 Peter 5
- ☐ **29** 2 Peter 1
- ☐ **30** 2 Peter 2

December

- ☐ **1** 2 Peter 3
- ☐ **2** 1 John 1
- ☐ **3** 1 John 2
- ☐ **4** 1 John 3
- ☐ **5** 1 John 4
- ☐ **6** 1 John 5
- ☐ **7** 2 John
- ☐ **8** 3 John
- ☐ **9** Jude
- ☐ **10** Revelation 1
- ☐ **11** Revelation 2
- ☐ **12** Revelation 3
- ☐ **13** Revelation 4
- ☐ **14** Revelation 5
- ☐ **15** Revelation 6
- ☐ **16** Revelation 7
- ☐ **17** Revelation 8
- ☐ **18** Revelation 9
- ☐ **19** Revelation 10
- ☐ **20** Revelation 11
- ☐ **21** Revelation 12
- ☐ **22** Revelation 13
- ☐ **23** Revelation 14
- ☐ **24** Revelation 15
- ☐ **25** Revelation 16
- ☐ **26** Revelation 17
- ☐ **27** Revelation 18
- ☐ **28** Revelation 19
- ☐ **29** Revelation 20
- ☐ **30** Revelation 21
- ☐ **31** Revelation 22

All scripture is given by inspiration of God, and is profitable for doctrine, for reproof, for correction, for instruction in righteousness:—2 Timothy 3:16

APPENDIX E 323

ONE-YEAR BIBLE READING SCHEDULE

January

☐	1	Gen. 1–3	Matt. 1
☐	2	Gen. 4–6	Matt. 2
☐	3	Gen. 7–9	Matt. 3
☐	4	Gen. 10–12	Matt. 4
☐	5	Gen. 13–15	Matt. 5:1–26
☐	6	Gen. 16–17	Matt. 5:27–48
☐	7	Gen. 18–19	Matt. 6:1–18
☐	8	Gen. 20–22	Matt. 6:19–34
☐	9	Gen. 23–24	Matt. 7
☐	10	Gen. 25–26	Matt. 8:1–17
☐	11	Gen. 27–28	Matt. 8:18–34
☐	12	Gen. 29–30	Matt. 9:1–17
☐	13	Gen. 31–32	Matt. 9:18–38
☐	14	Gen. 33–35	Matt. 10:1–20
☐	15	Gen. 36–38	Matt. 10:21–42
☐	16	Gen. 39–40	Matt. 11
☐	17	Gen. 41–42	Matt. 12:1–23
☐	18	Gen. 43–45	Matt. 12:24–50
☐	19	Gen. 46–48	Matt. 13:1–30
☐	20	Gen. 49–50	Matt. 13:31–58
☐	21	Ex. 1–3	Matt. 14:1–21
☐	22	Ex. 4–6	Matt. 14:22–36
☐	23	Ex. 7–8	Matt. 15:1–20
☐	24	Ex. 9–11	Matt. 15:21–39
☐	25	Ex. 12–13	Matt. 16
☐	26	Ex. 14–15	Matt. 17
☐	27	Ex. 16–18	Matt. 18:1–20
☐	28	Ex. 19–20	Matt. 18:21–35
☐	29	Ex. 21–22	Matt. 19
☐	30	Ex. 23–24	Matt. 20:1–16
☐	31	Ex. 25–26	Matt. 20:17–34

February

☐	1	Ex. 27–28	Matt. 21:1–22
☐	2	Ex. 29–30	Matt. 21:23–46
☐	3	Ex. 31–33	Matt. 22:1–22
☐	4	Ex. 34–35	Matt. 22:23–46
☐	5	Ex. 36–38	Matt. 23:1–22
☐	6	Ex. 39–40	Matt. 23:23–39
☐	7	Lev. 1–3	Matt. 24:1–28
☐	8	Lev. 4–5	Matt. 24:29–51
☐	9	Lev. 6–7	Matt. 25:1–30
☐	10	Lev. 8–10	Matt. 25:31–46
☐	11	Lev. 11–12	Matt. 26:1–25
☐	12	Lev. 13	Matt. 26:26–50
☐	13	Lev. 14	Matt. 26:51–75
☐	14	Lev. 15–16	Matt. 27:1–26
☐	15	Lev. 17–18	Matt. 27:27–50
☐	16	Lev. 19–20	Matt. 27:51–66
☐	17	Lev. 21–22	Matt. 28
☐	18	Lev. 23–24	Mark 1:1–22
☐	19	Lev. 25	Mark 1:23–45
☐	20	Lev. 26–27	Mark 2
☐	21	Num. 1–2	Mark 3:1–19
☐	22	Num. 3–4	Mark 3:20–35
☐	23	Num. 5–6	Mark 4:1–20
☐	24	Num. 7–8	Mark 4:21–41
☐	25	Num. 9–11	Mark 5:1–20
☐	26	Num. 12–14	Mark 5:21–43
☐	27	Num. 15–16	Mark 6:1–29
☐	28	Num. 17–19	Mark 6:30–56

March

☐	1	Num. 20–22	Mark 7:1–13
☐	2	Num. 23–25	Mark 7:14–37
☐	3	Num. 26–28	Mark 8
☐	4	Num. 29–31	Mark 9:1–29
☐	5	Num. 32–34	Mark 9:30–50
☐	6	Num. 35–36	Mark 10:1–31
☐	7	Deut. 1–3	Mark 10:32–52
☐	8	Deut. 4–6	Mark 11:1–18
☐	9	Deut. 7–9	Mark 11:19–33
☐	10	Deut. 10–12	Mark 12:1–27
☐	11	Deut. 13–15	Mark 12:28–44
☐	12	Deut. 16–18	Mark 13:1–20
☐	13	Deut. 19–21	Mark 13:21–37
☐	14	Deut. 22–24	Mark 14:1–26
☐	15	Deut. 25–27	Mark 14:27–53
☐	16	Deut. 28–29	Mark 14:54–72
☐	17	Deut. 30–31	Mark 15:1–25
☐	18	Deut. 32–34	Mark 15:26–47
☐	19	Josh. 1–3	Mark 16
☐	20	Josh. 4–6	Luke 1:1–20
☐	21	Josh. 7–9	Luke 1:21–38
☐	22	Josh. 10–12	Luke 1:39–56
☐	23	Josh. 13–15	Luke 1:57–80
☐	24	Josh. 16–18	Luke 2:1–24
☐	25	Josh. 19–21	Luke 2:25–52
☐	26	Josh. 22–24	Luke 3
☐	27	Judges 1–3	Luke 4:1–30
☐	28	Judges 4–6	Luke 4:31–44
☐	29	Judges 7–8	Luke 5:1–16
☐	30	Judges 9–10	Luke 5:17–39
☐	31	Judges 11–12	Luke 6:1–26

April

☐	1	Judges 13–15	Luke 6:27–49
☐	2	Judges 16–18	Luke 7:1–30
☐	3	Judges 19–21	Luke 7:31–50
☐	4	Ruth 1–4	Luke 8:1–25
☐	5	1 Sam. 1–3	Luke 8:26–56
☐	6	1 Sam. 4–6	Luke 9:1–17
☐	7	1 Sam. 7–9	Luke 9:18–36
☐	8	1 Sam. 10–12	Luke 9:37–62
☐	9	1 Sam. 13–14	Luke 10:1–24
☐	10	1 Sam. 15–16	Luke 10:25–42
☐	11	1 Sam. 17–18	Luke 11:1–28
☐	12	1 Sam. 19–21	Luke 11:29–54
☐	13	1 Sam. 22–24	Luke 12:1–31
☐	14	1 Sam. 25–26	Luke 12:32–59
☐	15	1 Sam. 27–29	Luke 13:1–22
☐	16	1 Sam. 30–31	Luke 13:23–35
☐	17	2 Sam. 1–2	Luke 14:1–24
☐	18	2 Sam. 3–5	Luke 14:25–35
☐	19	2 Sam. 6–8	Luke 15:1–10
☐	20	2 Sam. 9–11	Luke 15:11–32
☐	21	2 Sam. 12–13	Luke 16
☐	22	2 Sam. 14–15	Luke 17:1–19
☐	23	2 Sam. 16–18	Luke 17:20–37
☐	24	2 Sam. 19–20	Luke 18:1–23
☐	25	2 Sam. 21–22	Luke 18:24–43
☐	26	2 Sam. 23–24	Luke 19:1–27
☐	27	1 Kings 1–2	Luke 19:28–48
☐	28	1 Kings 3–5	Luke 20:1–26
☐	29	1 Kings 6–7	Luke 20:27–47
☐	30	1 Kings 8–9	Luke 21:1–19

May

☐	1	1 Kings 10–11	Luke 21:20–38
☐	2	1 Kings 12–13	Luke 22:1–30
☐	3	1 Kings 14–15	Luke 22:31–46
☐	4	1 Kings 16–18	Luke 22:47–71
☐	5	1 Kings 19–20	Luke 23:1–25
☐	6	1 Kings 21–22	Luke 23:26–56
☐	7	2 Kings 1–3	Luke 24:1–35
☐	8	2 Kings 4–6	Luke 24:36–53
☐	9	2 Kings 7–9	John 1:1–28
☐	10	2 Kings 10–12	John 1:29–51
☐	11	2 Kings 13–14	John 2
☐	12	2 Kings 15–16	John 3:1–18
☐	13	2 Kings 17–18	John 3:19–36
☐	14	2 Kings 19–21	John 4:1–30
☐	15	2 Kings 22–23	John 4:31–54
☐	16	2 Kings 24–25	John 5:1–24
☐	17	1 Chr. 1–3	John 5:25–47
☐	18	1 Chr. 4–6	John 6:1–21
☐	19	1 Chr. 7–9	John 6:22–44
☐	20	1 Chr. 10–12	John 6:45–71
☐	21	1 Chr. 13–15	John 7:1–27
☐	22	1 Chr. 16–18	John 7:28–53
☐	23	1 Chr. 19–21	John 8:1–27
☐	24	1 Chr. 22–24	John 8:28–59
☐	25	1 Chr. 25–27	John 9:1–23
☐	26	1 Chr. 28–29	John 9:24–41
☐	27	2 Chr. 1–3	John 10:1–23
☐	28	2 Chr. 4–6	John 10:24–42
☐	29	2 Chr. 7–9	John 11:1–29
☐	30	2 Chr. 10–12	John 11:30–57
☐	31	2 Chr. 13–14	John 12:1–26

June

☐	1	2 Chr. 15–16	John 12:27–50
☐	2	2 Chr. 17–18	John 13:1–20
☐	3	2 Chr. 19–20	John 13:21–38
☐	4	2 Chr. 21–22	John 14
☐	5	2 Chr. 23–24	John 15
☐	6	2 Chr. 25–27	John 16
☐	7	2 Chr. 28–29	John 17
☐	8	2 Chr. 30–31	John 18:1–18
☐	9	2 Chr. 32–33	John 18:19–40
☐	10	2 Chr. 34–36	John 19:1–22
☐	11	Ezra 1–2	John 19:23–42
☐	12	Ezra 3–5	John 20
☐	13	Ezra 6–8	John 21
☐	14	Ezra 9–10	Acts 1
☐	15	Neh. 1–3	Acts 2:1–21
☐	16	Neh. 4–6	Acts 2:22–47
☐	17	Neh. 7–9	Acts 3
☐	18	Neh. 10–11	Acts 4:1–22
☐	19	Neh. 12–13	Acts 4:23–37
☐	20	Esther 1–2	Acts 5:1–21
☐	21	Esther 3–5	Acts 5:22–42
☐	22	Esther 6–8	Acts 6
☐	23	Esther 9–10	Acts 7:1–21
☐	24	Job 1–2	Acts 7:22–43
☐	25	Job 3–4	Acts 7:44–60
☐	26	Job 5–7	Acts 8:1–25
☐	27	Job 8–10	Acts 8:26–40
☐	28	Job 11–13	Acts 9:1–21
☐	29	Job 14–16	Acts 9:22–43
☐	30	Job 17–19	Acts 10:1–23

July

☐	1	Job 20–21	Acts 10:24–48
☐	2	Job 22–24	Acts 11
☐	3	Job 25–27	Acts 12
☐	4	Job 28–29	Acts 13:1–25
☐	5	Job 30–31	Acts 13:26–52
☐	6	Job 32–33	Acts 14
☐	7	Job 34–35	Acts 15:1–21
☐	8	Job 36–37	Acts 15:22–41
☐	9	Job 38–40	Acts 16:1–21
☐	10	Job 41–42	Acts 16:22–40
☐	11	Ps. 1–3	Acts 17:1–15
☐	12	Ps. 4–6	Acts 17:16–34
☐	13	Ps. 7–9	Acts 18
☐	14	Ps. 10–12	Acts 19:1–20
☐	15	Ps. 13–15	Acts 19:21–41
☐	16	Ps. 16–17	Acts 20:1–16
☐	17	Ps. 18–19	Acts 20:17–38
☐	18	Ps. 20–22	Acts 21:1–17
☐	19	Ps. 23–25	Acts 21:18–40
☐	20	Ps. 26–28	Acts 22
☐	21	Ps. 29–30	Acts 23:1–15
☐	22	Ps. 31–32	Acts 23:16–35
☐	23	Ps. 33–34	Acts 24
☐	24	Ps. 35–36	Acts 25
☐	25	Ps. 37–39	Acts 26
☐	26	Ps. 40–42	Acts 27:1–26
☐	27	Ps. 43–45	Acts 27:27–44
☐	28	Ps. 46–48	Acts 28
☐	29	Ps. 49–50	Rom. 1
☐	30	Ps. 51–53	Rom. 2
☐	31	Ps. 54–56	Rom. 3

August

☐	1	Ps. 57–59	Rom. 4
☐	2	Ps. 60–62	Rom. 5
☐	3	Ps. 63–65	Rom. 6
☐	4	Ps. 66–67	Rom. 7
☐	5	Ps. 68–69	Rom. 8:1–21
☐	6	Ps. 70–71	Rom. 8:22–39
☐	7	Ps. 72–73	Rom. 9:1–15
☐	8	Ps. 74–76	Rom. 9:16–33
☐	9	Ps. 77–78	Rom. 10
☐	10	Ps. 79–80	Rom. 11:1–18
☐	11	Ps. 81–83	Rom. 11:19–36
☐	12	Ps. 84–86	Rom. 12
☐	13	Ps. 87–88	Rom. 13
☐	14	Ps. 89–90	Rom. 14
☐	15	Ps. 91–93	Rom. 15:1–13
☐	16	Ps. 94–96	Rom. 15:14–33
☐	17	Ps. 97–99	Rom. 16
☐	18	Ps. 100–102	1 Cor. 1
☐	19	Ps. 103–104	1 Cor. 2
☐	20	Ps. 105–106	1 Cor. 3
☐	21	Ps. 107–109	1 Cor. 4
☐	22	Ps. 110–112	1 Cor. 5
☐	23	Ps. 113–115	1 Cor. 6
☐	24	Ps. 116–118	1 Cor. 7:1–19
☐	25	Ps. 119:1–88	1 Cor. 7:20–40
☐	26	Ps. 119:89–176	1 Cor. 8
☐	27	Ps. 120–122	1 Cor. 9
☐	28	Ps. 123–125	1 Cor. 10:1–18
☐	29	Ps. 126–128	1 Cor. 10:19–33
☐	30	Ps. 129–131	1 Cor. 11:1–16
☐	31	Ps. 132–134	1 Cor. 11:17–34

ONE-YEAR BIBLE READING SCHEDULE

September

☐	1	Ps. 135–136	1 Cor. 12
☐	2	Ps. 137–139	1 Cor. 13
☐	3	Ps. 140–142	1 Cor. 14:1–20
☐	4	Ps. 143–145	1 Cor. 14:21–40
☐	5	Ps. 146–147	1 Cor. 15:1–28
☐	6	Ps. 148–150	1 Cor. 15:29–58
☐	7	Prov. 1–2	1 Cor. 16
☐	8	Prov. 3–5	2 Cor. 1
☐	9	Prov. 6–7	2 Cor. 2
☐	10	Prov. 8–9	2 Cor. 3
☐	11	Prov. 10–12	2 Cor. 4
☐	12	Prov. 13–15	2 Cor. 5
☐	13	Prov. 16–18	2 Cor. 6
☐	14	Prov. 19–21	2 Cor. 7
☐	15	Prov. 22–24	2 Cor. 8
☐	16	Prov. 25–26	2 Cor. 9
☐	17	Prov. 27–29	2 Cor. 10
☐	18	Prov. 30–31	2 Cor. 11:1–15
☐	19	Eccl. 1–3	2 Cor. 11:16–33
☐	20	Eccl. 4–6	2 Cor. 12
☐	21	Eccl. 7–9	2 Cor. 13
☐	22	Eccl. 10–12	Gal. 1
☐	23	Song 1–3	Gal. 2
☐	24	Song 4–5	Gal. 3
☐	25	Song 6–8	Gal. 4
☐	26	Isa. 1–2	Gal. 5
☐	27	Isa. 3–4	Gal. 6
☐	28	Isa. 5–6	Eph. 1
☐	29	Isa. 7–8	Eph. 2
☐	30	Isa. 9–10	Eph. 3

October

☐	1	Isa. 11–13	Eph. 4
☐	2	Isa. 14–16	Eph. 5:1–16
☐	3	Isa. 17–19	Eph. 5:17–33
☐	4	Isa. 20–22	Eph. 6
☐	5	Isa. 23–25	Phil. 1
☐	6	Isa. 26–27	Phil. 2
☐	7	Isa. 28–29	Phil. 3
☐	8	Isa. 30–31	Phil. 4
☐	9	Isa. 32–33	Col. 1
☐	10	Isa. 34–36	Col. 2
☐	11	Isa. 37–38	Col. 3
☐	12	Isa. 39–40	Col. 4
☐	13	Isa. 41–42	1 Thess. 1
☐	14	Isa. 43–44	1 Thess. 2
☐	15	Isa. 45–46	1 Thess. 3
☐	16	Isa. 47–49	1 Thess. 4
☐	17	Isa. 50–52	1 Thess. 5
☐	18	Isa. 53–55	2 Thess. 1
☐	19	Isa. 56–58	2 Thess. 2
☐	20	Isa. 59–61	2 Thess. 3
☐	21	Isa. 62–64	1 Tim. 1
☐	22	Isa. 65–66	1 Tim. 2
☐	23	Jer. 1–2	1 Tim. 3
☐	24	Jer. 3–5	1 Tim. 4
☐	25	Jer. 6–8	1 Tim. 5
☐	26	Jer. 9–11	1 Tim. 6
☐	27	Jer. 12–14	2 Tim. 1
☐	28	Jer. 15–17	2 Tim. 2
☐	29	Jer. 18–19	2 Tim. 3
☐	30	Jer. 20–21	2 Tim. 4
☐	31	Jer. 22–23	Titus 1

November

☐	1	Jer. 24–26	Titus 2
☐	2	Jer. 27–29	Titus 3
☐	3	Jer. 30–31	Philemon
☐	4	Jer. 32–33	Heb. 1
☐	5	Jer. 34–36	Heb. 2
☐	6	Jer. 37–39	Heb. 3
☐	7	Jer. 40–42	Heb. 4
☐	8	Jer. 43–45	Heb. 5
☐	9	Jer. 46–47	Heb. 6
☐	10	Jer. 48–49	Heb. 7
☐	11	Jer. 50	Heb. 8
☐	12	Jer. 51–52	Heb. 9
☐	13	Lam. 1–2	Heb. 10:1–18
☐	14	Lam. 3–5	Heb. 10:19–39
☐	15	Ezek. 1–2	Heb. 11:1–19
☐	16	Ezek. 3–4	Heb. 11:20–40
☐	17	Ezek. 5–7	Heb. 12
☐	18	Ezek. 8–10	Heb. 13
☐	19	Ezek. 11–13	James 1
☐	20	Ezek. 14–15	James 2
☐	21	Ezek. 16–17	James 3
☐	22	Ezek. 18–19	James 4
☐	23	Ezek. 20–21	James 5
☐	24	Ezek. 22–23	1 Peter 1
☐	25	Ezek. 24–26	1 Peter 2
☐	26	Ezek. 27–29	1 Peter 3
☐	27	Ezek. 30–32	1 Peter 4
☐	28	Ezek. 33–34	1 Peter 5
☐	29	Ezek. 35–36	2 Peter 1
☐	30	Ezek. 37–39	2 Peter 2

December

☐	1	Ezek. 40–41	2 Peter 3
☐	2	Ezek. 42–44	1 John 1
☐	3	Ezek. 45–46	1 John 2
☐	4	Ezek. 47–48	1 John 3
☐	5	Dan. 1–2	1 John 4
☐	6	Dan. 3–4	1 John 5
☐	7	Dan. 5–7	2 John
☐	8	Dan. 8–10	3 John
☐	9	Dan. 11–12	Jude
☐	10	Hos. 1–4	Rev. 1
☐	11	Hos. 5–8	Rev. 2
☐	12	Hos. 9–11	Rev. 3
☐	13	Hos. 12–14	Rev. 4
☐	14	Joel	Rev. 5
☐	15	Amos 1–3	Rev. 6
☐	16	Amos 4–6	Rev. 7
☐	17	Amos 7–9	Rev. 8
☐	18	Obad.	Rev. 9
☐	19	Jonah	Rev. 10
☐	20	Micah 1–3	Rev. 11
☐	21	Micah 4–5	Rev. 12
☐	22	Micah 6–7	Rev. 13
☐	23	Nahum	Rev. 14
☐	24	Hab.	Rev. 15
☐	25	Zeph.	Rev. 16
☐	26	Hag.	Rev. 17
☐	27	Zech. 1–4	Rev. 18
☐	28	Zech. 5–8	Rev. 19
☐	29	Zech. 9–12	Rev. 20
☐	30	Zech. 13–14	Rev. 21
☐	31	Mal.	Rev. 22

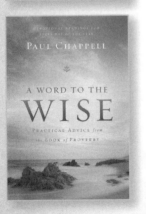

Visit us online

strivingtogether.com

wcbc.edu